The *Other* Public Lands

Giant City State Park, Illinois (Photo by author)

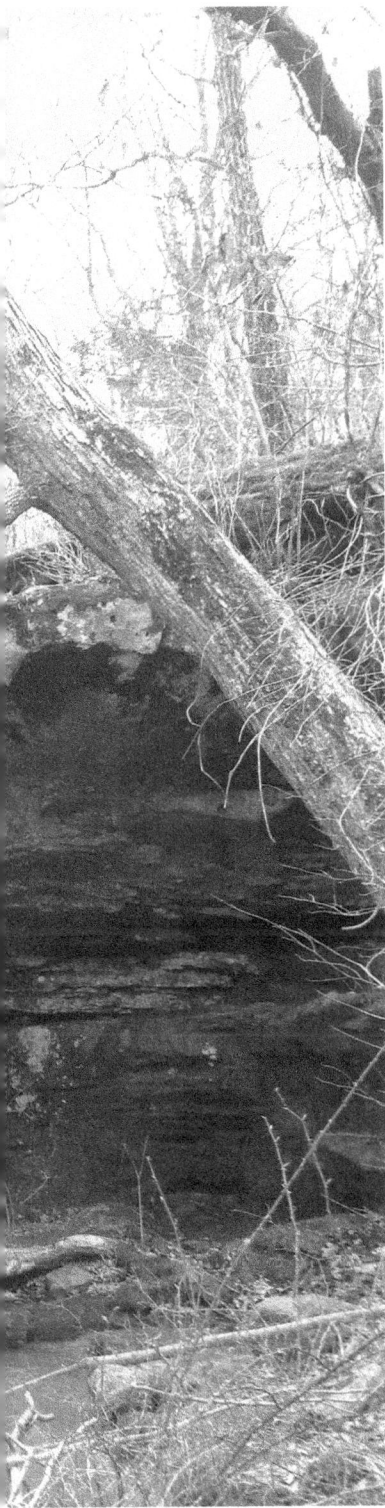

STEVEN DAVIS

The *Other* Public Lands

Preservation, Extraction, and Politics on the Fifty States' Natural Resource Lands

TEMPLE UNIVERSITY PRESS
Philadelphia • *Rome* • *Tokyo*

TEMPLE UNIVERSITY PRESS
Philadelphia, Pennsylvania 19122
tupress.temple.edu

Library of Congress Cataloging-in-Publication Data

Names: Davis, Steven, 1964– author.
Title: The other public lands : preservation, extraction, and politics on
the fifty states' natural resource lands / Steven Davis.
Description: Philadelphia: Temple University Press, 2025. | Includes
bibliographical references and index. | Summary: "A comprehensive
comparative study of state public land management and politics"—
Provided by publisher.
Identifiers: LCCN 2024027577 (print) | LCCN 2024027578 (ebook) | ISBN
9781439925539 (cloth) | ISBN 9781439925546 (paperback) | ISBN
9781439925553 (pdf)
Subjects: LCSH: Public lands—United States—States—Management. | Natural
areas—United States—States—Management. | Conservation of natural
resources—United States—States. | Public lands—Government
policy—United States—States. | Land use—Poliical aspects—United
States—States.
Classification: LCC HD216 .D386 2025 (print) | LCC HD216 (ebook) |
DDC 354.3/42130973—dc23/eng/20241121
LC record available at https://lccn.loc.gov/2024027577
LC ebook record available at https://lccn.loc.gov/2024027578

To Jen, Samuel, Julian, Zola,

and my parents.

And in memory of Russ Tooley (1943–2024),

public-spirited citizen scientist and

all-around good guy.

Contents

Preface

In March 2020, normal life across the world came to a screeching halt as the COVID-19 pandemic began to sweep across the globe. All at once, businesses, restaurants, workplaces, and schools closed from coast to coast as the country went on lockdown. As it was spring break, I had a week before remote teaching began, and my kids were home from college and high school, so we hunkered down and pondered this strange new world we found ourselves in.

By the middle of the first week, cabin fever set in, and so, on a sunny weekday, we all set out for Gibraltar Rock State Natural Area about thirty miles north of where we live in south-central Wisconsin. This several-hundred-acre tract of state-owned public land features a dense oak-basswood forest that rises to a dramatic lone bluff capped in dolomite, which for millennia allowed it to resist the forces of glaciation and erosion that smoothed the surrounding land into gently rolling hills. At the sheer craggy edge of the bluff, ancient wind-sculpted junipers grow at weird angles and frame dramatic views of the bogs and fields and farms of the Wisconsin River valley hundreds of feet below. Vultures often float lazily at eye level near the top of the bluff as they ride the thermals that rise off the cliff face. Gibraltar has always been one of my favorite places—beautiful and dramatic. And, as a low-profile state natural area (rather than a state park) with absolutely no facilities and a bit off the beaten path, it always seemed to me to be a dependably serene and contemplative spot.

That is, until that March day in the early pandemic as I approached the tiny gravel parking lot and saw it packed with cars, some double parked, parked on the grass, and lined up on both sides of the road as far as the eye could see. Everyone, it seemed, got the same idea at once, and I wondered what happened to my quiet, under-the-radar hiking spot. What happened was that when faced with the fear, confusion, uncertainty, and abundant free time of the COVID lockdown, people naturally fell back on that which brought comfort, inspiration, and continuity in one of the few settings we were told was relatively safe. The pandemic, then, brought into high relief the extent to which accessible wild parks are utterly essential life-affirming amenities that many Americans rely greatly upon. "State parks are," according to one professional park advocate, "what got many of us through the pandemic and these issues of climate, public health, and access really converged."[1]

Beyond just my little corner of Wisconsin, the pandemic brought state and national park visitation to unprecedented levels. William Rice and Bing Pan find an across-the-board 20.2% increase in 2020, while the National Park Service reported a 25% visitation increase in 2021.[2] Meanwhile, in densely populated Maryland, state park visitation soared 45% in 2020, and an astonishing 182% for just March and April of that year,[3] while it rose 30% in Michigan.[4] Thus, it became quite clear that with life wildly upended, the natural world was one of the few things to dependably offer the succor that we all so desperately needed.

People flocked to the state parks in Maryland, just as I did 850 miles to the west, because they were relatively close in distance. This easy availability is the reason that state public lands are perhaps the most important of public lands, at least as far as serving people is concerned. They exist in the sweet spot between conservation and access; bigger, wilder, and more biodiverse than most city or county parks but far more accessible and evenly dispersed geographically than federal lands. This is especially critical east of the Mississippi River, which contains only 4% of the vast federal public land estate.[5] As such, they offer, in the words of biologists James Miller and Richard Hobbs, "conservation where people live and work."[6] Evidence of this vital role can be seen by the fact that state parks serve nearly triple the number of visitors as the national park system on just 16% of the land.[7]

Another important reason to more deeply understand state public lands is that from the granting of Yosemite to the State of California in 1864 (before it switched back to federal control a few decades later) to the federal land transfer movement of today, there has long been political agitation to shift control of at least some federal lands to the states, specifically in the

West. If this political debate is to be fully joined and we are to comprehensively assess likely outcomes, then it would certainly help to have a less opaque and more nuanced and clear-eyed view of state public land management than we currently do. Despite the importance and, at least to park visitors, the centrality of state public land to American conservation and recreation, the literature is surprisingly thin. This becomes especially noticeable when compared with the scholarship on the federal lands, which is as extensive and prolific and varied as that focused on the states is scant. According to renowned public lands scholar Sally Fairfax, "The absence of research on state lands limits us to only the most tentative generalizations about even such basic facts as the extent of state land ownership."[8] Not only do the federal lands tend to dominate the focus of public land scholars, but they also dominate the public's imagination and the cultural narrative as well. It is Yosemite, Yellowstone, Acadia, the Everglades, and the Smoky Mountains that enjoy the spotlight and crowd our imagination, much more than equally dramatic state lands like Maine's Baxter, Michigan's Porcupine Mountains, Big Basin Redwoods in California, the Jocassee Gorges of South Carolina, or Wisconsin's Devil's Lake.

While public lands scholars have profiled certain parts of state land systems, like trust lands (Jon Souder and Sally Fairfax), state parks (Ney Landrum, Freeman Tilden, Rebecca Conard, and Thomas Cox), and state forests (Tomas Koontz), there does not exist in the public lands literature any comprehensive book-length profile of the full breadth and scope of state natural resource lands and the political dynamics that swirl around their management.[9] And this, despite the fact that they comprise nearly a quarter of all public land in America and, at 200 million acres, are nearly a third the size of the federal estate. This book, then, sets out to help fill that gap by offering a wide-angle overview of the entire state public land enterprise in all its remarkable range and variation. As a political scientist, I am most interested in how states approach the management of their public lands, especially in terms of how they prioritize competing claims related to conservation, equity and access, resource development, recreation, and finance.

This accounting of state land attempts to do two somewhat contradictory things at once: describe the significant variation between states and regions in how values and priorities get expressed as policy but also look for patterns common to fifty diverse states that distinguish state land management from the federal system. Now, of course, with fifty unique and increasingly polarized states, there are limits as to how much detailed description and individualized analysis this volume can (or would even want to) achieve. Instead, the goal is to describe diversity and find common patterns by identifying issues and themes at a broader level and single out states, not so much to exhaustively recount their policy minutiae but rather to tell stories that illustrate these larger points.

Plan of the Book

This book, then, strives to serve as a sort of sophisticated primer on state public lands and the political dynamics that underlie their management. Chapter 1 introduces the reader to the complex infrastructure of state public lands, a (very brief) history of how this infrastructure came about, and the differences between states in both the composition of their holdings and what goals and values are prioritized and how this determines the uses to which the lands are put. In doing so, a preservation/resource extraction/recreation framework is introduced and utilized. Chapter 1 also describes some of the structures and patterns marking state land management agencies as well as the differences between them, especially regarding the degree to which they are centralized or not.

Chapter 2 focuses on state parks and the tensions between recreation and the preservation of biodiversity and natural landscapes. As perhaps the most beloved, high-profile, and heavily used elements of state land holdings, state park systems are under tremendous strain caused by a combination of heavy usage and severe financial constraint, which to some critics stems from the indifference and neglect of policymakers. The proposed solutions to these problems (privatization, commercialization, external support, new funding sources, etc.) raise all sorts of issues about equity, access, appropriate development, and ecological health.

Chapter 3 turns the focus to perhaps the only element of state lands that is strictly geared toward biodiversity and preservation: state natural areas programs and state wilderness systems. Despite tending to be tiny, poorly funded, and overlooked systems, they play an especially critical environmental role, at least in those states where they exist. That, in itself, becomes a crucial indicator of various states' priorities and values.

In Chapter 4, state forests and other similar multiple use lands are examined. Such lands are primarily geared toward resource production, though preservation and recreational uses have legitimate claims here as well. As multiple use doctrine also underlies the bulk of federal management, it is very important to explore the similarities and differences between state and federal forest management. In doing so, one must also consider the external political environment, as multiple use management tends to engender the greatest levels of political conflict. As such, factors like the interest group environment, the role of courts, and agency culture/behavior are compared and analyzed both between states and the federal government and among specific states that approach certain issues somewhat differently.

State wildlife management areas (WMAs), the subject of Chapter 5, are, for many states (specifically the majority without trust lands), the largest category in their inventory. As with multiple use lands, they face competing claims for extraction, recreation, and preservation. This chapter explores the nature of those conflicts as they pertain to the states—specifically issues of game versus nongame priorities in wildlife management; state agency values, culture, and behavior (and differences with federal wildlife managers); and the conundrum posed by the outsized role that hunting licenses play in funding the entire system, especially as participation in hunting slowly declines in the U.S. Chapter 5 also considers the extent to which this funding regime distorts wildlife management priorities, especially in the case of endangered and/or nongame species and high-profile, politicized species like wolves and sage grouse.

Chapter 6 tackles the largest category of state lands in terms of acreage—the trust lands. These lands have a unique and complicated history and legal status. They are the lands granted to states by the federal government upon statehood in order to support public schools and occasionally other institutions, and they still exist in twenty-three states. This chapter explains how they are very different from regular state land (like parks, forests, WMAs, etc.), mostly due to the *trust doctrine*, which requires them to produce the highest revenue from the top bidder. This keeps them from being truly *public* in the way other public land is. The aggressive revenue generation that the trust doctrine seems to mandate has led to all manner of debate and calls for reform or at least reinterpretation of what public trust doctrines truly require. This is especially relevant given trust lands' controversial role as a model for the transfer of federal land to state control if it were ever to happen.

Finally, Chapter 7 reviews what is most important about state land and tries to offer an honest appraisal of state land systems' suitability for handling the mass transfer of hundreds of million acres of federal lands, as was explicitly stated in the 2016 Republican Party platform. More broadly, this conclusion also offers some notions on rethinking state lands in this post-pandemic era, including how to assure adequate access in an era of increased demand. This would include questions about the funding of state lands, the better use of ecosystem service frameworks, the prioritization of biodiversity and sustainability, and the treatment of state public lands as the public goods they are. Since various research has begun to firmly connect people's time spent in nature to their physical and mental well-being,[10] the issue of how readily and equitably wild lands are accessed can increasingly be seen as one of fundamental social importance.

Acknowledgments

This book is the culmination of a project begun many years ago to bring together a comprehensive portrait of state public lands. Over the last two and half years, I became determined to turn what had been an extensive article into a book, which required much additional research and digging around. I would like to thank my institution, Edgewood College, for supporting me in this endeavor, especially through a sabbatical grant in the fall of 2022 that allowed me to make great progress on research and writing. I also want to thank Edgewood's Rennebohm Library for helping me track down and access many crucial sources and David Wells and the Art Department for allowing me to write so productively at the Painted Forest facility in the beautiful, quiet, and isolated splendor of rural Sauk County.

Closer to home, I want to thank Jen Tooley, my dear love, for her endless encouragement, interest, and excitement regarding this obsession of mine. There is absolutely no one I would rather conduct "field observation" with in state natural areas far and wide.

Finally, I want to thank all the scholars who toil away in this rather obscure but important corner of public lands research for their contributions and insights, which made my own work possible, as well as all the public servants in state agencies across the country who dutifully and patiently answered my constant deluge of emails and phone calls to ferret out exact numbers and clarify opaque things.

The *Other* Public Lands

Tettegouche State Park, Minnesota (Photo by author)

1

State Public Lands

At Once Familiar and Obscure

> Taking states seriously as land managers and evaluating their
> constraints and potential is a contribution to the [public lands]
> dialogue in and of itself.
>
> —Sally Fairfax, "Thinking the Unthinkable:
>   States as Public Land Managers"

State Lands in a Federally Dominated Realm

America's federal lands—that is, its national parks, national forests, wildlife refuges, and wilderness areas—dominate our collective imagination regarding public lands. They are the subjects of lavishly photographed coffee-table books, Ken Burns documentaries on public television, bumper stickers denoting all the national parks the driver has visited, and, most relevant here, massive amounts of scholarly research. The U.S. Forest Service, for example, just might be the most heavily studied agency in the entire federal government. Every federal land management agency, every era in the history of federal lands, and every contentious issue and political battle has been subject to intense and well-deserved scrutiny by generations of scholars. And all this is for good reasons. The federal estate, at two-thirds of a billion acres, or more than a quarter of the United States' land mass, is a one-of-a-kind aggregation of priceless resources with outsized economic, social, cultural, and ecological importance.[1]

However, there is another assemblage of public lands—those owned and managed by the 50 states—that has received, by comparison, only a modicum of attention despite its own importance and even greater ubiquity. This ubiquity stems from the fact that unlike the federal lands, which are overwhelmingly situated from the Rocky Mountains westward, state public lands are found in every state and near every city, from one coast to the other and from the Gulf to the Canadian border. As a consequence of this geo-graphic dispersal, state lands have far greater levels of use and visitation than their federal counterparts. This is especially true in places like New York, which has not a single national park or national forest and is a mere 0.8% federally owned (ranked 46th)[2] and yet enjoys, nonetheless, millions of acres of public land from modest state parks to the massive backcountry wilder-ness of the Adirondacks.

While the amount of state land is not nearly as large as the federal estate, it is still quite extensive at roughly 200 million acres, or nearly 9% of the U.S.—a bit less than a third of what the federal government owns.[3] While they are as familiar to residents of any given locale as the state park down the road, they are also, in the aggregate, something of a mystery. Taken as a whole, this terra incognita holds some surprises. Would one ever guess that, at least in the state sphere, New Jersey, Hawaii, New York, Florida, or Pennsylvania are public land "superpowers"? Or that some states actually allow logging or drilling in their *state parks*, while others have certain parks' perpetual protection as wilderness written into their state constitution? In this state realm, one learns of innovation and clever adaptation alongside neglect and indifference, privatization schemes in some states and programs of furious public land acquisition in others. According to public lands schol-ar Sally Fairfax, echoing Justice Louis Brandeis, "States could and do, fre-quently act as 'little laboratories'; sites of experimentation with tools and approaches that spread to other states and occasionally even to the federal government."[4] Failure to give the states their due as coherent actors in the public land management realm, Fairfax argues, terribly impoverishes our understanding of public land issues and debates.[5]

Scholars like Fairfax and Robert Nelson are, in fact, quite bullish on state land management, finding it more innovative and responsive than that of their federal counterparts.[6] Fairfax, in particular, complains that one legacy of the Progressive Era conservation movement was that it besmirched states as the "bad guys," a notion that, even today, "leaves us thinking there is no other option" for public land.[7] She especially takes issue with public land scholar Marion Clawson's characterization of the states' "incompetence and venality," which he felt was justified based on their resistance and in-terference with the progressive goals of federal land retention and scientific management, ideas she feels have not quite worked out as promised and have run roughshod over local actors.[8] For more than a century, periodic waves of so-called Sagebrush Rebels have arisen and agitated for a transfer of at least some federal lands to the states.[9] Should this ever come to pass, then fully appreciating this debate and understanding the real-world implications of state management and control becomes all the more important.

The Lay of the Land: State-Owned Natural Resource Lands

Table 1.1 ranks the 50 states by the percentage of each that is comprised of state-owned natural resource land.[10] It is worth noting that the nearly 200 million acres of state land are perhaps not what they might be assumed to be at first glance. First, as Figure 1.1 shows, almost half of this total is in Alaska, while the 49 other states account for the other half. Alaska's bounty of state land has to do with the enormous grant of unassigned federal land that Alaska was given at statehood in 1959. Much of this land is still held in trust with rather vague guidelines as to its use. The other approximately 112 million acres of state lands (including Alaska's agency-owned lands) are roughly split in half again, with 49.2 million acres of institutional (mostly school) trust lands also granted at statehood and about 60.9 million acres of agency-owned conservation lands such as state parks, state forests, and wildlife management areas. Each of these types of state land are explored in detail in subsequent chapters.

While the overall figure for state ownership of land in the U.S. is 8.8%, Alaska's massive holdings skew state averages to such an extent that the median percentage of state-owned land—4.4%—might offer a clearer picture. The data in Table 1.1 show that the top 12 states own more than 10%

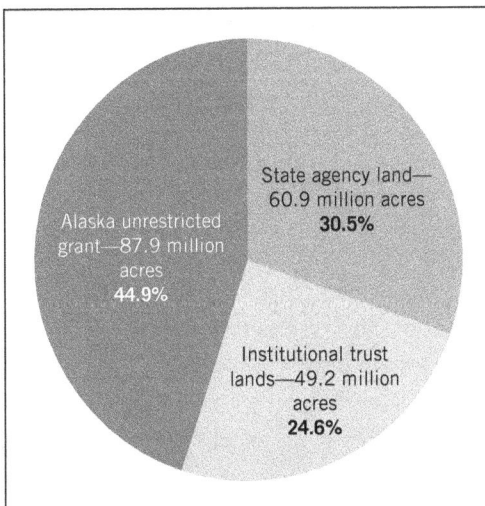

Figure 1.1 State-owned land by category
(Data sources: See Tables 1.1 and 6.1 and appendix.)

Rank	State	Percentage of land state owned	Acres of state-owned land (in thousands)	Trust lands make up more than 90% of total state land
			TABLE 1.1 ACREAGE AND PERCENTAGE OF STATE-OWNED NATURAL RESOURCE LANDS	
1	Hawaii	37.0%	1,521.0[1]	
2	Alaska	27.6%	100,623.0[2]	X
3	New Jersey	17.6%	837.2	
4	Minnesota	16.4%	8,400.0[3]	
5	Florida	15.4%	5,316.9	
6	New York	14.1%	4,271.4	
7	Pennsylvania	13.9%	4,000.0	
8	Arizona	12.8%	9,337.7	X
9	Michigan	12.6%	4,593.5	
10	New Mexico	12.0%	9,292.4	X
11	Massachusetts	11.6%	584.3	
12	Utah	10.3%	5,439.2	
13	Delaware	9.2%	114.5	
14	Washington	9.1%	3,856.7	
	U.S. overall	8.8%	199,843.8	
15	Rhode Island	8.3%	55.8	
16	Maryland	8.0%	500.6	
17	Connecticut	7.8%	243.2	
18	Wyoming	6.2%	3,853.1	X
19	Montana	6.1%	5,647.0	X
20	Vermont	5.9%	350.0	
21	Maine	5.2%	1,028.3	
22	Idaho	5.1%	2,687.2	
22	Louisiana	5.1%	1,432.9[4]	
22	Colorado	5.1%	3,406.4	
	U.S. overall (minus Alaska grant)	4.9%	110,143.8	
23	Wisconsin[5]	4.6%	1,586.4	
24	New Hampshire	4.1%	233.1[6]	
25	Tennessee	3.6%	961.2	
25	Mississippi	3.6%	1,081.0	
25	West Virginia	3.6%	556.6	
26	Nebraska	3.1%	1,535.6	X
27	North Carolina	3.0%	920.5	
28	California	2.9%	2,938.0	

Rank	State	Percentage of land state owned	Acres of state-owned land (in thousands)	Trust lands make up more than 90% of total state land
28	Oregon	2.8%	1,725.3	
29	Oklahoma	2.5%	1,105.0	
30	South Carolina	2.4%	463.0	
31	Ohio	2.3%	590.0	
31	South Dakota	2.3%	1,139.6	
32	Missouri	2.2%	975.4	
33	Georgia	1.9%	714.6	
33	North Dakota	1.9%	825.0	X
34	Indiana	1.8%	413.2	
35	Virginia	1.7%	431.4	
36	Alabama	1.6%	528.8	
37	Arkansas	1.5%	510.7	
38	Illinois	1.1%	398.8	
38	Iowa	1.1%	390.7	
39	Kentucky	1.0%	243.5	
39	Texas	1.0%	1,718.1	
40	Nevada	0.5%	325.6	
41	Kansas	0.3%	145.0	

Data sources: See appendix.

[1] Includes all state-owned lands, not just natural resource lands.

[2] Approximately 89.7 million acres of this figure (or 89%) is an unrestricted grant of land from the federal government upon statehood in 1959 and held in trust, though it is not traditional institutional trust land.

[3] Includes 2,285,588 acres of tax-forfeited land owned by the state but managed by counties as county forests.

[4] This figure includes some state-owned lands that are not necessarily natural resource lands.

[5] Wisconsin also has a unique and massive 2.4-million-acre county forest system made up of tax-forfeited lands that stayed under county ownership, albeit with very tight state guidance and regulation. Therefore, with state and county ownership combined, Wisconsin has nearly 4 million acres of non-federal public land, or 11.5% of the state, which would rank it #12.

[6] In addition to this state-owned land, New Hampshire has an extensive 272,098-acre system of conservation easements on private lands.

of land in their respective states. The top 2, Hawaii (37.0%) and Alaska (27.6%), have the advantage of having received the huge, previously mentioned federal land grants.[11] As for the other top states, all but 3 are east of the 100th meridian where federal land is scarcer. In fact, the near-total absence of federal land in northeastern states like New Jersey, New York, and Massachusetts has probably forced those states to conceive of the provision of public land as primarily a state responsibility. This seems to be true as well for Florida, which, although it has a rather decent complement of federal land, has felt obliged, nevertheless, to embark on an aggressive program of land acquisition starting in the 1960s.

As for Arizona, New Mexico, and Utah, the only western states in the top 12, their abundance of state lands is almost solely due to school land grants at statehood, the bulk of which these states, unlike many of their neighbors, carefully held onto. However, if one was to look only at state lands acquired through means other than statehood grants, these western states actually have rather minuscule holdings. For example, without including trust lands, the percentage of state land in Arizona is only 0.15%, which would move it from eighth place to dead last behind Kansas. These nontrust lands would include things like state parks and state forests, which are public land types that exist in abundance at the federal level in many of these western states, and so, perhaps the impetus to acquire such lands is much weaker than in the East. The last column in Table 1.1 denotes which states have more than 90% of their state lands made up of trust lands. One of the highest-ranked states for public ownership (ranked fourth at 16.4%) is Minnesota, which has uniquely combined its retention of large school trust grants (like many western states) with an abundance of land it went on to acquire on its own (like many eastern states).

At the opposite end of the rankings in Table 1.1 are the states with very limited public land holdings, and while they are from a mix of regions, the South and Great Plains are most heavily represented, as can be seen in Figure 1.2. While they too lack an abundance of federal lands, unlike their northeastern counterparts, this fact does not seem to have inspired them to make land acquisition a priority in the last century. This might be due to well-documented regional differences in cultural and political orientations (greater libertarianism, less institutional trust, less environmental concern)[12] and perhaps greater resource and institutional capacity constraints. As has become abundantly clear in other policy areas, like COVID-related public health measures or abortion rights, cultural and ideological differences at the state and local levels can create vastly disparate policy environments

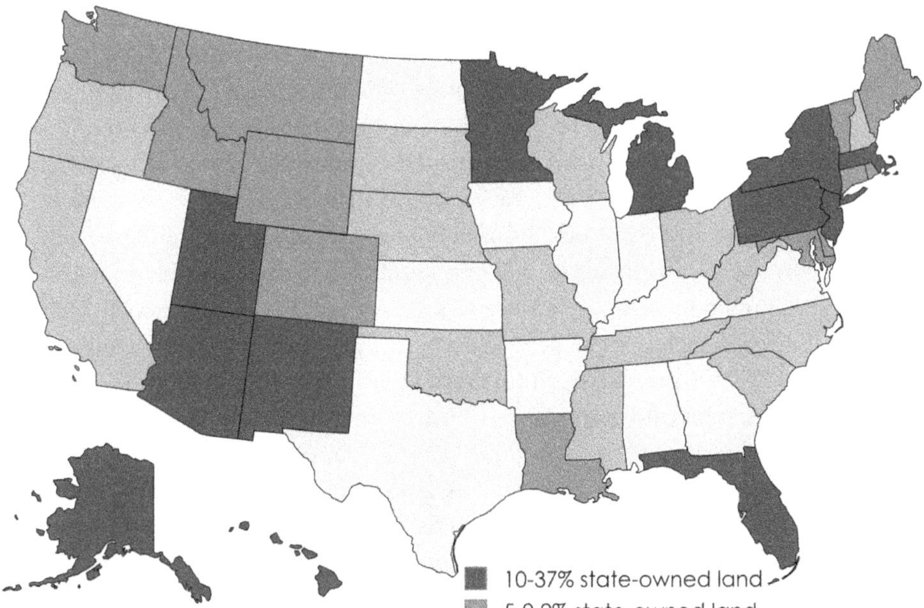

Figure 1.2 State-owned public land as percentage of all land in state
(Data sources: See Table 1.1 and appendix.)

Legend:
- 10-37% state-owned land
- 5-9.2% state-owned land
- 2-4.9% state-owned land
- <2% state-owned land

between and among states. That said, it should also be noted that general support for and enjoyment of public lands counts as one of the relatively few areas of clear bipartisan agreement among the broader public.[13]

A Very Brief History of State Lands

State lands can be traced back to America's earliest days. The colonial land charters that extended west beyond the original 13 colonies and over the Appalachians were federalized after the American Revolution.[14] This frontier land was later augmented by waves of purchase, annexation, native displacement, and conquest that eventually enlarged this mass of federal land all the way to the Pacific. It is obvious, but important nonetheless, to note that all these lands, public or private—homesteaded, granted to states, or retained by the federal government—had belonged to the native inhabitants who lived on them for millennia until they were pushed aside and their lands informally grabbed or more formally ceded.[15]

While the bulk of federally controlled land was destined to be home-steaded, Congress planned to put some aside for the new states. The General Land Ordinance of 1785 and the Northwest Ordinance of 1787 laid out a process by which the frontier was to be demarcated, settled, and eventually moved into statehood.[16] A key part of this process (and one explored in more detail in Chapter 6) was the provision that one square-mile section (and later two, and then four) of each 36-square-mile township "shall be reserved," in the words of the General Land Ordinance, "for the maintenance of public schools."[17] Because Congress thought an enlightened and well-governed society to be dependent on the presence of universal education, and because new states on the frontier lacked any kind of existing tax base, these school land grants were seen as an important tool for equity and social improvement.[18]

Unfortunately, this legislation was quite vague as to how states were obliged to use these trust lands, and so the first wave of recipients, starting with Ohio in 1803, largely sold off or otherwise squandered their grants in short order.[19] It was not until Congress wrote more restrictive language into subsequent statehood acts and states themselves wrote protections into their constitutions that state trust lands became more secure.[20] This is the reason trust lands tend to be concentrated in states west of the 100th meridian, even though all states since 1803, east and west, received substantial granted acreage.[21]

For most of the 19th century, these trust lands were essentially the only form of state land. However, by the end of the century, states were beginning to be swept by the same currents of Progressive Era reform that were sweeping national politics. And few policy areas felt this impact more keenly than conservation. As a result, there was a great shift nationally from the disposal of federal lands to their retention as national parks, national forests, wildlife refuges, and rangelands began to be put aside to be "scientifically managed" in the public interest. Many states, especially in the Northeast and Upper Midwest, were not immune to this same siren song of conservation and reform, albeit with a decade or so lag and considerably less financial wherewithal. This period gave birth, then, to what state parks historian Ney Landrum calls "the state parks movement"[22] (explored in much greater detail in the next chapter).

Inherent limitations notwithstanding, states, especially those with no trust lands and in areas lacking in federal lands, began the painstaking process of acquiring scenic or biologically important tracts of land, often parcel by parcel. However, in some states, the Great Depression helped turbocharge this process as large tracts of cutover and abandoned stump fields and failed farms became tax delinquent and reverted through forfeiture to state or county ownership. This is how Minnesota, Wisconsin, Michigan, and Pennsylvania, for example, came to accumulate huge tracts of land that were destined to become their respective state forest systems.[23]

The next period of growth in state public lands came during the post–World War 2 boom times as increased motorization, suburbanization, and standards of living led to greater tourism and demand for recreation. Many states responded by picking up the pace of land acquisition, while latecomers like Kansas, Arizona, Utah, and Arkansas were finally joining in, for the first time, by establishing state park systems.[24] This phase of rapid growth continued into the 1970s, especially helped along by the enactment of the Land and Water Conservation Fund (LWCF) in 1965, which created a pool of acquisition and park infrastructure funds from royalties paid to the federal government from offshore oil production. In order to qualify for these funds, states have had to engage in a level of comprehensive planning and assessment (which many had never previously done) according to a standardized framework (the so-called SCORP Reports).[25]

By the early 1980s, however, the halcyon days of state land expansion and generous budgets ended abruptly as recession, recurrent state budget crises, and the increasing prevalence of "free market" approaches to public services put the squeeze on state public land systems. Meanwhile, some states lost their fervor for land acquisition to meet the needs of growing populations. To make matters even worse, the LWCF very much fell out of favor during the Reagan administration—and later, from a hostile Congress—as $22 billion in trust funds went unallocated over several decades.[26]

In more recent times, state lands have faced a mixed bag of challenges and opportunities. On the one hand, periodic funding crises, and the neglect they spawn, have grown worse and, in many places, endemic. This problem reached epic proportions in the years that followed the mortgage crisis and the so-called Great Recession of 2008–2010, with park closures, mothballing, outsourcing, and devolution to local governments becoming relatively commonplace (discussed in much greater detail in the next chapter). On the other hand, parks and recreation have rarely been more popular, in demand, and vigorously supported by organized interests and in public opinion. This widespread support is, at least in part, what led Congress in 2020 to pass, with large and unusually bipartisan majorities, the

Great American Outdoors Act, which permanently reauthorized the expired LWCF and guaranteed $900 million in annual allocations for land acquisition and park operation (protected from diversion). At least 40% of this money must go to the states.[27] Furthermore, generous COVID stimulus grants to states have been used by some states to shore up state park budgets, undo the damage of the previous retrenchment, and meet the explosion of new demand unleashed by the pandemic.[28]

Even well before the pandemic, many states and their voters had come to view their public land systems as irresistible assets that they have been willing to support with a substantial commitment of resources. According to the Trust for Public Land, between 1988 and 2007, voters approved $46 billion in over 1,500 state and local conservation and land acquisition initiatives, which represents a 76% success rate.[29] Indicative of this support would be Missouri, whose voters first approved a 0.1% sales tax for parks and conservation in 1988 with 68.7% voting yes and then reauthorized it three more times, with the most recent vote in 2016 hitting 79.9% yes.[30] Sometimes, as in the case of Alabama and its 1992 Forever Wild initiative (which passed with a 84% yes vote), resounding victories have germinated in what might seem to be the most politically infertile soil.[31] Likewise, successful constitutional amendments in Texas in 2019 to tax sporting goods for conservation and in Montana, where 50% of marijuana tax revenues are similarly earmarked, seem to be signs of state conservation's near-universal appeal.[32] A small sampling of other successful referenda and acquisition funds include New Jersey's Green Acres program from 1961, Connecticut's 1998 Open Space and Watershed Land Acquisition Program, Minnesota's 2008 Legacy Fund earmarking a $0.0375 sales tax, and most recently the $40 million Land for Maine's Future program created in 2021.[33]

Perhaps no state in the country, though, has embarked on a program of land acquisition more aggressively than Florida. Through its succession of legislatively mandated acquisition programs—the Land Acquisition Trust Fund (1963), Endangered Lands Program (1972), Conservation and Recreational Land Program (1979), Preservation 2000 (1990), and Florida Forever (1999)—Florida has accumulated an impressive 3.8 million acres of conservation lands.[34] According to Nelson, in the decade from 2008 to 2018, Florida has spent more on land acquisition than the LWCF allocated to all 50 states.[35]

Despite this relatively clear and consistent support, the fact remains that because American politics is so extremely polarized and ideologically fraught, the very idea of state public land has nevertheless been called into question from time to time. This has been especially true in the years following the 2010 midterm elections, which coincided with the ascent of the so-called Tea Party movement. For example, in Michigan, a leading state for public land, free market think tanks and GOP legislators began to ask why the state needed so much land. The libertarian Mackinac Center argued that public land and its recreational facilities "directly harm the livelihoods of people who voluntarily provide the same services at a reasonable cost and involve government in recreational programs enjoyed by a few but paid for by nearly everyone."[36] Their solution is full-on privatization—to sell the best tracts to private conservancies and release the rest for development by private entities. While this might seem an extreme position, it soon found some support within the Michigan legislature's Republican caucus, many of whose members have come to see Michigan's public land as harming local economic development and starving tax rolls.[37] According to a leading state senator on the issue, "the state owns too much land . . . it is more than the department is able to care for and meet its obligations on." Therefore, he concludes, "A primary objective should be to return land to private ownership."[38] In response, the Michigan legislature passed a land acquisition moratorium in 2012 for the northern half of the state (despite having previously established a trust fund for just that purpose), which remained in place until the Michigan Department of Natural Resources (DNR) came up with a new management vision and land acquisition strategy.[39]

In neighboring Wisconsin, the very same geopolitical forces in the very same period led to an even starker backlash—a fairly arbitrary order in the 2013 state budget for the DNR to identify and sell off 10,000 acres of state land, almost as if it were to be some sort of ritual sacrifice.[40] This directive was combined with a full decoupling of the state park system from all general budget support. Meanwhile, annual land acquisition spending in Wisconsin plummeted from $61.6 million in 2007 to $2.9 million in 2018.[41] Other states that have toyed with privatization in the last decade or so (whether full-on divestment of some public land or outsourced operations) include Mississippi, Oklahoma, West Virginia, Alabama, Tennessee, and California.

The Three Purposes of Public Land

Specific units of public land in the United States, whether federal, state, or local, are generally managed to achieve one or more of three broad purposes:

1. Preservation—To safeguard native ecosystems, natural landscapes, and the biodiversity contained within them as well as protect places with exceptional aesthetic, historical, cultural, or wilderness values.
2. Resource extraction—To utilize public land to produce marketable commodities such as timber, minerals, ores, energy, or livestock to support local economies and produce revenue for agency operations, the broader state government, or local jurisdictions (or some combination of all three).
3. Recreation—To provide various forms of passive and active recreational opportunities to the general public as both a public service and a source of economic development through enhanced tourism and revenue generation for the managing agencies.

Mostly, these broad purposes get articulated through legislative mandate or executive rulemaking, or perhaps through the enabling legislation of a given agency or department tasked with managing a certain type of land. In some cases, this guidance is explicit and direct, and at other times, it is characterized by vagueness and opacity. To use two examples of well-known federal laws, the Wilderness Act of 1964 offers a nice illustration of the former, laying out with precision and clarity what can and cannot be done in a designated wilderness area, while the Multiple-Use Sustained-Yield Act of 1960, which invites managers to weigh between legitimate opposing uses, might be a good example of the latter, vaguer sort of law.[42]

Sometimes, as might be the case with state natural areas established to protect some exquisitely rare and delicate ecological feature or state trust lands obligated to raise revenue for schools, a single, dominant use is prioritized over the others. Other public land categories, however, are explicitly intended to be managed as multiple use, whereby managers must weigh and prioritize competing claims and uses in order to maximize utility without completely shutting down other uses or degrading or negating future opportunities for these alternative uses. This is, of course, easier said than done and represents perhaps the most challenging, delicate, and consequential task facing any public land manager.

Going forward, this *preservation-extraction-recreation* framework provides the analytical basis for the ensuing chapters of this book. Indeed, these chapters are organized to examine each of the major categories of state public land and explore the policy conflicts, management dilemmas, and political dynamics inherent to each and that stem from the different ways these three broad purposes are prioritized and operationalized. For example, with state parks (as seen in the next chapter), profound conflicts largely arise between the impetus to protect and preserve the natural landscape versus the demands for the provision of public recreation, which, incidentally, serves as a crucial source of operational revenue. For instance, should campground facilities and campground roads be plopped down right in the center of an especially shady, attractive, and biologically important mature forest? The recreation priority suggests they should, while the preservation priority would push such facilities far away from this spot. With state wildlife areas, a different version of this clash plays out between pressure to enhance biodiversity across the board versus the demands for maximized recreational hunting opportunities of an extremely limited range of game species. How, for example, should a state wildlife agency respond if endangered wolves prey on the elk that are so popular to hunt?

With state forests, meanwhile, battles are often waged between demands for ecological integrity (such as water quality, biodiversity, and old-growth forests) versus the need and mandate to produce important commodities. To the extent that recreation becomes impacted (i.e., clear-cuts alongside hiking trails or fracking activity scaring off game species), this third purpose gets thrown into the mix as well. Meanwhile, state trust lands, despite being a largely dominant-use jurisdiction mandated to produce revenue through commodity production, increasingly find themselves facing persistent and vocal demands for both recreational access and at least some form of preservation of the most fragile sites.

State Natural Resource Agencies: Patterns on a Theme

In many ways, the state natural resource agencies that manage public conservation lands for the variety of purposes outlined previously are a mirror of their federal counterparts. There are state forest services (or divisions) staffed with trained foresters, state park agencies tasked with balancing recreation and resource protection, and state wildlife agencies managing game populations and (hopefully) all faunal biodiversity. The four major federal land management agencies—the U.S. Forest Service, the National Park Service, the U.S. Fish and Wildlife Service, and the Bureau of Land Management—are famously decentralized, split across two different departments in the cabinet and marked by very distinct mandates, histories, professional backgrounds, and organizational cultures. This bureaucratic fragmentation has long been the target of reformers who see it as inefficient, duplicative, and very much at the expense of good policy coordination.[43]

For their part, state land management agencies run the gamut from being much more centralized than their federal counterparts to even less so. Table 1.2, which categorizes states by the level of centralization of their natural resource agencies, shows the incredibly wide range that exists. In total, 18 states are classified as *highly centralized*, which denotes that a single department-level "superagency" administers all aspects of land management (and sometimes air and water pollution control as well). Typically, such a large and complex agency will feature within it divisions or bureaus to focus on specific functions like forestry, parks and recreation, and wildlife.

An additional 6 states are *somewhat centralized*, meaning there are two agencies independent of each other, with one dominant and the other managing a much more modest subset of public land. For example, in Wisconsin, the DNR approaches superagency status as it manages 1.4 million acres of state parks, forests, scenic waters, natural areas, and wildlife areas, but then there is also the Board of Commissioners of Public Lands, which manages a much smaller inventory of 77,000 acres of school trust lands that remain in Wisconsin. Another 6 states are considered *somewhat decentralized* in that they also feature two departments/agencies wholly independent of each other, but with each managing an equally significant portfolio of lands. A good example of this category is Massachusetts, where the Department of Conservation and Recreation is responsible for managing over 400,000 acres of state parks, forests, and watershed reserves, while the Department of Fish and Game manages a further 230,000 acres of state wildlife areas.

The final category, *highly decentralized*, is also the largest. These 20 states have at least three independent entities managing different types of public land. California provides a good illustration of this, as it splits authority between four agencies—the Department of Parks and Recreation, the Department of Forestry and Fire Protection, the Department of Fish and Game, and the State Lands Commission (which oversees trust lands). It should be noted that in states with trust land, decentralization might be at least partly driven by the fact that such lands, so distinct in their history and mandate, are almost always managed by independent boards or commissions.[44]

TABLE 1.2 LEVEL OF CENTRALIZATION AMONG STATE NATURAL RESOURCE AGENCIES			
Highly centralized[1]	Somewhat centralized[2]	Somewhat decentralized[3]	Highly decentralized[4]
Alabama	Delaware	Hawaii	Alaska
Colorado	Georgia	Massachusetts	Arizona
Connecticut	Mississippi	Missouri	Arkansas
Illinois	South Dakota	Montana	California
Indiana	Texas	Nebraska	Florida
Iowa	Wisconsin	Nevada	Idaho
Kansas			Kentucky
Maryland			Louisiana
Michigan			Maine
Minnesota			New Mexico
New Hampshire			New York
New Jersey			North Carolina
Ohio			North Dakota
Pennsylvania			Oklahoma
Rhode Island			Oregon
Utah			South Carolina
Vermont			Tennessee
West Virginia			Virginia
			Washington
			Wyoming

[1] *Highly centralized* refers to states with a single natural resource agency at the department level whose various divisions manage all categories of state-owned conservation lands.

[2] *Somewhat centralized* refers to states with two natural resources agencies independent of one another, of which one is the dominant agency with responsibility for most of the public land portfolio while the other manages only a modest subset of public land.

[3] *Somewhat decentralized* refers to states with two agencies independent of one another in which each has a significant responsibility for managing various categories of state conservation land.

[4] *Highly decentralized* refers to states with at least three agencies independent of one another with responsibility for managing state conservation lands.

In further chapters, the roles and behaviors of various state land management agencies are examined in much more detail, but at this juncture, it is important to point out that a state's level of administrative centralization has complex and sometimes unexpected effects. Decentralization, especially when some of the entities are commissions with set terms, can enhance an agency's autonomy and insulate it, to some extent, from political pressure, whether legislative, executive, or external. Conversely, such agencies can also grow into isolated and out-of-touch fiefdoms cut off from policy innovation or public preferences. Just such an accusation is often hurled by critics at what they see as the "old boys" networks that dominate some states' fish and game commissions to the detriment of ecologically sensitive wildlife policy. Administrative centralization, on the other hand, tends to improve cooperation and efficiency, whereby, for example, ecological restoration initiatives, invasive species control policies, or biodiversity goals can be standardized and coordinated across all units of a single department. But this might also present a bigger, more singular, and more accessible prize to capture and manipulate should a state's political leadership turn hostile to the goals of conservation.

It is hard to draw any firm conclusions about the relationship between a state's position on the centralization–decentralization continuum in Table 1.2 and its orientation toward public land. The most centralized states contain both public land behemoths (Minnesota, Michigan, and Pennsylvania) and laggards (Kansas, Alabama, and Iowa). Likewise, the ranks of the most decentralized include titans (California, New York, and Florida) but also lightweights (Kentucky, Oklahoma, and North Dakota) in the realm of public lands. Nor does there seem to be any regional patterns at play; instead, individual states, each reflecting their own unique political context and institutional and organizational histories, have either produced waves of consolidation or else institutional solidification and the hardening of boundaries with few overarching patterns.

The seeming randomness of whether state agencies are centralized or not is not meant to suggest that a state's administrative architecture for public land management never tells us anything important about that state's values, priorities, and orientations toward their public land. How else to interpret the fact that state parks are embedded in the Department of Energy, Minerals, and Natural Resources in New Mexico; the Department of Tourism and Recreational Development in Oklahoma; or the Department of Culture, Recreation, and Tourism in Louisiana? In West Virginia, meanwhile, all natural resource agencies, including parks, wildlife, and forestry, are located within the Department of Commerce. Similarly, does the explicitness of the Wisconsin DNR's Bureau of Endangered Resources tell us anything about the priorities of an agency that happens to administer one of the nation's largest and oldest state natural areas programs that vigorously protects biodiversity in rare ecological communities? In sum, how states view their acquired public lands, prioritize their policy goals, and structure their land management can seem at once to conform to certain patterns across 50 states and yet be infinitely variable. This should be kept in mind as the ensuing chapters delve more deeply into the public land portfolios of the states.

Twin Falls State Park, Washington (Photo by author)

2

The State Park Idea

The Vision and the Reality

> It is becoming increasingly difficult for men and women in great cities
> to go back to the great outdoors and there renew the springs which
> nourish and sweeten their lives . . . city parks do not fill the gap. . . .
> National Parks partly fill this need, but they are remote from the great
> masses of population; consequently, the great movement for *State Parks*
> in recent years has come from a realization of the need and of the
> remedy. The *State Park* has come to stay. It is a growing factor in
> American life and it is among the most hopeful, for it is a reaction from
> the inner instincts of humanity against a wholly new and artificial
> environment which threatens not only the impairment of its life but
> the mutilation of its soul. Modern man was building himself a prison.
> The *State Park* is one way out.
>
> —Introduction, Proceedings of the Second National Conference
>   on State Parks, May 22, 1922, quoted in Ney Landrum,
>   *The State Parks Movement*

State Park Systems across the U.S.

Although state parks make up but a small fraction of all state public lands,[1]
they are what people most readily associate with the very notion of *state land*,
perhaps to the point of being almost synonymous. As such, they tend to serve
as the *crown jewels* of most states' public lands inventory, with the most visitation, the most vigorous marketing, and, consequently, the greatest visibility and name recognition. For the last decade, total annual state park visitation has averaged around 800 million, which is 2.7 times greater than the
national parks despite having just one-sixth of the acreage.[2] Collectively, the
2.4 billion hours spent annually in the parks are estimated to account for
roughly one-third of all nature-based recreation in the U.S.[3] No other type
of public land—local, state, or federal—comes close to these use statistics.
According to historian Thomas Cox:

State Parks are far more important than is generally recognized. They are visited by more people each year than are national parks, even though their collective budgets are far smaller. They play a major role in the tourist trade, which is a key element in the economy of many states. Their history tells us much about changing patterns of recreation and much else in American society.[4]

State park systems are typically composed of lands earmarked for some combination of recreational use and natural or historic preservation. This would include state parks, state recreation areas, state trails, state historic sites, and, in some places, state natural areas.[5] As discussed in the last chapter (see Table 1.2), some states' park systems are embedded within larger multijurisdictional natural resource agencies, while others are administered by stand-alone agencies. While the latter arrangement might prevent a park system from getting lost and forgotten in a larger DNR or Department of Tourism, it can also have the opposite effect, especially if it is a state that that is not fully committed to the park ideal. A 2009 report on Arizona's state parks, for example, found that their independent, stand-alone status in this case actually worked to their disadvantage since they were generally perceived as a small, weak, and isolated agency that the legislature could roll over quite easily.[6] Their history of being on the receiving end of routine and painful budget cuts and diversions of dedicated lines of funding that were supposed to be earmarked for parks would seem to bear this out.

Special Status State Parks

Two states, New York and Maine, also have extensive acreage in a parallel system of parkland that is administered apart from those states' regular park systems.[7] These rather large special status parks, specifically New York's Adirondack and Catskill preserves and Maine's Baxter State Park, have unique and idiosyncratic histories and governance structures (discussed later in this chapter). In the case of New York's special parks, their inviolable protection is actually written into the state constitution,[8] and in Maine's case, it is the result of a deed left by former Governor Percival Baxter to govern his massive land donation (which includes the famed Mt. Katahdin) and caretaking trust.[9] At 2.9 million mostly wilderness acres, New York's special parklands make up nearly two-thirds of all public land in the state and are nearly 10 times larger than the state's fairly extensive regular park system.[10] The presence of these special parklands has vaulted New York into the top echelons of state public land holdings among the 50 states. Similarly, Maine's 210,000-acre Baxter State Park is nearly triple the size of its regular state park system.

State Parks as an Element of State Lands

State park systems in the U.S. contain 11.8 million acres, or 14.9 million acres if the special status parks are included. As is clear from Table 2.1, all 50 states have park systems, though some are modest and others quite extensive. The mean system is 236,500 acres, while the median is roughly 118,000 acres. Table 2.1 ranks state park systems by absolute acreage, and in this regard, the "big five" are Alaska, New York (if its special parklands are included), California, Florida, and Texas. However, one might instead consider the extent to which a given state's overall public land inventory consists of state parks in order to compare states. Here, one finds that New York,[11] California, Nevada, and Indiana all have more than 40% of their state-owned land as state parks, as compared to a mean of only 7.5%.

At the opposite end of the spectrum tend to be mostly western states with large trust land holdings that seriously dilute their often relatively small park systems. Such states include Arizona (0.6%), Montana (0.8%), New Mexico (2%), and Utah (2.2%). Similarly, states with huge state forest systems like Hawaii or Minnesota also have proportionally less land in their state parks. A final way to view the relative size of state park systems would be as a percentage of the entire land mass of a state (see Table 2.1 and Figure 2.1)—in some ways, this might be the ultimate measure of a state's commitment to the state park ideal. While New York, not surprisingly, dominates this measure with an astonishing 10.7% of the state as state park or special parkland, the runner-up, New Jersey (at 4.6%), is perhaps an even bigger surprise. No other states come close, though Delaware, Florida, and Maryland are all above 2% of their land mass. It is also worth mentioning that the physically enormous state of California maintains an impressive 1.5% of its land as state park, more than double the national mean of 0.7%. At the bottom end, at least five states, Arizona, North Dakota, Kansas, Montana, and Mississippi, have less than one-tenth of 1% of their land protected as state parks.

Along with wildlife areas, state parks are one of the jurisdictions of state land where it is relatively common to lease land, often from the federal government. Although the bulk of state park land is in public ownership, there are a few states, like Kansas, Nebraska, North Dakota, Oklahoma,

State	State park system[1] acreage (in thousands)	State parks as percentage of all state public lands	State parks as percentage of total state land	Visits per capita 2017	Park agency as division of larger department or stand-alone (SA)	No entrance fee
Alaska	3,357.0	3.3%	0.9%	4.98	Division	
New York (including special status parks)	3,237.0	75.8%	10.7%	NA	SA	
California	1,500.0	51.1%	1.5%	2.06	SA	
Florida	800.0	15.0%	2.3%	1.54	Division	
Texas	630.0	36.7%	0.4%	0.34	Division	
Michigan	359.8	7.8%	1.0%	3.23	Division	
New York	350.0	8.2%	1.2%	3.58	SA	
Pennsylvania	300.0	7.5%	1.0%	3.13	Division	X
Maine (including special status park)	295.9	28.7%	1.5%	NA	Both[2]	
North Carolina	250.0	27.2%	0.8%	1.86	Division	
Tennessee	240.8	25.1%	0.9%	5.80	Division	X
Minnesota	232.0	2.8%	0.5%	1.84	Division	
Colorado	220.4	6.8%	0.3%	2.67	Division	
New Jersey	220.2	26.3%	4.6%	1.75	Division	
New Mexico	190.0[3]	2.0%	0.2%	2.40	Division	
Indiana	183.3[4]	44.4%	0.8%	2.61	Division	
Ohio	180.0	30.5%	0.7%	3.67	Division	X
Nevada	162.7	50.0%	0.2%	1.26	Division	
Missouri	160.4	16.4%	0.4%	3.53	Division	X
Illinois	152.2[5]	38.2%	0.4%	3.01	Division	X
Washington	142.4	3.7%	0.3%	4.76	SA	
Maryland	141.6	28.3%	2.3%	2.39	Division	
Virginia	127.0	29.4%	0.5%	1.23	Division	
Wyoming	120.0[6]	3.1%	0.2%	8.38	SA	
Utah	119.3	2.2%	0.2%	1.68	Division	
Wisconsin	117.2[7]	7.4%	0.3%	3.12	Division	
South Dakota	103.0	9.0%	0.2%	8.83	Division	
Oregon	100.0	5.8%	0.2%	12.71	SA	
Nebraska	97.2[8]	6.3%	0.2%	6.65	Division	
West Virginia	91.3	16.4%	0.6%	4.18	Division	
Maine	86.2	8.4%	0.4%	2.10	Division	
Georgia	85.0	11.9%	0.2%	0.86	Division	
South Carolina	85.0[9]	18.4%	0.4%	1.60	SA	
Massachusetts	77.3	13.2%	1.5%	3.97	Division	
New Hampshire	77.0[10]	33.0%	1.3%	0.96	Division	

Vermont	74.3	21.2%	1.3%	1.53	Division	
Oklahoma	68.4[11]	6.2%	0.2%	2.48	Division	X
Iowa	67.3	17.2%	0.2%	4.91	Division	X
Arizona	64.4	0.6%	< 0.1%	0.42	SA	
Idaho	58.9	2.2%	0.1%	2.90	SA	
Arkansas	54.4	10.7%	0.2%	2.34	Division	X
Alabama	48.0	9.1%	0.1%	1.01	Division	
Montana	46.5	0.8%	< 0.1%	2.56	Division	
Kentucky	45.0	18.5%	0.2%	1.46	SA	X
Connecticut	34.0	14.0%	1.1%	2.63	Division	X
Kansas	32.2[12]	22.2%	< 0.1%	2.40	Division	
Hawaii	30.0	2.0%	0.7%	2.06	Division	X
Louisiana	29.2	2.0%	0.1%	0.38	Division	
Delaware	26.5	23.1%	2.1%	6.15	Division	
Mississippi	23.6	2.2%	< 0.1%	0.35	Division	
North Dakota	21.3[13]	2.3%	< 0.1%	1.98	SA	
Rhode Island	8.2	14.7%	1.2%	7.68	Division	
Total U.S.	11,790.5	5.9%; not including trust lands 19.4%	0.5%	NA	NA	
Total U.S. (including special status parks)	14,887.2	7.4%; not including trust lands 24.5%	0.7%	NA	NA	

Data sources: See appendix.

[1] Includes state parks, state recreation areas, state trails, and state historical sites.

[2] The regular park system is embedded within the Department of Agriculture, Conservation, and Forestry, but Baxter, the very large special status park, is governed by a stand-alone agency, the Baxter State Park Authority.

[3] Of the acreage, 71,032 acres is leased.

[4] Indiana's state park system prominently includes state reservoirs, many of which are leased from the Army Corps of Engineers. Overall, 56% of the system's acres are leased.

[5] Includes 18,300 leased acres

[6] Only 6,235 acres of this is state owned; the rest is leased.

[7] Includes 3,863 acres of easements on private land.

[8] Of this total, 57,845 acres are leased, much of it from the federal government.

[9] About 14,000 acres of South Carolina state park land is leased, much of it from the Army Corps of Engineers.

[10] Includes 7,209 acres of easements. State parks and state forests in New Hampshire are all part of the same system of state reservations, and because many parks allow logging, the differences between the two categories are far more subtle than in most states. In fact, the Division of Forestry, rather than the Division of Parks, is the lead administrator in some New Hampshire state park units.

[11] Approximately two-thirds of Oklahoma's state park system is leased, much of it from federal lands.

[12] Almost the entire Kansas state park system is on leased land.

[13] About half of the North Dakota park system is leased.

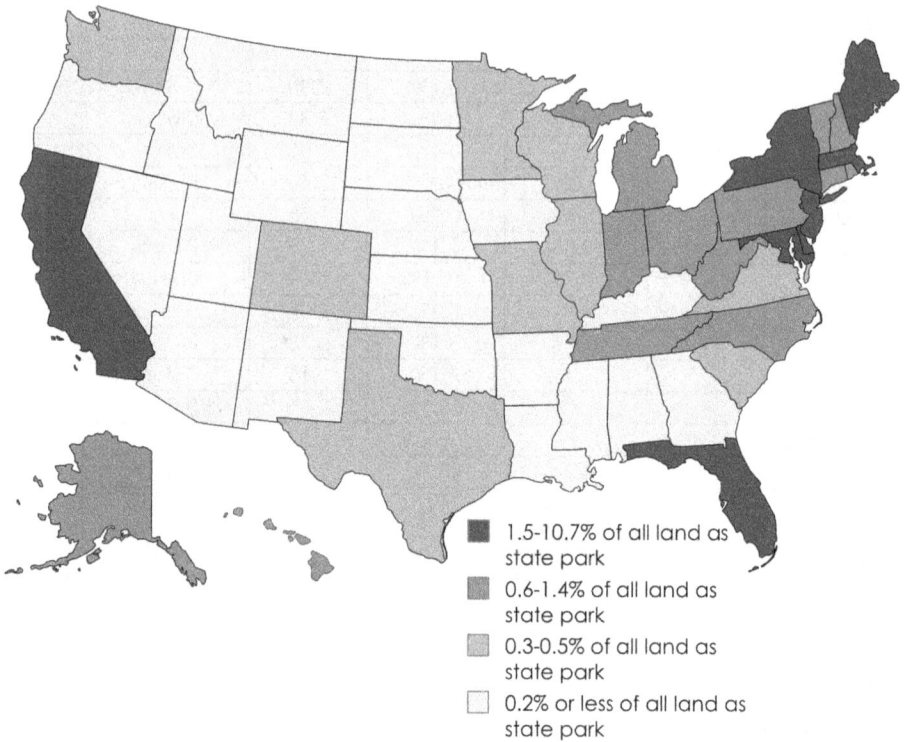

Figure 2.1 State park systems as percentage of all land in state
(Data sources: See Table 2.1 and appendix.)

Wyoming, and Indiana, with substantial leased acreage that accounts for between half to nearly all of their park system's land (details are noted within Table 2.1 and its notes).

A Brief History of the State Park Movement

The history of state parks has an arc quite similar to that of the national parks. In fact, these histories directly intersect in the case of Yosemite, which in 1864 became one of the very first places the federal government ever set aside to preserve before it was promptly ceded to the state of California.[12] The latter's disastrous mismanagement, however, led to an eventual refederalization, which was completed by 1906. Much like the federal government, some states in the post–Civil War era began to set aside certain lands that retained outstanding natural beauty or historical significance. Because so much land in the East was in private hands, this often meant acquisition rather than mere retention of land already owned—a much more complicated, expensive, and ambitious task. Also, like the federal government in those early days, these reserved lands existed in a sort of limbo: a hodgepodge of individual sites with no official status, managing agencies, or clear political mandates. According to Landrum, when it dawned on the states how expensive and complicated it would be to run a state park system, many held off and clamored instead for new national parks in their states.[13]

It was not until Niagara Falls State Park was formally created in 1885 that state parks came to assume the form we recognize today.[14] States found themselves, at the cusp of the new century, poised to move beyond their haphazard collection of individual tracts and consider building more coherent park systems. All this park-building ferment was tapping into the same river of progressive political reformism that was flowing through the national conservation movement. "The tie that binds state park advocates, who often were widely separated by geography and sometimes unaware of activities outside their own states," notes historian Rebecca Conard, "was political progressivism; that is, positive state interference to improve society."[15] In a country in which private property was considered an exalted and sacred right, this call for collectively held lands to be scientifically managed in the public interest was something of a revolutionary idea. Since progressivism was strongest as a political movement in the Northeast and Midwest, states in those regions, like Michigan, Minnesota, Wisconsin, Pennsylvania, and New Jersey, were the most active early adopters of the state park idea.[16] None proved more of a leader, however, than New York.

In 1885, the same year that it established the first official state park, New York also created the boundaries of the Adirondack and Catskill forest preserves in response to the rapid despoliation of these rugged wilderness lands by lumber interests. Unfortunately, this rather weak designation did little to stop the logging in these areas, especially given the lawlessness and intimidation that were rampant in the region.[17] In 1892, the Adirondack Park was formally created by the state legislature, but continuing controversies over logging and development within its boundaries led to the adoption two years later of Article XIV in the New York State Constitution[18] pertaining to the Adirondack and Catskill preserves:

> The lands of the state, now owned or hereafter acquired, constituting the forest preserve as now fixed by law, shall be forever kept as wild forest land. They shall not be leased, sold, or exchanged, or be taken by any corporation, public or private, nor shall the timber thereon be sold, removed, or destroyed.[19]

To this day, this article is considered perhaps the strongest, clearest, and most preservation-oriented land protection mandate in the world. It is also a document that could only have come out of the Progressive Era.

By 1900, the state park movement really began to pick up momentum, and within two decades, the number of established state park systems climbed to around 19.[20] Much like the efforts of John Muir, Stephen Mather, and Horace Albright in relentlessly advocating for the national parks, state park entrepreneurialism depended heavily on the obsessive focus of a diverse band of civic-minded visionaries drawn from business, academia, and public service.[21] Where state parks' growth flourished, it was often due to these patrons and activists like Thomas McBride in Iowa, Ralph Smith in California, Robert Sawyer in Oregon, and Richard Lieber in Indiana.[22]

The first annual National Conference on State Parks held in 1921 in Des Moines is considered by many state park historians as the most important catalyst of the state parks movement and a real watershed.[23] Within a decade after the conference, the number of established state park systems, according to Landrum, had risen to 30, with most of the remaining states in various planning stages.[24] The event was organized by Stephen Mather, the first director of the National Park Service (NPS), and he had several motivations to push for such a meeting. He sincerely wanted the NPS to be the "big sibling" to state park systems by consulting, sharing know-how, and acting as an information clearinghouse.[25] As such, the state park idea and the national park idea were to form a complementary partnership. But Mather was also under constant pressure from congressmen wanting new national parks in their districts, something many state governments coveted as well. He felt this would overwhelm and dilute the top-tier, world-class park system he was trying to create.[26] And because national parks tended to be isolated and distant, something else was needed to fill the gaps and more readily serve the people—and that something was state parks. In fact, one of the rallying cries of the conference came to be "a state park every hundred miles."[27] Although the vision dominating the conference in 1921 was firmly progressive and preservationist, from this slogan one can, incidentally, glimpse the future as the seeds of the idea of parks as tools of economic development and mass tourism would take root from this slogan.

After the 1921 conference, state parks could largely be seen as emulating the NPS model and mirroring its mission and organizational philosophy, albeit on a less grand scale. At this tail end of the Progressive Era, they also found themselves, not surprisingly, subject to and influenced by the very same political and social undercurrents that shaped the NPS. Both Conard in her study of Iowa parks and Cox in his history of the parks of the Pacific Northwest, though, point out that the state parks were not merely the "lesser clones"[28] of national parks but also the product of rather unique and particular sets of influences "shaped by the purely local."[29] As an example, Cox explains why the South was such a latecomer to the parks movement:

> In the South, poverty, traditions of limited government, the weakness of transcendentalism . . . and the pastoral-plantation idea that extolled the country estate rather than unsullied nature, combined to discourage participation in the state parks movement.[30]

Southern state park systems were distinct not only in their grudging adoption of the very state park idea but also in their fervent application of racial apartheid to those parks in the Jim Crow era.[31] At first, African Americans were categorically excluded from most state parks in the South. So egregious was this exclusion that it could not even be expected to satisfy even the most cynical application of the *separate but equal* doctrine, a fact that the NAACP thought made state parks especially vulnerable to legal challenge. And so, in the face of mounting legal pressure, southern states began, decades later, a parallel park system for black people—one that was vastly inferior by every metric of quantity, quality, and infrastructure.[32]

By the 1930s, control of the state parks movement began to shift from its earlier visionary patrons to professional bureaucratic organizations as institutional capacity built. The Great Depression of that era proved at first to be an obvious financial curse but then a far greater blessing for state parks as New Deal relief programs came to channel huge amounts of labor and resources for infrastructure and park improvement.[33] The projects of the Civilian Conservation Corps (CCC) were the perfect marriage of need and opportunity. Although coordinated by the NPS, CCC projects benefited states to a far greater extent, with 475 CCC camps toiling away in state parks at the peak in 1935.[34] The CCC spent a third of a billion dollars at the time on building trails, roads, lodges, cabins, and campgrounds, many of which are still in use today.[35] Not only did the CCC experience radically change and modernize the parks' physical infrastructure, but it also forced the parks to professionalize and get more organized in order to meet the requirements imposed by the funding.[36]

While World War 2, with its gas rationing and wartime restrictions, put a temporary halt to this explosion in park development and expansion, this subdued period would not last long as the postwar era would soon usher in an age of increased mobility, suburbanization, and prosperity that would see demand for state parks skyrocket.[37] The period between the 1950s and

1970s saw unparalleled growth for the state parks, with even the last reluctant stragglers, like Arizona, Utah, Alaska, and Kansas, creating new parks and park systems.[38] The last vestiges of Jim Crow were also rooted out of southern park systems during this era due to court rulings and the federal Civil Rights Act. This acquisition bonanza was partly driven, as previously mentioned, by yet another program of cooperative federalism—the Land and Water Conservation Fund, which pumped several billion dollars into acquisition until it was mothballed during the Reagan administration.[39]

This "golden age" for parks was to come to an abrupt and painful end with the recession of 1981 and the dramatically changing ideological and budgetary climate. Almost instantly, vigorous park expansion and mostly adequate budgets gave way to financial crisis, austerity, outsourcing, neglect, and disinvestment.[40] Throughout all this, the state parks were no less loved and no less used, it is just that the commitment to the ideal seems to have weakened among policymakers as ideological winds shifted and political polarization grew. The ramifications of these changes on the financing and operation of state parks are explored further on in this chapter.

The unprecedented explosion in demand for state park recreation during the pandemic may offer an opening for change as policymakers are reminded what popular and irreplaceable assets their park systems are. Meanwhile, the massive transfers of unrestricted federal aid to the states in the American Rescue Plan Act of 2021 have offered, at least to those states that have applied any of those funds to their parks, a reprieve from the starvation budgets of the last decade and a much-needed jolt of maintenance and infrastructure funding.[41] Whether this reprieve proves to be temporary respite or the start of a new era for state parks remains to be seen.

Paying for Parks—Budgets, Revenue, and Austerity

State park finances are difficult to summarize as there is wild variation in how the 50 states fund their systems. The budget processes that underlie these finances are also, according to Landrum, the single most important external political influence on park management.[42] Overall, in 2018, states collectively spent $2.85 billion on operations plus an additional $1.1 billion on capital expenditures.[43] They offset this with $1.4 billion in revenue, much but not all of which is earmarked to go back to the park systems' budgets.[44] This is a far greater ratio of revenue to expenditure than at the NPS, which brings in only $1 for every $10 it spends.[45] One of the reasons that revenues are so much higher on state land is to make up for the collapse of budget support from states' general funds. In 1990, general fund support made up 59.1% of state park budgets across the U.S., but by 2015, this had dropped to 31.2%.[46] On the other side of the ledger, park-generated revenues went from 30.6% to 42.5% of park budgets during that same period.[47]

Adjusting for inflation, total state-contributed funding for operations and capital declined from $3.74 billion in 2006 to $2.59 billion in 2017, or 30.7%.[48] At least 3 states, New Hampshire, South Carolina, and Wisconsin, have gone a step further and ended all state funding for operational park budgets.[49] Wisconsin, which had long been on the vanguard of the state parks movement, offers an especially dramatic case study of this trend in declining state support. It went from a legally mandated general fund support level of 50% in the 1990s to 21% in 2013 after the mandate was repealed down to zero today.[50] At the other end of the spectrum, 14 states, including New York, North Carolina, Kentucky, Tennessee, Massachusetts, and Connecticut, still fund at least 50% of their state parks' budgets through general revenue, though this is not necessarily a guarantee against severe cuts.[51]

As previously mentioned, there are all sorts of variations in what combination of funds states use to support their parks. On average, park-generated revenue is now the single largest piece at 42.5%, followed by 31.2% general fund support, 18.6% dedicated funds, 1.4% federal grants, and 6.4% made up of other things such as donations or leases.[52] Dedicated funds offer states a potentially attractive alternative to general fund support. Whether through legislation or voter-approved referenda, the majority of states have created at least some dedicated lines of funding earmarked for parks.[53] These can be a share of general sales tax (Minnesota, Arkansas, and Missouri) or, more typically, excise taxes or fees on things like real estate transfers, sporting goods, vanity license plates, plastic bags, tobacco, gasoline, tax return check-off boxes, oil leasing, and ATV, snowmobile, and boat registrations.[54] Minnesota, Oregon, Arizona, and Colorado earmark a share of lottery proceeds.[55] An interesting proposal in Arizona, meanwhile, would have the state park system named as an official institutional beneficiary of the state's extensive trust land revenues along with the K–12 schools, universities, hospitals, and prisons that are already named.[56]

Dedicated funds are not a panacea in terms of expanding the amount of overall park funding. In fact, at least seven states have used their dedicated funding lines to completely withdraw from general fund contributions.[57] And even where this has not occurred, there has still generally been, according to Margaret Walls, a "dollar for dollar" swap with the general fund. Instead, their benefit has been to stabilize and secure funding and make it less vulnerable to the unpredictably wild swings that characterize general funding.[58] One observer notes that Oregon, with its lottery revenues, was one of the few states whose parks did not suffer in the Great Recession due to this sort of insulation.[59] Certainly, if a legislature is craven or desperate enough, they can raid and divert a dedicated funding line, as happened to Arizona's lottery-fed Heritage Fund in the 1990s,[60] but policymakers tend to be far more loath to do this than simply turn down the flow of general funds. This is especially true of dedicated funding lines that were established by voters through referenda or constitutional amendment such as in Arkansas, Colorado, Michigan, Minnesota, and Missouri.[61]

Special taxing districts are another idea that deserves consideration as they are perhaps the gold standard for dedicated funds and the stability and predictability they bring. Although they do not exist at the state level, there are 1,440 special park districts at the county and local level in the U.S. that have been granted their own property tax levying powers.[62] Perhaps the most prominent of these are the county forest preserve districts of northeastern Illinois around Chicago. These districts were authorized by Illinois law in 1893, and they have used these stable and politically insulated taxing powers to build one of the largest and most beloved urban wildlands systems in the U.S. at 178,000 acres.[63]

Critics of dedicated funds come at them from several angles. Some do not like the seemingly random disconnect between a focused tax or fee and the beneficiary, which they claim harms the broader public's "buy-in."[64] Why should lottery players or smokers or those with vanity plates have to bear a disproportionate burden for the parks all can enjoy? Also, even if the tax or fee is more logically connected to public land but too narrowly targeted (i.e., ATV licenses or hunting equipment), according to Walls, this might create a loud and focused sub-constituency who feels their extra taxation gives them greater say (as in, "What do you mean I can't ride my ATV across these fragile dunes? I pay for this park!").[65] For this reason, if dedicated funds must be raised, she prefers they be broadbased, like a guaranteed cut of general sales tax revenue.[66] Finally, free market economists do not like dedicated funding lines because they feel that a guaranteed levy interferes with society's decision-making on what the optimal provision level of some good should be.[67] However, as obvious public goods, state parks are likely already subject to a disconnect between demand and level of provisioning whereby their adequate supply requires government action. Therefore, the underprovisioning of parks (specifically, the deep cutting of general fund support despite rising visitation) already is a fundamentally *political*, not economic, consideration.

Park-Generated Revenue and Equity

While dedicated funds offer policy analysts a tempting array of possible alternatives, it is park-generated revenue that has been the fastest growing segment of park budgets, and this has had severe ramifications on the park experience. This solution, long the favorite of free market–aligned policymakers, requires that park managers run their parks more like a business and attempt to monetize as many aspects of their parks as possible through entrance fees, trail passes, enhanced lodging, and other amenities. While the average annual park pass in the U.S. was $59 in 2018, some states, like Kansas, California, and Alabama, charge close to $200.[68] On the other hand, 11 states charge no entrance fee at all (see Table 2.1 for details). Other states have tried to be even more creative. In New Hampshire, with no general or dedicated fund support, internally generated revenue is the main source of the budget, and a full 30% of that comes from a network of retail stores selling a wide variety of goods in parks, campgrounds, and beaches.[69] In Wisconsin, an idea was floated, but never ultimately adopted, to sell corporate naming rights and sponsorships for revenue.[70]

The two problems with the revenue-only model, according to critics, are its overall unsustainability and its costs to equity and access. Regarding the former, critics assert that "no state park system has been able to fund operations and capital development through park revenue over the long term."[71] Any system that attempts to do so will inevitably fail, either requiring eventual inputs of public funding or else floundering and limping along only through the added efforts of volunteers, nonprofits, and local communities. This is because parks are not *just* consumer attractions but also quality-of-life amenities and storehouses of tremendous ecological service. As such, they are *public goods*, like schools, libraries, or lighthouses, which, by definition, cannot be provided by the market alone. Much as fire departments cannot be expected to raise their own revenue, state parks offer many extremely valuable but hard-to-monetize benefits and services and involve, according to critics, "capitalism-resistant" activities like hiking, biodiversity protection, or wild solitude.[72] To *truly* pay for themselves through revenue alone and capture all costs without turning themselves into something that is decidedly *not* a state park (but rather a mall, amusement park, or resort), they would need to charge exorbitant entrance fees, especially for the more isolated or lesser used parks, that would, according to one analyst's study, run into the many hundreds of dollars just to get in.[73]

This brings us to the second criticism regarding equity and access. Charging fees, especially high ones structured to meet budget needs, unavoidably rations use, and this burden, of course, falls most heavily upon the less affluent. As such, argues Thomas More, "fees are socially regressive. . . . As fees rise, the remaining public money simply subsidizes the already comfortably well-off; fees sap the social importance of parks."[74] The state parks movement at the turn of the 20th century most certainly did not articulate a vision of scenic beauty, recreation, and rejuvenation for just the upper middle class and rich people who could afford it, a point made by Landrum when referring to a total free market approach to setting fees:

> Such specious ideas miss the point of having a public park system in the first place, and, if actually implemented, would do great violence to the concept of maintaining a balanced park system (including areas with no revenue-producing potential) readily accessible to all people (the deprived as well as the affluent).[75]

This former director of the Florida State Park system goes on to declare that "state parks are not a business; they do not exist to make money."[76] A Tennessee state senator, in a debate over whether to allow outsourcing of park operations and the fee increases that were nearly certain to follow, agrees with Landrum, arguing that state parks "should not have that impersonal, profiteering kind of feeling. . . . If we make it overly expensive for working families to enjoy it, we're neglecting one of the primary purposes of state parks."[77]

Walls notes that the rationing of use through increased entrance fees is also inefficient if it keeps people out of parks that have spare capacity.[78] In response, some argue for demand pricing whereby people are charged higher fees to use certain immensely popular park units while keeping the quieter parks' fees lower.[79] It should be noted, however, that high-demand state parks tend to be near more crowded urban areas, and this raises a whole different set of equity issues around race and class and mobility. This becomes an especially urgent topic given the history of racial segregation and exclusion in certain state park systems in decades past. A parallel issue can be found regarding the price of park lodging where straight-on supply-and-demand pricing has long prevailed and it is not now at all unusual to have to pay many hundreds of dollars per night for cabins and lodge rooms.[80] Needless to say, this amenity and the experience that goes with it is currently off-limits to a great many, perhaps most, park users.

Hard Times in a New Ideological Landscape

Looking back at the history of state parks, changing macroeconomic conditions can only explain part of the shift from relatively stable budgets to the near-perpetual crisis of the last few decades. There has also been a clearly discernible ideological shift in attitudes among legislators and policymakers (much more so than the general public) toward market-based pieties and away from commitments to the collective provision of public goods. There has been, therefore, movement away from the ideal that state parks, like schools and libraries, are profoundly valuable community resources and not mere luxuries to be jettisoned or handed over to private markets at the first sign of budget stress.

State parks make up a minuscule 0.16% of all state budget outlays,[81] and yet they are routinely one of the very first areas to be cut, and often to an extent disproportionate to overall budget reductions. As such, state park systems perpetually find themselves as the "low-hanging fruit" at budget reduction time instead of the bigger-ticket items that account for the other 99.84% of the states' budgets. This seeming expendability of valuable state park systems does not seem to make much sense in light of their heavy ongoing usage and tremendous popularity. Perhaps, though, this could be at least partly explained by the fact that the base of support for parks is overly broad and diffuse. A narrow and focused constituency, on the other hand, might have a much easier time organizing and mobilizing and extracting direct political costs if their demands go unheard, as Mancur Olson and others have long argued.[82] Despite all they may mean to people, state parks do not seem to rise to a level of immediate issue salience and potency of the sort that gives legislative budget cutters pause or any fear of political retribution. Instead, they seem to have become a go-to place for cuts.

Since the 1980s, the state park budget situation has ranged from bad to worse. Declining budgets have coupled with rising demand and increased maintenance costs as old infrastructure from the New Deal or the 1960s boom begins to deteriorate. We are "coasting on the fumes of the investments we made in the '60s and 70's," claims Michigan's DNR director.[83] On top of this, climate change promises to impose even greater costs. Jordan Smith and colleagues calculate that every 1% increase in visitation adds approximately $26.16 of costs per acre of parkland while every 1% increase in average annual mean temperature will bring another $11.51 in costs per acre.[84] Because the budget trend has been flat or declining, he and his co-authors forecast a "dire" outlook for state park systems.[85]

In good economic times, this situation is barely tenable, but in economic downturns, it is downright catastrophic and has resulted in a relentless decline in park systems' human capital, infrastructure, and the visitor experience. The estimated $95 billion backlog in state park maintenance that has developed is just the tip of the iceberg.[86] This downward spiral reached its nadir between 2009 and 2012, the years bracketing the Great Recession and the severe budget crises that ensued. No state was hit harder than California, with a 40% reduction in general fund contributions, a $75 million budget cut in 2012 alone, and an estimated $1 billion in deferred maintenance.[87] Staffing, meanwhile, was cut to 1979 levels even though the system had grown by 500,000 acres and 10 million users since then.[88] In the 2011–2012 budget, after a referendum to increase vehicle fees (for parks) was defeated, Governor Brown put forward a proposal to indefinitely close 70 state parks, a quarter of the system.[89]

Meanwhile, in the state of Washington, the 2009 state park operating budget was slashed from $100 million to $48 million as general fund support dropped from $97 million to $17 million in just three budget cycles.[90] "The future," according to a member of the Washington Parks Commission, "is not in public funding."[91] If this is true, then Wisconsin parks, cut off from all general and dedicated funds, offer a glimpse into that future. At High Cliff, a fairly large and popular state park, six full-time employees have been whittled down after the cuts to a single person who serves as both the superintendent and the only ranger.[92] According to this lone permanent employee, this has led to a "constant triage" of dealing with litter, uncut lawns in picnic and camping areas, and deferred maintenance on pipes and electrical systems.[93] He goes on:

> The quality isn't there. There's a lot of stuff that falls through the cracks. It's just the ripple effect of that. If you don't have people to do the job, then things don't get done.[94]

Similarly, Rhode Island park staff between 1989 and 2018 declined from 123 full time equivalent (FTE) to 42, or 67%.[95] Since 2000, Mississippi has cut spending by 60% and staffing by 70%.[96] Meanwhile, most Iowa state parks, like the one in Wisconsin, currently have only one FTE. Making matters worse, the Iowa legislature cut park budgets but would not allow any increases in park-generated revenue to compensate.[97] Research by environmental economists has long identified labor as the "key input" in assuring recreational productivity and satisfaction; without an adequate labor supply, they argue, the entire system breaks down.[98]

Some park systems have responded to budget crises with proposals even more dire than staff cuts or deferred maintenance. In addition to California, the states of Oklahoma, Mississippi, and Alaska have all seriously considered permanently closing parks, while other states authorized or proposed energy development or logging projects that might be appropriate for multiple use lands but are generally unheard of for state parks. For example, in 2011, Colorado leased St. Vrain State Park to Anadarko for oil production.[99] Ohio allows coal mining in Barkcamp State Park, while West Virginia, Ohio, and Pennsylvania have all employed horizontal drilling beneath some of their state parks.[100] West Virginia legislators also recently proposed a bill to allow logging in their state parks to raise revenue for maintenance, but this was defeated after strong public backlash.[101] Perhaps the most extreme case has been North Dakota, where exemptions granted at the highest levels of state government allowed Conoco-Phillips to drill six oil wells inside Little Missouri State Park. The wells have overwhelmed the park with the noise, infrastructure, floodlights, and pollution of their 24/7 operation. "They've trashed it," said one local conservationist.[102]

Nice Park You Got Here—Shame if Something Happened to It

In the face of such debilitating challenges, state parks have come to lean heavily on an important asset—the love and binding commitment that ordinary people feel toward their favorite parks. This support manifests itself most prominently in the form of so-called "Friends" groups, which consists of ordinary citizens who organize around their local state park and volunteer with upkeep, campgrounds, educational programming, and fundraising for capital expenses and supplies. As park staff numbers continue to decline to completely unsustainable levels, superintendents have come to increasingly rely on Friends groups. Nowhere is this trend further along, not surprisingly, than Wisconsin, which is the only state to have an organized Friends group for every single state park unit.[103] In Wisconsin, this volunteer labor equals 70 full-time employees and has resulted in over $100 million in donations over the years.[104] In the face of Wisconsin's audacious defunding of its state park system, it is clear that without volunteers, the whole thing would fall apart. The High Point superintendent notes the critical role of volunteers but also the inherent limitations of this setup:

> I can't express the gratitude I have for volunteers because they are keeping it going . . . but it's just not reliable. You can't run a business on volunteers. And there's only so much you can do as a volunteer.[105]

Friends groups are now so ubiquitous and vital to the functioning of Wisconsin parks that the DNR's parks division has even come to incorporate a process of tight coordination that includes running these groups through a kind of accreditation program and training for fundraising.[106]

From one angle, this can play as a feel-good story of civic-minded good citizens rushing to the defense of their beloved state parks and toiling for love and not money to keep them whole. But viewed from a different angle, this can be seen as a deeply cynical ploy by legislators to cut spending and foist what should be an accountable and collective responsibility onto unpaid labor. They do this by leveraging peoples' deep emotional attachment and then holding the much-loved parks hostage until those same people agree to provide this free labor. As Jodi Peterson puts it,

> These strapped state governments appear to be relying on the fact that everyone loves parks and that it's much more likely that communities and donors will pitch in to keep a park open than to pay for, say, road repair. A state dollar saved on parks is a dollar that can be used to plug a hole elsewhere.[107]

A variation on this theme is when local governments are put in a position to pitch in for or even fully take over the operation of parks they feel are vital to their well-being. Indeed, when Oklahoma announced the closing of seven state park units in 2011, municipal and tribal governments stepped up to rescue all of them.[108] And yet, what town or county or reservation, especially in rural areas, has more solid finances than their state does? It is simply passing along the burden to pay for public goods further down the food chain to the level of government with probably the least capacity to take on added expenses.

Likewise, California's threat to close 70 of its state parks in 2012 was defused for some of those units only after various nonprofits and local governments entered into operating agreements with the state.[109] In Alaska, the state had slated to close three parks in the Valdez area in 2015 but ended up signing a contract with a nonprofit, Valdez Adventure Alliance, to run the parks and keep the estimated $5 million that the parks pumped annually into the local economy flowing. Funding the operation, however, was quite a challenge for a small nonprofit, and it took quite a bit of fundraising and grant writing.[110]

For last-ditch efforts to save beloved parks and keep local recreational economies afloat, local government, nonprofits, or Friends group interventions are crucial, but they are not a sustainable solution or any kind of substitute for the sort of budget fixes that would bring stability and accountability back to state park finances. These local actors simply do not have the financial wherewithal to permanently run chunks of our failing state park systems. And even if they did, this would still create the precedent of private money not just supplementing or enhancing public funds but replacing them altogether, thereby allowing state governments to essentially wash their hands of the matter. To make matters worse, this would most likely lead to a two-tiered park structure whereby parks in places with "Friends" who have access to resources get saved while those serving poorer, more isolated, or less politically mobilized communities get neglected or shut down.

STATE PARKS: *Spotlight on New York*

When it comes to state parks, New York, the home of America's first state park at Niagara Falls, is in a class by itself. Its regular park system, with 350,000 acres spread across 250 units (and 178 actual state parks), is the sixth-largest system in the U.S. in terms of absolute acreage. Add to this a one-of-a-kind, 2.9-million-acre parallel system of wilderness parks in the Adirondacks and Catskills and New York can be considered nothing less than a parks juggernaut with nearly 11% of the state's entire land mass covered by state-owned park land—a figure no other state comes close to.

The Regular Park System

New York's conventional state park system is administered by an independent parks agency, the Office of Parks, Recreation, and Historical Preservation (OPRHP), which in turn is overseen by a 14-member State Council of Parks. This independent commission style of administration has most likely shielded the agency to some extent from political interference and perhaps enhanced its political clout within New York state government. With 2,087 full-time and 4,500 seasonal employees,[1] the agency has a mission statement that commits it to "be responsible stewards of our valuable natural, historical, and cultural resources,"[2] and this has required a very tricky balancing act of recreation and access on one hand and preservation on the other. In service to the former goal, the OPRHP maintains 26 golf courses, 36 swimming pools, 27 marinas, 40 boat launches, 25 nature centers, 958 cabins and cottages, and 8,555 campsites.[3]

The New York state park system stands out among its peers for its strong emphasis on accessibility and equity. In fact, according to the park council's annual report, its strategic priorities are as follows:

> To expand diverse and equitable access to parks so that people from all communities and across all ages and abilities are included and can fully experience parks and historic sites . . . we support the agency's diversity, equity and inclusion initiative which seeks to reach new park users, promote access, and diversify the workforce. Additionally, we support the . . . effort to ensure that the state's historic sites embrace narratives that reflect the diversity of our state and nation's history.[4]

These efforts include the "Get Outside and Get Together," "Connect Kids to Parks," and "Ladders to the Outdoors" initiatives, which all seek to expand the park experience to diverse, underserved, and younger segments of the population.[5]

The attempts to enhance accessibility in the state parks seem to have paid off, with visitation growing from 57.9 million in 2011 to 79.5 million a decade later in 2021—the second-highest visitation figure in the country. In fact, Niagara Falls State Park logs more visits than Yosemite and Grand Canyon combined.[6] This upward trend might have also been helped by the passage in 2015 of NY Parks 2020, a huge multiyear $900 million infusion of capital investment earmarked to rebuild and expand park infrastructure.[7] Overall, New York has shown a much more steadfast and durable commitment to its state parks than many other states. In 2022, New York had an all-funds (operating and capital) budget of $462 million,[8] one of the highest in the country. According to Walls, it is also one of only a handful of states in which general funds make up more than 50% of the park system budget,[9] reflecting a fairly strong and consistent statewide commitment to the ongoing vitality of what is seen as an essential public good. The rest of New York's park system budget comes from revenue generation (mostly entrance and recreation fees), a real estate transfer tax, a plastic bag fee, and some very strong support from private foundations, conservancies, and other partnerships. In fact, New York (and New York City) have long been at the forefront of cultivating donor relationships in the private sector that have benefitted park finances.[10] It is important to point out, however, that even a state so generally supportive of its parks suffered through the very same period of severe budget crisis in 2009–2010 that afflicted so many other states and their park systems. By the spring of 2010, New York had temporarily closed some parks and had drawn up plans to shut down a further 40% of the parks in the system through the summer. Only a last-minute funding deal in the legislature just before Memorial Day kept the parks open that year.[11]

Another way that New York stands out regarding its parks is the extent to which the state government seems to be fully cognizant and appreciative of the broader economic value generated by the system. In fact, this might explain why New York still maintains as much general fund budget support as it does while so many other states have backed away. A 2017 study measuring the economic spin-off value (but not ecosystem service value) of just the regular 350,000-acre park system found that the impact of both visitor spending and state funding together created 54,000 jobs, $5 billion in spending, and $2.9 billion in increased GDP (or $3.7 billion in 2024 dollars).[12]

Special Status Parks

While its popular and well-supported regular park system would alone make New York a leader, it also is blessed with a unique and quite massive parallel system containing millions of acres of wild land in the Adirondack and Catskill Mountains. As discussed earlier in this chapter, the New York legislature created the massive Adirondack Park in 1892 in an attempt to get a grip on the widespread and ruinous deforestation that was spreading throughout the region. When that did not seem to do enough to halt the destruction, the New York Constitution was subsequently amended to permanently protect the forest from logging and keep it "forever wild."[13] Over the years, Adirondack Park's boundaries have been enlarged to now include 5.8 million acres in a unique public-private matrix that forms one of the largest individual parks in the whole country. Within the famed "blue line" delineating the park boundary is about 2.7 million constitutionally protected acres of state land, while the rest is private land, though more heavily zoned and regulated than outside the boundary. About 130,000 permanent residents and 200,000 seasonal ones live in farms and towns scattered within the park's boundaries.[14] In 1904, a similar park (also with constitutional protection) was established in the Catskills with a combination of wild state land (288,000 acres), New York City watershed lands, and private lands within its roughly 700,000-acre boundary area.[15]

While New York's conventional state park system heavily stresses access and recreation, its special status parks (because of their size, wildness, and the state constitution) are all about preservation and very traditional low-impact forms of recreation that do not require much infrastructure. In fact, of Adirondack Park's 2.7 million acres of state-owned land, about half exist as stringently protected statutory wilderness areas (see Chapter 3) and the other half as slightly less restrictive *wild forest* (which allows for motorized conveyance). For these reasons, the Adirondack and Catskill Parks have considerably smaller budgets than the regular park system as there is not nearly as much to actively "manage." They each draw about 12 million annual visitors, which, while impressive, pales in comparison to the regular park system, which draws 3 times the people on 10 times less land.[16] However, one area of recreation that is well developed on the special status parks are campgrounds, with roughly 7,000 campsites, which, when combined with the OPRHP's 8,555 sites, makes New York the undisputed champion of state park camping.[17]

While Adirondack Park is not exactly a state park in the traditional sense, it is certainly not any kind of multiple use land given its stringent ecological protections and wilderness character. Its management is split between the Adirondack Park Agency (APA), a small, independent bureau created in 1971, and the Department of Environmental Conservation (DEC), a large agency that also manages state forests and state wildlife areas. The APA is responsible for comprehensive planning, permitting, and land use, while the DEC manages the park at ground level regarding things like trails, camping, hunting and fishing, and boating regulations.[18] The Catskill Park, meanwhile, is run entirely by the DEC. Interestingly, the OPRHP plays no role in managing either special status park.

NOTES

1. New York State Council of Parks, Recreation, and Historic Preservation, *Annual Report 2022* (Report, February 2023), p. 5.

2. Office of Parks, Recreation, and Historic Preservation, *Mission Statement and Guiding Principles* (Policy Directive GOV-POL-001, October 7, 2014), available at: https://parks.ny.gov/documents/inside-our-agency/PublicDocuments/GuidancePolicies/MissionStatement.pdf.

3. New York State Council of Parks, Recreation, and Historic Preservation, p. 5.

4. *Ibid.*, p. 3.

5. *Ibid.*, pp. 3, 10.

6. *Ibid.*, p. 5.

7. Office of Parks, Recreation, and Historic Preservation, *Building Better Parks: Update on NY Parks 2020 Progress* (Report, May 3, 2018), p. 1.

8. New York State Council of Parks, Recreation, and Historic Preservation, p. 5.

9. Margaret Walls, *Paying for State Parks: Evaluating Alternative Approaches for the 21st Century* (Resources for the Future Report, January 28, 2013), pp. 6, 10.

10. *Ibid.*, pp. 12, 15, 17–18.

11. Parks and Trails New York, *Protect Their Future: New York's State Parks in Crisis* (Report, November 2010), p. 3.

12. Heidi Garrett-Peltier, *Economic Benefits of the New York State Park System* (Parks and Trails New York Report, August 2017), p. 2.

13. New York Department of Environmental Conservation, *Birth of the Blue Line in the Adirondack and Catskill Parks* (Webpage, undated), available at: https://dec.ny.gov/nature/forests-trees/forest-preserve/birth-of-blue-line-in-adirondack-catskill-parks.

14. Adirondack Council, *About the Adirondack Park* (Webpage, 2023), available at: https://www.adirondackcouncil.org/page/the-adirondack-park-19.html.

15. Catskill Advisory Group, *Catskill Advisory Group Report 2022* (Report, January 4, 2023), p. 2.

16. *Ibid.*, p. 3; Adirondack Council.

17. New York Department of Environmental Conservation, *2023 Summer Recreation Campground Summary* (Fact Sheet, June 29, 2023), available at: https://extapps.dec.ny.gov/docs/permits_ej_operations_pdf/2023facilityinfo.pdf.

18. Adirondack Park Agency, *More about the Adirondack Park . . .* (Webpage, undated), available at: https://apa.ny.gov/About_Park/more_park.html.

Privatization in the State Parks

One of the reasons state parks have been under such budgetary stress has to do with the political winds in the resource management realm shifting since the 1980s toward free market ideologies. It should come as no surprise, then, that for many state policymakers, privatization has become an attractive alternative for their park systems. The term *privatization* can refer to anything from a full-scale sell-off of public assets to contracting with private entities to operate and manage entire state parks to a much more modest outsourcing of various aspects of park operations like food service, retail, campgrounds, or maintenance.[111] The first, most drastic variety has been the least common for state parks, though this remains a coveted goal for the most libertarian-minded legislators and their think-tank allies who worry that state parks "crowd out" private sector provision of recreational opportunities and starve local tax rolls.[112]

On rare occasions, though, proposals do arise to privatize a particularly valuable piece of park that a developer wants or perhaps arrange a land exchange. One example of this would be the periodic efforts of well-connected developers and political donors to gain control of all or parts of New Jersey's Liberty State Park, with its iconic shoreline views of New York City and five million annual visitors; apparently many influential people consider it too valuable a piece of real estate to be "wasted" as a state park.[113] In Wisconsin, meanwhile, the state recently agreed to exchange a forested section of valuable Lake Michigan dunes habitat in a popular state park to a politically powerful donor for a planned golf course on adjacent land for a biologically desolate tract of developed land alongside a road.[114]

At the other end of the spectrum, the softest forms of privatization, such as outsourcing of food and beverage operations and golf course or ski resort amenities, are quite common and have been going on for decades. They tend to not be overly controversial as they involve peripheral functions and the external control of these aspects of park operations does not tend to impact the crucial issues of public access and conservation. It is the remaining form of privatization—a contract to fully operate an entire publicly owned state park (often referred to as the public-private partnership, or PPP, model)—that is both controversial and increasingly put forward as a solution to the perennial problems of state park finances.[115]

To state governments where this has been tried, or at least proposed, including Alabama, West Virginia, Mississippi, Oklahoma, and California, PPP outsourcing is seen as a potentially advantageous way to take the seemingly intractable and ongoing problem of state park funding off their plate. To PPP advocates, unleashing the talents and innovations of market actors will necessarily lead to better-managed parks as they "will figure out ways to provide [park services] once the government gets out of the way," according to one supporter of privatization.[116]

To its advocates, then, PPP is a "win-win" scenario for all concerned. By taking parks off the states' books, it supposedly achieves the financial self-sufficiency that would keep park systems from having to beg hat in hand before the legislature for adequate funding each year. "The less we have to rely on money from the General Assembly," according to one park director, "the more we insulate ourselves."[117] Instead, all financial risk would supposedly shift onto the concessionaire and the state would gain a portion of revenue as "rent" while keeping its parks open and operating well. Privatizers argue that this optimization of operations is because private management is far less top heavy and inefficient than the public sector and brings with it "an infusion of knowledge and capital."[118] Finally, PPP advocates believe that their model has superior accountability in that fully public management is responsible for both service provision and oversight, which inevitably creates a conflict of interest. In a PPP arrangement, on the other hand, the state would retain oversight functions in an outsourcing contract.[119]

Research on outsourcing generally finds mixed results with actual savings quite dependent on the details of the arrangement and what exact service is being outsourced.[120] Also, Argentino Pressoa notes that costs associated with the process of arranging contracts as well as proper oversight are often neglected when evaluating the efficiency of outsourcing.[121] Furthermore, for-profit contractors must not only cover their operating costs but also return dividends to their owners or shareholders. So, if they are actually going to save the state money, this extra profit margin would need to come from somewhere, and that is usually, at least according to critics, at the expense of the quality of service or investments in the physical assets being managed.[122] This is what many jurisdictions' experiences with privatized water or transit systems have shown.[123]

Outsourcing the provision of straightforward services like food, kayak rentals, or lodging seems to offer greater potential for efficiency than outsourcing anything related to public goods and what economists call "natural monopolies" like sewer systems, electricity, or, according to economist Greg Mankiw, the parks themselves, where the initial costs of the infrastructure are prohibitive, rendering true competition illogical, impractical, and largely unattainable.[124] Concessionaires are willing and able to handle food service, souvenir sales, and boat rentals but not those other and more critical aspects of a park like biodiversity, solitude, ecological health, and equitable access. According to Walls, it would be unlikely that any outsourcing contract that was designed to truly take account of and actively protect a park's natural assets and public access would allow a concessionaire to raise enough revenue to make it worth their while.[125] There is really no such thing, then, as a profitable, privately run state park that is focused primarily on natural resource management or any larger public mission. And without these things, Landrum wonders, why would they even still be "regarded as *state* parks anyway?"[126] Indeed, he questions whether privatization initiatives in some states have more to do with ideological compulsions than fiscal prudence.

Another complaint from state park supporters is that concessionaires profit from public amenities acquired and/or built with taxpayer dollars. In one anti-privatization activist's analogy, it is as if "mom and dad are going to give me a stand and a pitcher and some lemonade, some ice and some cups, and I'm going to keep all the money."[127] West Virginia had some prior experience with private operators of their lodges, and, according to a former park superintendent, so little was invested in maintenance that the state later had to replace some buildings. "Concession-run private parks don't work," he claims. "They will leave a broken facility. They get all the revenue and take none of the costs."[128] Since that earlier period of PPP management, the state reinvested heavily in their park system, spending $151 million in capital upgrades since 2017, and as a result, visitation and revenue have surged.[129] And then, almost like clockwork, after all this taxpayer-funded investment, the concessionaires came knocking again. A thus-far-unsuccessful privatization bill (S 485) was introduced in the state senate in 2022 to reintroduce private operations to West Virginia parks. This bill offered few limits or requirements upon the contractors, and its vague language, critics feared, could lead to grossly inappropriate developments inside the parks, such as casinos, racetracks, and amusement parks. It also set no guidelines for lodging or entrance fees.[130] Similarly, a firestorm of protest arose when Tennessee proposed handing over the extremely popular Fall Creek Falls State Park to a private operator. State Senator Janice Bowling responded by reminding her colleagues that they were the "stewards of the real assets of the people of Tennessee. These are not our properties to sell."[131]

A final fear that critics of outsourcing express is that private park operators would cherry-pick the most lucrative and economically viable state parks with high visitation and already developed infrastructure and ignore the rest, which would stay public but languish and perhaps eventually be closed.[132] The reason for this worry is that publicly run systems tend to pool all their revenues so that the "profitable" parks subsidize the rest. In Wisconsin, for example, most of the 74 fee areas in the state park system cost more to run than they make in revenue and are supported by the small handful of parks that pile on the revenue.[133] In a partial outsourcing scheme, those profitable parks' excess revenue would go straight into the contractors' pocket rather than support the whole system.

A 2010 report from the Arizona State Parks Foundation bears out this concern, finding that physically remote parks with low visitation as well as parks with deteriorated or nonexistent infrastructure have very poor prospects for privatization.[134] In the cherry-picking scenario, they become unwanted orphans without a bit of attention paid to whatever non-revenue-generating but still magnificently valuable assets they possess in terms of biodiversity, wilderness values, or aesthetic or historical values. These latter values however are what make parks public goods instead of just revenue-generating investment schemes, and some would argue that providing them is among the core functions of government—exactly the argument of one Mississippi state senator debating a recent park privatization bill in that state:

> We give billions and billions and billions of dollars away to the well-connected, and billions of dollars to out-of-state corporations, but when was the last time we focused on the core functions of government? The pattern plays out—we neglect something, then let a bunch of big boys come in and take over and make a bunch of money.[135]

For all these reasons, then, the critics of privatization claim that what this PPP boosterism offers is far more peril than promise.

Andrew Mowen and colleagues argue that for privatization to ultimately be successful, there must be broad political and public support and buy-in. In a survey of 1,477 Pennsylvania state park visitors, they set out to measure this support and found only the faintest traces of it.[136] Mowen and his colleagues measured peoples' attitudes toward eight potential targets of privatized park management and found that only 1% of respondents wanted all eight areas privatized while 24% wanted none of them privatized.[137] Specifically, between 81% and 94% opposed outsourcing in five of the eight categories: maintenance, environmental education, pool and beach staff, campgrounds, and recreation. The other three areas, watercraft rental, special events, and food and beverage sales, were more evenly split, but only the last category had a majority of support at 55%.[138] Incidentally, the park users were also asked to rate their satisfaction with state parks staff on a 5-point scale. For the categories related to stewardship of the environment and sensitive natural areas and opportunities for public access, the parks scored a collective 4.3 points, which perhaps goes a long way toward explaining people's general hostility to park privatization.[139]

Commercialization or Preservation?
The Dual Mission of State Parks

State parks, like their national counterparts, have always been guided by a dual mandate—preserving nature and wildness while also providing recreation for the people. The official NPS mission statement from 1916 lays out this goal poetically, if also a bit ambiguously, as it instructs the agency to "preserve unimpaired the natural and cultural resources . . . of the national park system for the enjoyment, education, and inspiration of this and future generations."[140] Weighing careful and ecologically sensitive stewardship of park land with access and adequate provision of recreation for the people who collectively own the land has always been a delicate balancing act for all park systems. And it is, of course, a bit of a conundrum in that all park "enjoyment" will, at least to some extent, unavoidably "impair" the natural resources. It takes, therefore, a lot of restraint and care and thoughtfulness to pull off such a complex mandate.

Even if the organizational mission was split, however, it was abundantly clear where state park managers' hearts lay in those early years and at the first state parks conference in 1921. State parks officials were much more enthusiastic about and focused on the preservation side of their mission than the recreation side.[141] In a report for the 1947 state park conference, Indiana parks official Cap Sauers argued that state parks were no place for heavily developed recreation or even flush toilets; he felt that only the most primitive and passive recreation was compatible with the state park mission.[142] Richard Lieber, one of the giants in the state parks movement, likewise warned to not let the "destructive hand of commercialism" damage the state parks.[143] Meanwhile, in 1955, NPS director Conrad Wirth's similar admonition led the National Conference on State Parks to create so-called "vigilance committees" to red-flag "incongruous" developments in any state park systems.[144]

While the NPS, with great difficulty and extended periods of backsliding, has largely pulled off this dual mandate and honored its commitments to preservation, states have been far less successful. Despite their clear preservationist heritage, the strong and unmistakable trend starting in the 1950s and 1960s has been toward the *commercialization* of state parks in which management decisions have tended to favor forms of recreation that are tourism oriented, have high revenue potential, and generally require highly developed infrastructure that negatively impacts the natural systems the park was originally formed to protect. "By the mid-1960s," reports Conard, "park management was geared to accommodate mass recreation, preferably tied to water."[145] And by the 1980s, parks fully entered the era Landrum has coined "Anything Goes."[146] It is now not uncommon to find marinas, resorts, conference centers, restaurants, golf courses, ski facilities, swimming pools, sports facilities, elaborate RV-oriented "improved" campgrounds, and retail stores in state parks across the country. Between just the years 1980 and 2000, there was a 59% increase in lodge rooms, a 65% increase in cabins, and a 33% increase in improved campsites, despite an overall increase in overnight visitation of just 4%.[147] Only five states now have no cabins or lodges in their park system.[148]

According to Landrum, there has been a huge shift in many park systems from traditional *resource-based* recreation (hiking, fishing, camping, photography, birding) to *user-based* recreation (golf, boating, resort stays).[149] The problem is that while the former is inherently related to the places and features the park was created to protect, the latter is a more generic and interchangeable form of recreation (a pool or golf course being pretty much the same anywhere) and related to a brand of mass tourism that caters to a more affluent and comfort-seeking market. According to resource management specialist J. Mark Morgan, "such facilities bear little or no resemblance to the natural resources present at the site."[150] Landrum notes this as well:

> In due course, parks that started out as relatively simple, minimally developed natural areas may undergo a complete transmogrification through the constant addition of new facilities and the introduction of new forms of play. . . . The extraordinary natural and cultural resources that justified creation of the state parks may be all but superseded by an artificially constructed environment like that of a recreational theme park such as Disneyland or Six Flags.[151]

There are a number of underlying reasons for this shift toward commercialization in which park visitors are now seen primarily as consumers and parks as revenue-generating marketplaces. Perhaps most important has been the huge decline in state budget support and the resultant push for park-generated revenue and self-sufficiency discussed earlier in this chapter. This has created a desperate scramble for park managers to monetize everything they can, cut expenses unrelated to revenue, and create new revenue-generating facilities and opportunities as well. In Texas, this incentive structure for park managers is officially known as "entrepreneurial budgeting."[152] Since biodiversity, ecological restoration, or wild solitude cannot effectively raise much or any revenue, they are deprioritized. Making matters worse, notes Morgan, is the fact that in some places, legislators are doing the prioritizing and facilities/infrastructure selection themselves and foisting it upon now subordinate park managers whether they are comfortable with the policy decisions or not.[153] Finally, the previously discussed park privatization schemes that outsource management to concessionaires tend to turbocharge this bias toward revenue generation and high-impact development even more as public sector managers are completely removed from the scene. Beyond the usual resorts and golf courses, one Oklahoma concessionaire even proposed things like movie nights, concerts, farmers' markets, and retail stores,[154] none of which would be out of place in any city's downtown business district. Along those same lines, a federal advisory panel appointed by President Trump, which included representation from a number of private park management firms, recommended Wi-Fi, food trucks, and Amazon delivery hubs.[155]

It is not just budget woes creating this shift, though, as broader historical and cultural factors are also at play. The postwar era, specifically, saw increased affluence and near-universal automobile-based mobility, which has led to the explosive growth of a tourism industry that revenue-conscious park managers now see themselves in competition with.[156] Meanwhile, cultural changes have profoundly altered recreational tastes among an easily bored and distracted populace with a strong taste for fast-paced, high-volume entertainment. So, to state park officials, the competition for the tourist dollar is not a different state or national park down the road but rather the water parks, outlet malls, adventure parks, corn mazes, rock climbing gyms, resorts, and the like, and in the minds of those seeking revenue, primitive camping and quiet hikes are just not going to snag the passing motorist. Not coincidentally, state parks have been integrated into and heavily promoted in state tourism campaigns, and in a few states, the parks themselves have been subsumed into the tourism departments of state government.

To Morgan, this has not expanded the market as much as exchanged it for a different one. In a process he describes as "invasion and succession," Morgan argues that once a park gets commercialized and full of development and noise and traffic and crowds, self-reliant traditional visitors who sought wild nature and solitude flee to other quieter spots (a state forest or wildlife area, perhaps) and get replaced by modern visitors who demand entertainment and services.[157] And because the latter are already conditioned to accept congestion and noisy crowds, they report no loss of satisfaction.[158] Furthermore, the introduction of fees and expensive lodging creates a vicious cycle of sorts whereby the dominant modern user now has a consumer stake that needs to be catered to and gets to dictate the pace and intensity of future park development. As Morgan puts it,

> Through commercialization, politicians may have conveyed the following messages: "the only good park visitor is one that spends money." In their zeal to increase revenue, legislators may have unwittingly narrowed the constituency of state parks, rather than broadened the base of public support.[159]

In this scenario, Morgan wonders if parks have simply responded to changing tastes and needs "or instead created an artificial demand structure based on recruitment and retention of 'modern' park visitors?"[160]

More importantly, if the traditional user has been ignored and replaced, does that imply that the traditional preservationist mission of natural resource protection and biodiversity has been replaced as well? It is undeniable that the heavy development that comes with a park full of amenities comes at a profound cost not only to the traditional visitor's experience but to the natural systems present in that park as well.[161] Even more impactful than the facilities themselves and their often oceanic parking lots are the roads that cut across parks to access all the features and that cause extensive habitat fragmentation, the severe ecological consequences of which are documented by a significant scientific literature.[162] In national parks, which have a mean acreage of 200,946 acres,[163] this intense level of development can more easily be absorbed by the sheer size of their pristine, wild backcountry; the traditional user can escape the modern user and yet they can still share the same park. Conversely, state parks, with an average unit size 100 times smaller at 2,126 acres,[164] and nearly 18 times more visitor hours per acre,[165] have no such luxury; heavy development tends to impact the park and park experience from one end to the other, making management decisions more of a zero-sum game. Figure 2.2, which features a map of Elk City State

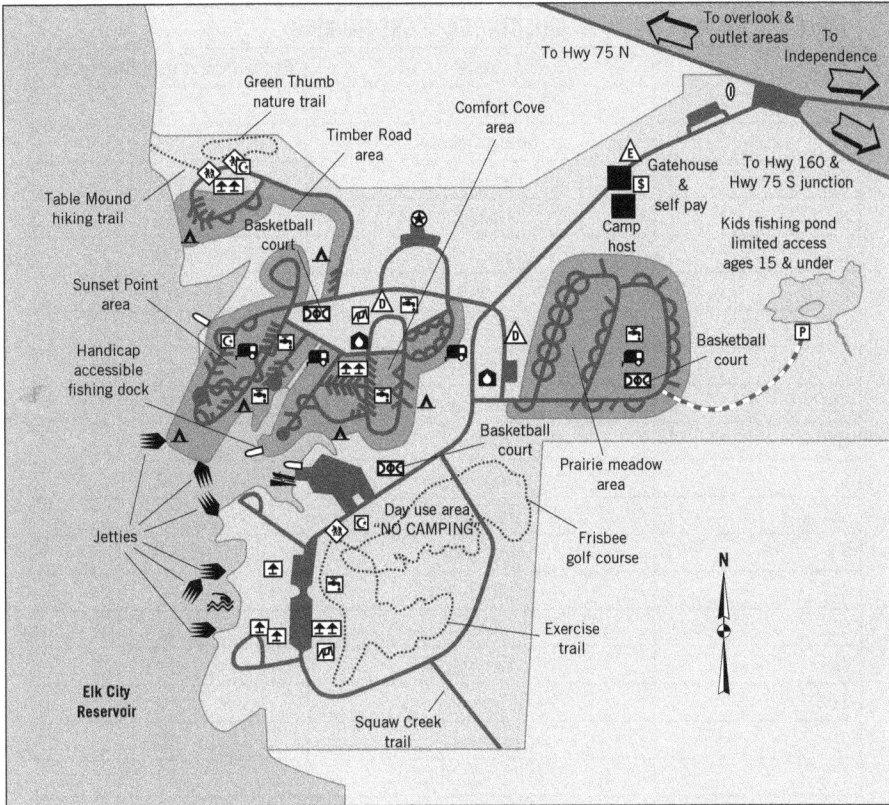

Figure 2.2 Elk City State Park, Kansas (Source: Kansas Department of Wildlife and Parks.)

Park, an 857-acre unit in Kansas, illustrates how intense and all encompassing this level of development and fragmentation can be.

Fifty Divergent States on the Recreation-Preservation Spectrum

When discussing general trends and themes, it is easy to forget all the disparities and variability regarding how the 50 states operate their parks and balance preservation, recreation, and rampant commercialization. Consequently, facilities and development are not evenly distributed across the country. Some of the states traditionally identified with having less developed parks and very modest facilities include Wisconsin, Maine, Minnesota, Alaska, and Florida. For example, Wisconsin's park system has only 10 cabins, compared to its neighbor Michigan's 208.[166] It also has one of the lowest proportions of "improved" campsites and is the only state with a law

TABLE 2.2 STATE RECREATION ORIENTATION SCORE RANKING

Rank	State	Recreation orientation score[1]
1	Kentucky	.92
2	South Dakota	.78
3	Oklahoma	.61
4	Alabama	.60
4	Indiana	.60
5	Ohio	.59
5	West Virginia	.59
6	Tennessee	.47
7	Arkansas	.41
8	Kansas	.40
9	Mississippi	.39
10	Louisiana	.37
11	New York[2]	.36
12	Virginia	.34
13	Illinois	.32
14	Georgia	.29
15	Missouri	.28
16	Delaware	.27
17	North Carolina	.26
18	Wyoming	.25
18	California	.25
19	Nebraska	.24
20	Texas	.23
21	Nevada	.21
21	Rhode Island	.21
22	South Carolina	.20
22	New Jersey	.20
22	Massachusetts	.20
23	Maryland	.19
23	Pennsylvania	.19
24	Iowa	.17
24	Florida	.17
25	Michigan	.16
25	New Hampshire	.16
26	Colorado	.14
27	Oregon	.13

28	Vermont	.12
28	Idaho	.12
29	North Dakota	.11
30	Minnesota	.09
30	Connecticut	.09
31	Washington	.08
32	Wisconsin	.07
32	Utah	.07
32	New Mexico	.07
33	Hawaii	.06
34	Maine[3]	.04
35	Arizona	.03
36	Montana	.02
37	Alaska	.01

Data sources: Yu-Fai Leung, Jordan Smith, and Anna Miller, *Statistical Report of State Park Operations: 2014-2015 Annual Information Exchange* (National Association of State Park Directors, Vol. 37, March 2016), pp. 6–17, available at: https://cnr.ncsu.edu/news/wp-content/uploads/sites/10/2016/05/NASPD-AIX-2014-15-Data-Report-Final-copy.pdf, and data in Tables 1.1 and 2.1.

[1] A state's recreation orientation score is calculated adjusted to a 0–1 scale using the following variables: facilities (improved campsites [thousands], cabins [tens], lodges, restaurants, golf courses, marinas, pools, stables, and ski facilities) per 1,000 acres of parkland, facilities per number of system units, and percentage of total state land composed of state park system acreage. These are weighted at a 4:4:1 ratio.

[2] New York's score is calculated from data that includes its special status state parks along with its regular park system.

[3] Maine's score is only for its regular state park system and excludes Baxter, its special status park.

capping the total proportion of electrified campsites.[167] Alaska, meanwhile, has not a single electrified site on one of the largest systems in the U.S. At the other end of the scale are Alabama, Kentucky, Ohio, and West Virginia with an extensive array of "resort parks" featuring restaurants, conference facilities, sports facilities, and more. Kentucky alone has 18 lodges, while 23 states have none.[168]

Table 2.2 attempts to provide some quantitative comparison regarding how heavily developed each state's park system is and to what degree the state's overall public land system is oriented toward recreation. These scores are calculated largely based on the number of facilities per acre and unit, and they show some strong regional disparities. The highest-scoring states (most developed) are generally clustered in the South, the Ohio Valley, and the Great Plains, while the lowest scoring states tend to be in the Northeast, the Upper Midwest, and the West. As for these low-scoring states, the question arises as to whether this is due to purposeful management philosophy (eastern and northern states?) or low capital budgets and indifference (Rocky Mountain states?).

To the extent that an overt management principle determines how developed a park system is allowed to become, state park systems' divergent mission statements might provide some clues. For example, Pennsylvania's explicitly spells out that while recreation is important, "the conservation of the natural, scenic, aesthetic, and historical values of the park should be given first consideration."[169] Likewise, North Carolina's park management guidelines clearly spell out the importance of ecosystem restoration and give instructions to manage the parks with a minimum of intrusions and disturbance.[170] Many more states, however, have mission statements that are overly vague and nondirective, like Utah's guidance "to enhance the quality of life in Utah through parks, people, and programs."[171] However, Landrum claims that "mission statements, however derived, also appear to be far less controlling in actual practice than the term might imply."[172] Lowell Caneday and his colleagues find evidence for this same conclusion in their cluster analysis of state park types, which finds that neither mission statements nor administrative set-ups predicted the actual orientation of park operations: "It appears as though the reality of a given management approach is dependent upon the realities 'in the field' . . . rather than a well-intentioned mission statement."[173]

Back to Basics

While we often celebrate the "laboratories of democracy" model of state policy divergence, when it comes to the state parks, Landrum bemoans this diversity as a "hodge-podge" that causes state parks as a whole to suffer an "identity crisis."[174] For that reason, he yearns for a set of principles that are "universal and timeless, and steadfastly defended as such."[175] No other function of state government, he complains, is "so amorphous and so malleable as state parks."[176] Both he and Morgan separately use the same exact words in giving voice to their policy recommendations: "get back to basics," and do what parks do best, what they were designed for, and what will reach the widest spectrum of the public.[177] When free market advocates claim that highly developed parks are a response to the demands of recreational markets and thus are merely giving the people what they want, Landrum responds by stressing that this was never what they were created or intended for.[178] Going back to the earliest days of the state parks movement, it is clear that parks were created as a refuge from the things found in everyday life, not as just another, more luxurious or entertaining aspect of it. As the great naturalist Aldo Leopold put it, "Recreation is valuable in proportion . . . to the degree to which it differs from and contrasts with workaday life."[179]

However, this free market notion that park commercialization merely represents the satisfaction of market demand is rejected by others, as well, who stress it is actually a very poor and even inaccurate measure of what the public really wants and thinks. For example, Christos Siderelis and his colleagues, in their extensive production analysis, find that adding more intensive recreation facilities to parks does not enhance their utilization and that where park systems did experience overcapacity, it tended to be more likely in those that were more traditional and preservation oriented in their management:

> Evidently, the quality of added facilities to broaden parks' appeal to the public (ie recreation orientation) is not important in explaining . . . utilization capacities of the states' systems. . . . In fact, those state systems experiencing an overcapacity in park utilizations are 35% more likely to be associated with a state park system being oriented towards public lands preservation. If the primary objective of a state park system is to increase attendance, our results . . . would suggest that the states' officials continue focusing on the preservation and protection of native ecosystems.[180]

These findings are corroborated by a 2008 survey done as part of Arizona's mandatory park planning assessment (as required by the federal LWCF process). In that survey, recipients were asked which park descriptions matched their preferences on a 5-point scale. While the choice of "large, nature-oriented parks with few buildings primarily used for hiking, picnicking or camping" scored 4.27 and "open spaces in natural settings with very little development" scored 4.25, the choice of "large, developed parks with many facilities and uses" only had a rating of 3.87.[181] Anecdotally, the crush of visitation to state parks at the height of the pandemic, when most park facilities were closed out of precaution but hiking trails remained open, would seem to bear out that connection to the natural world is what people most value and desire from their state parks. The only flaw of traditional visitors, then, is not that they are out of step or a weird minority but simply that not enough revenue can be wrung out of them.

The True Value of State Parks

The biggest problem for state parks as budget time rolls around is that so many legislators view their economic costs and benefits from the most primitive and one-dimensional angle possible—operating costs plus capital costs on one side versus revenues on the other. By this measure, most state parks can be said to "lose" money and not pull their weight. If seen as a budgetary drain and an unaffordable luxury, then it is little wonder that parks face seemingly endless cuts and austerity and privatization. But in reality, this view of the economic value of parks is not only impossibly narrow and shortsighted but also empirically wrong. State parks, as it turns out, are magnificently valuable state assets, and if treated in accordance with the economic benefits they bestow, they ought to be fully and gladly supported as the kind of pivotal investments that pay off way more than they cost—qualities that states usually associate with roads, bridges, ports, and development projects. And this does not even directly include the vast amounts of intangible, noneconomic value—aesthetic, ecological, historical, cultural, social, and psychological—that state parks bestow upon society. Instead, we consider here only their direct and indirect economic value.

Economists use a host of widely accepted tools to widen the lenses and measure broader economic impact beyond merely expenses and revenues, such as analyzing return on investment (ROI) and multiplier (spin-off) effects. ROI simply measures how much economic value is generated for each dollar spent (in the case of public land, for either operations or acquisition). Previous studies of various jurisdictions of public land by the Trust for Public Land found the ROI for land acquisition to be between 400% and 1,100%.[182] For specific state park *operations* ROIs, Michigan reports 400%, West Virginia 1,300%, and Maine an incredible 4,000%.[183] According to Nelson, Florida seems acutely aware of statistics such as these, as it uses an "amenities" argument to justify its many bond issues for land acquisition—that is, state parks and protected land help draw people to Florida, which fuels growth and strengthens the economy and thus provides a positive ROI for the acquisition costs.[184]

Similar to the ROI concept is the idea of multiplier effects, or the measurable ripple effect that a state park has on the surrounding region's economy. John Bergstrom and his colleagues examined visitation to state parks in four southern states (North Carolina, South Carolina, Georgia, and Tennessee) and found a mean employment *multiplier* of 1.58.[185] In other words, for every one job directly created by state park recreation, another 0.58 jobs were created in the regional economy by these ripple effects—for example, the person hired at the counter of a sandwich shop to serve the people brought to the area by the park. The total income multiplier they calculated was even more pronounced at 2.39, while the gross output multiplier (for all other aspects of economic activity) was 2.08, which, they note, is roughly on par with other leading industries in Georgia (one of the four states in the case study), such as wood products (2.42), agriculture (2.66), and miscellaneous other industries (ranging from 1.92 to 2.70).[186] The conclusion to be drawn here is that state parks, producing no commodities, only recreational visitation, could hold their own and directly contribute to the regional economy on par with most other industries. Jeffrey Prey, David Marcouiller, and Danya Kim come to similar conclusions in their exhaustive study of the economic impacts of the Wisconsin State Park System. Finding the parks to be "linchpin regional assets to economic vitality," they report a multiplier effect of 1.65 for total economic output and 1.62 for income.[187]

Economist Juha Siikamäki, using the different methodology of time valuation analysis, concludes that America's state parks together annually contribute $14 billion to the nation's economy.[188] Table 2.3 summarizes the findings of selected state-level analyses of park systems' contributions to state economies. Although some of the studies use measures that are not perfectly comparable (for example, economic activity generated vs. value added), in general, one finds that state parks contribute hundreds of millions to billions of dollars to individual state economies, create thousands to tens of thousands of jobs, and add tens to hundreds of millions of dollars in tax revenues. And that last point refers just to sales and income tax; other studies have measured the increased property tax valuation for homes in proximity to state parks. A University of Connecticut study, for example, found a high-end estimate of $5.4 million in enhanced property tax revenue in Connecticut from homes bordering state parks.[189] What all these disparate measures show are figures that dwarf the collective $2.55 billion annual state spending on parks (operating and capital funds not offset by revenue). From this angle, state park austerity does not display prudence or fiscal responsibility but rather a reckless and self-defeating case of being "penny-wise and pound-foolish."

Focus the lenses of economic value out even more broadly and the foolishness compounds. A growing number of environmental economists today go beyond the traditional measures of economic impact, like the ROIs and multiplier effects discussed previously, and incorporate the value (as best they can calculate) of the services that functioning ecosystems provide society and that currently go completely unvalued in the traditional approach

TABLE 2.3 SELECTED STUDIES MEASURING ECONOMIC IMPACTS OF STATE PARK SYSTEMS

Year of study	State park system	Total economic impact (millions of $)	Total visitor spending (millions of $)	Jobs created	Tax revenue generated (millions of $)
2011	Alabama	375.0	152.4	5,340	NA
2019	Washington	786.0	1,600.0	10,000	16.0
2020	Tennessee	1,840.0	NA	NA	121.8
2020	Florida	2,272.0	2,577.8	31,810	150.0
2011	Connecticut	1,250.0	544.0	9,000	NA
2019	Virginia	343.0	286.2	4,180	25.3
2019	Texas	688.0	NA	6,801	NA
2020	Arizona	272.0	NA	4,200	NA
2006	Maine	95.7	21.9	1,449	NA
2021	Kansas	287.4	NA	3,039	NA
2013	Wisconsin	626.9	765.7	8,251	NA
2016	Rhode Island	311.9	315.8	3,709	38.8
2010	California	4,300.0	6,900.0	56,000	NA

Data sources: Kelli Dugan, "State Parks Pump up Alabama Economy" in *AL.com* (Webpage, March 21, 2014), available at: https://www.al.com/business/2014/03/state_parks_pump_up_alabama_ec.html; Tennessee Department of Environment and Conservation, *Tennessee State Parks Had $2.1 Billion Economic Impact in 2021* (Press Release, March 7, 2022), available at: https://www.tn.gov/environment/news/2022/3/7/tennessee -state-parks-had--2-1-billion-economic-impact-in-2021.html; Washington State Parks, *Economic Benefit of Parks* (Webpage, 2022), available at: https://www.parks.wa.gov/971/Economic-benefits-of-parks; Florida Department of Environmental Protection, *2020 Annual Economic Impact Assessment Report for the Florida State Park System* (Memorandum, September 25, 2020), available at: https://floridadep.gov/sites/default/files/2019-2020 %20EIA%20Report%20FINAL%20and%20COVER%20MEMO.pdf; Jan Spiegel, "Economic Value of State's Parks Is More than $1 Billion" in *The Connecticut Mirror* (December 9, 2011), available at: https://ctmirror .org/2011/12/09/economic-value-states-parks-more-1-billion/; Vincent Magnini, *Virginia State Parks: Economic Impacts Report 2019* (Virginia Tech Report, 2019), available at: https://www.dcr.virginia.gov/state-parks/docu ment/virginia-state-parks-2019-economic-impact-study.pdf; Ji Youn Jeong and John L. Crompton, *The Econom- ic Contributions of Texas State Parks* (Texas Park and Wildlife Report, January 2019), available at: https://www .tpwf.org/wp-content/uploads/2019/02/The-Economic-Contributions-of-State-Parks-2018-Report.pdf; Dari Du- val, Ashley Bickel, and George Frisvold, *Economic Contributions and Impacts of Arizona's State Parks FY 2020* (University of Arizona Cooperative Extension Report, June 2021), available at: https://arizona-content.usedirect .com/storage/pages/20220628105240State%20Park%20Econom ic%20Contribution%2006212021%20(2) .pdf; Maine Department of Agriculture, Conservation, and Forestry, *The Case for Maine State Parks* (Webpage, January 2021), available at: https://legislature.maine.gov/doc/5156; Robert Roper, Charles Morris, Thomas Al- len, and Cindy Bastey, "Maine's State Parks: Their Value to Visitors and Contribution to the State Economy" in *Maine Policy Review* (Vol. 15, No. 1, 2006); Center for Economic Development and Business Research, *Kansas State Parks: Economic Contributions to Regional and State Economies* (Report, 2021), available at: https:// ksoutdoors.com/State-Parks/Kansas-State-Parks-Economic-Contributions-to-Regional-and-State-Economies Mi- chail Fragkias, Zeynep Hansen, Don Holley, Rob Humphrey, and Scott Lowe, *Economic Impact and Importance of State Parks in Idaho: A Park-Level Study* (Idaho State Parks and Recreation Report, January 2018), available at: https://parksandrecreation.idaho.gov/wp-content/uploads/Economic-Impact-and-Importance-of-State-Parks -in-Idaho.pdf; Jeffrey Prey, David Marcouiller, and Danya Kim, *Economic Impacts of the Wisconsin State Park System: Connections to Gateway Communities* (Wisconsin Department of Natural Resources Report PR-487- 2013, November 2013), pp. 7, 9; Thomas Sproul, *The Economic Impact of Rhode Island State Parks* (Univer- sity of Rhode Island Report, 2017), available at: https://dem.ri.gov/sites/g/files/xkgbur861/files/programs /bnatres/parksrec/pdf/econ-impact-parks.pdf; Katherine Litzy, *California State Parks: Economic Impact of Visitor Expenditures* (Master's Thesis, University of California, Sacramento, 2006), available at: https://csu-csus.esploro .exlibrisgroup.com/esploro/outputs/graduate/California-state-parks-economic-impact-of/99257831108101 671#file-0; California State Parks, *Meeting the Park Needs of All Californians: 2015 Statewide Comprehensive Outdoor Recreation Plan* (Webpage, undated), available at: https://www.parksforcalifornia.org/scorp/2015.

to economics. Simply put, *ecosystem services* refer to the many processes and systems by which the natural world produces the things upon which humans and all life on earth depend, including climate regulation, carbon sequestration, water quality and quantity, soil retention and formation, nutrient cycling, and pollination, to name a few.[190] While estimating ecosystem service value is notoriously difficult and imprecise, David Holzman offers a midrange estimate of $44 trillion annually in 2012 dollars (or roughly $60 trillion today).[191]

One way that valuation can be assessed is to estimate what it would cost to replace these services if they were impaired or distorted by human activity. In fact, the best-known case study of this would be New York City's municipal water, which is supplied by the huge watershed within the boundaries of the Catskill Park.[192] The costs imposed if that watershed was not protected as public land and functioning to hold and filter water are estimated to be $6–8 billion to build water filtration facilities and another quarter-billion dollars annually to operate them.[193] Yet nowhere does that value end up on any New York state park ledger sheet as a credit; at budget time, state legislators only seem to see the costs. One 2016 study, however, did try to isolate and measure the value of explicit ecosystem service provision in several Washington State parks. Cape Disappointment State Park, a 2,023-acre coastal unit, was found to annually provide, if extrapolated to 2024 dollars, $23.9 million in ecosystem services along with $44.7 million in other economic benefits not related to ecosystem services, for a total return on investment (for operational expenses) of 2,373%. Federation Forest State Park, a 619-acre old-growth unit near Tacoma, meanwhile, was found to have a 7,021% ROI based on $11.9 million (in 2024 dollars) of total annual economic benefit, of which $6.9 million was specifically ecosystem services.[194]

Some observers call for public land managers to more aggressively try to identify, market, and sell the ecosystem services that emanate from their state parks, but this is not easy. Markets for ecosystem services are very underdeveloped, where they exist at all, and since parks are already protected land, it is harder to find a buyer for a service that will be protected nonetheless. The more important point regarding ecosystem services is not that they should be used and marketed to provide yet another source of revenue but rather that they should be seen as outrageously valuable public goods that make state parks and all state natural resource land a massive storehouse of precious value for the state's people and economy that should be supported and invested in at a level that recognizes the extent of this wealth.

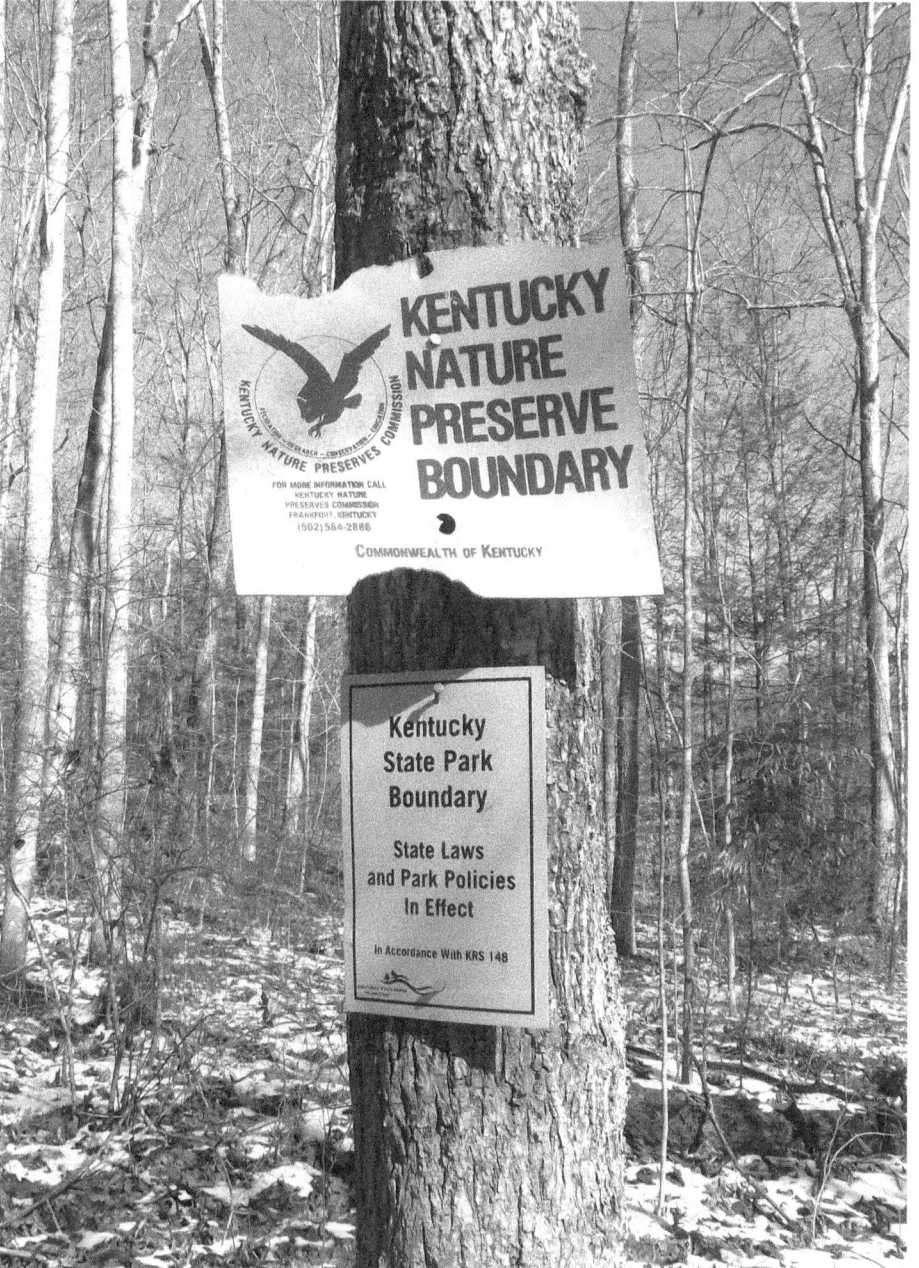

Pine Mountain State Nature Preserve, Kentucky (Photo by author)

3

Taking Preservation Seriously

State Natural Areas and Wilderness Areas

> Natural lands and waters together with the plants and animals living
> thereon in natural communities are a part of the heritage of the people.
> They are of value for scientific research, for teaching, as reservoirs of
> natural materials not all of the potential uses of which are now known,
> as habitats for rare and vanishing species, as places of historic and natural
> interest and scenic beauty and as living museums of the native landscape
> wherein one may envision and experience primeval conditions in a
> wilderness-like environment. They also contribute generally to the
> public health and welfare and the environmental quality of the State.
> —Illinois Natural Areas Preservation Act (525 ILCS 30)

While state parks might be seen as doing an imperfect job in living up to
their founders' largely preservationist ideals, there are other much smaller
and more overlooked corners to be found within the realm of state public
lands that focus more exclusively and comprehensively on biodiversity and
wildness. State natural areas (SNA) programs and, to a lesser extent, state
wilderness systems are two state land management categories that have developed to focus as much as possible on rare plant and animal communities
and endangered landscapes as well as the remaining scraps of exceptionally
wild, roadless land within certain states. Perhaps it is exactly this undivided
focus on preserving ecosystems and natural landscapes that makes them as
obscure, incomplete, and underresourced a category as they tend to be.

As one of the three broad purposes of public land outlined in Chapter
1, preservation, broadly conceived, most often has its roots traced back to
naturalist, Sierra Club founder, and indefatigable wilderness advocate John
Muir. His brand of preservationism found in nature something approaching
the divine, and his philosophy held that nature's worth was inherent; it did
not require human utility to justify itself:

> The world, we are told, was made especially for man—a presump-
> tion not supported by all the facts. A numerous class of men are

painfully astonished whenever they find anything, living or dead, in all God's universe, which they cannot eat or render in some way what they call useful to themselves.[1]

New Deal–era Forest Service official and wilderness advocate Bob Marshall, meanwhile, found in preserved wildland "perhaps the best opportunity for . . . pure esthetic rapture."[2] But it was not until another forester and later University of Wisconsin professor Aldo Leopold wrote *A Sand County Almanac* in 1949 that the conservation ideal was given its clearest articulation in terms of where moral imperative and science meet to create a *land ethic* with its notions of ecological stewardship. "When we see land as a community to which we belong," writes Leopold, "we may begin to use it with love and respect."[3] As a wilderness advocate but also an ardent restorationist and healer of broken landscapes, Leopold united all aspects of the preservationist tradition.[4] As an inveterate ecological tinkerer who tended to work at intimate, rather than grandiose, levels, he is perhaps the true patron saint of the preservation impulse in the state realm. At the state level, after all, such preservation also happens at a more intimate scale (especially compared to the federal lands) and tends to involve so much ecological restoration work and the participation of a dedicated and knowledgeable community of what Leopold would consider ethical "biotic citizen[s]" and park managers might call volunteer stewards.[5]

State Natural Areas Programs

It was around Leopold's time in the 1930s and 1940s that these new ideas about ecology began to slowly filter down to state public land managers as at least some of them began to think of the land in their care in more biologically informed ways and with an eye toward what we now call biodiversity. "To keep every cog and wheel is the first precaution of intelligent tinkering," as Leopold tells it.[6] Taking this notion to heart, New York's law regarding state nature preserves specifically instructs managers to regard them "as reservoirs of natural materials and ecological processes that contribute to the state's biological diversity."[7] If states were to save all the cogs and wheels, then they would first need to inventory these parts, down to the most obscure plant and animal populations and last remaining scraps of rare landscapes like alkaline fens and pine barrens and oak savannas and sphagnum bogs. And indeed, by the mid to late 20th century, some states began scouring their land holdings, and sometimes private lands as well, in order to compile natural heritage inventories and eventually registries. These inventories would often form the basis for future designations as official natural areas and, when on private land, perhaps a priority list for future acquisition.[8] In Conard's opinion, states were finally beginning to try to live up to the preservationist ideal that animated the early state parks movement but never fully took hold. She notes that Iowa's 1965 State Preserves Act "accomplished what the 1917 State Park Act intended but failed to fulfill: protect significant natural and cultural features in perpetuity."[9]

What is unique about state natural areas is that unlike other land management categories like parks, forests, recreation areas, wildlife areas, and wilderness, SNAs have no real analog in the vast federal system—they are essentially unique to state lands.[10] In 1951, Wisconsin became the first state to create an official state natural areas program in which tracts of mostly state-owned land (but also, with cooperation, local, federal, and private land) with exceptional natural communities and geological features were given special recognition and protection. This system is not only the nation's oldest but also the largest and most comprehensive (with 406,000 acres in 694 units).[11] In 1963, neighboring Illinois became the second state to create such a program with the passage of the Illinois Natural Areas Protection Act, which authorized the designation of nature preserves, which are analogous to SNAs. Within the next two decades, more than half the states in the U.S. followed suit in creating some version of a natural areas and/or natural heritage program. However, that rapid progress eventually stalled around the same time as state parks began having their own crises, and some states like Connecticut, Massachusetts, Kansas, and Montana allowed their programs to go inactive while other states like New York barely added any acreage to the systems for long periods.[12] It should also be noted that not all these SNA programs have been the result of state legislation; some programs and their process for designating preserves, even robust ones like Missouri's, were created through administrative rulemaking, which, of course, makes them more politically vulnerable.[13]

According to Table 3.1, there are 3.2 million acres of state natural areas on mostly state-owned land.[14] This is not a large portfolio of lands by any means, but it does pack a punch ecologically, representing some of the finest remnants of various natural communities found anywhere in their respective states. The relatively modest scale of these holdings can also be seen as speaking volumes about the extent of habitat degradation in the wider countryside. While some of these 3.2 million acres exist as stand-alone

State	Acres of state natural areas or equivalent (in thousands)	Official state natural areas program?	Overlay or stand-alone units[1]	Private, local, or federal land included as managed units?	SNA acreage as percentage of all state public land acreage[2]	Percentage of land in state protected as SNA
Wisconsin	406.0	Yes	Both	Yes	25.6%	1.2%
Georgia	336.6	Yes	Both	No	47.1%	0.9%
California	286.7[3]	Yes[4]	Stand-alone	No	9.8%	0.3%
Minnesota	192.0	Yes	Both	Yes	2.3%	0.4%
Colorado	180.0	Yes	Overlay	Yes	5.3%	0.3%
Washington	167.0[5]	Yes	Both	No	4.3%	0.4%
Michigan	130.0	Yes	Both	Yes	2.8%	0.4%
Tennessee	130.0	Yes	Both	No	13.5%	0.5%
South Carolina	128.5[6]	Yes	Both	No	27.8%	0.7%
Hawaii	123.8	Yes	Stand-alone	No	8.1%	3.0%
Kentucky	123.8	Yes	Both	Yes	50.8%	0.5%
Illinois	115.1	Yes	Both	Yes	28.9%	0.3%
Massachusetts	111.2[7]	Inactive	Overlay	No	19.0%	2.2%
Missouri	98.0	Yes	Both	Yes	10.0%	0.2%
Pennsylvania	90.5[8]	Yes	Overlay	No	2.3%	0.3%
Maine	90.0[9]	Yes	Overlay	No	8.8%	0.5%
Arkansas	73.4	Yes	Both	Yes	14.4%	0.2%
Virginia	60.3	Yes	Stand-alone	Yes	14.0%	0.2%
Indiana	54.6	Yes	Overlay	Yes	13.2%	0.2%
Louisiana	52.3	Yes	Overlay	Yes	3.6%	0.2%
New Jersey	40.0	Yes	Both	No	4.8%	0.8%
New York	35.2[10]	Yes	Both	No	0.8%	0.1%
North Carolina	33.3	Yes	Stand-alone	Yes	3.6%	0.1%
Arizona	27.6	Yes	Stand-alone	Yes	0.3%	< 0.1%
Oregon	25.6[11]	Yes	Both	Yes	1.5%	< 0.1%
Maryland	22.5[12]	Yes	Overlay	No	4.5%	0.4%
Vermont	19.5	Yes	Both	No	5.6%	0.3%
Ohio	13.4	Yes	Both	Yes	2.3%	< 0.1%
Iowa	10.0	Yes	Both	Yes	2.6%	< 0.1%
Delaware	7.0	Yes	Both	Yes	6.1%	0.6%
Connecticut	6.8	Inactive	Both	Yes	2.8%	0.2%
West Virginia	5.0[13]	Yes	Overlay	No	0.9%	< 0.1%
New Hampshire	3.4	Registry only	Stand-alone	No	1.3%	< 0.1%
South Dakota	2.8	No	Stand-alone	No	0.2%	< 0.1%

TABLE 3.1 STATE NATURAL AREAS

Mississippi	0.7	Registry only	Stand-alone	No	0.1%	< 0.1%
North Dakota	0.4	No	Stand-alone	No	< 0.1%	< 0.1%
Alabama	0	Registry only	NA	NA	0.0%	0.0%
Montana	0	Registry only	NA	NA	0.0%	0.0%
Total U.S.	3,200.2	NA	NA	NA	1.6%; not including trust lands 5.3%	0.1%

Data sources: See appendix.

Note: Texas, Nevada, Kansas, New Mexico, Utah, Rhode Island, Oklahoma, Idaho, Nebraska, Wyoming, Alaska, and Florida have neither state natural areas programs or any land holdings that qualify as a state natural area or equivalent.

[1] This refers to whether an SNA unit exists as its own discrete preserve (stand-alone) or as an SNA designation embedded within a larger preserve, such as a state park, state forest, or state wildlife area (overlay).

[2] This is intended to provide ratio/perspective rather than be a literal percentage, as some states have private, county, and federal land in their SNA programs. Also, this category is often an overlay status within existing state parks, state forests, and wildlife management areas (WMAs).

[3] This acreage comprises the total of two distinct SNA programs in California. The California Department of Fish and Wildlife has a system of ecological reserves totaling 239,722 acres on its WMA lands, while the University of California administers a separate 47,000-acre research natural area system.

[4] The California Natural Landmarks Program is the state's official program, but it is only empowered to make a registry of significant sites and not designate protected areas. The 284,100 acres listed in Table 3.1 are actually ecological reserves on California Fish and Wildlife lands as well as research natural areas run by the University of California system.

[5] The natural area system in Washington includes 40,816 acres of natural area preserves and 125,848 acres of natural resource conservation areas, which have greater public access and perhaps some limited facilities.

[6] This acreage consists of 95,661 acres of state heritage preserves and a single 32,874-acre unit, Jocassee Gorges, that is termed a state natural area.

[7] These acres are not technically state natural areas but rather the portion of the state reserves (forests) that are protected from active forest management to protect natural communities and, as such, serve a similar purpose.

[8] In Pennsylvania, there are separate designation processes depending on if the SNA is embedded within a state forest or state park. There are 78,600 acres designated within state forests and 11,857 acres in the state park system.

[9] Maine has an ecological reserve system within its larger system of reserved lands.

[10] New York's specially protected areas consist of two different types of classification: 21,765 acres of state nature and historic preserves and 19,900 acres of so-called unique areas, which are primarily found in the state forest system. About 6,436 of these unique areas acres are also nature preserves.

[11] This figure is only for state-owned, dedicated, and registered SNAs. Oregon has a very complex system with numerous levels of protection.

[12] Maryland's specially protected areas consist of two different types of classification: 12,751 acres of natural environmental areas and 9,757 acres of heritage conservation sites, which are more explicitly geared toward rare plant and animal populations.

[13] Roughly another 10,000 acres of designations within WMAs have been nominated and await consideration.

preserves, many more are embedded within larger units of state parks, state forests, or state wildlife areas. There is wide variation in how states arrange their SNA programs, what sorts of lands qualify, and who (agency or legislature) is actually responsible for designating them. The acreages reported in the table generally do not include the many more acres of land (often private) on natural heritage registries, which are inventoried but do not benefit from any added legal protection; thus, only official SNA units and/or designated SNAs with legally protected status are included. In those states that allow designation on private, local, and federal land, it is always with the willing cooperation of those other parties. More often than not, the private holdings are those of conservation organizations and land trusts, like the Nature Conservancy, who gladly seek such status for their preserves.

Table 3.1 also includes lands with special protected status outside of formal SNA programs. For example, the California Department of Fish and Game manages some of their more valuable preserves as *ecological reserves*, which serve the same functions for many of the same reasons and enjoy as much protection as any SNA. Likewise, Massachusetts, which lacks an SNA program, nevertheless has a management category for its state forests called *reserves* that prohibits logging and aims to manage for biodiversity and carbon storage. New York similarly uses the protective designation *unique areas* for ecologically important state forest tracts, despite also having a separate SNA program. Other states, like Connecticut, New Hampshire, South Dakota, Mississippi, and North Dakota, also lack active SNA programs but have small scattered units that are referred to as state natural areas and managed more protectively, so these were included in Table 3.1 as well.

As one can see in Figure 3.1, states with SNA holdings are not generally confined to any one region. If one looks at SNAs as a proportion of all state public land, the top states would be Kentucky, Georgia, Illinois, South Carolina, and Wisconsin, with the equivalent of a quarter to half of their public lands inventory protected as SNAs.[15] The national average looking only at nontrust lands is slightly over 5%. Looking at this in terms of how much of an *entire* state is composed of natural area acreage, SNAs, as such a small category of state land, barely register a blip. However, three states— Hawaii, Massachusetts, and Wisconsin—stand out as having between 1% and 3% of their overall land mass protected as SNAs or a functional equivalent. Georgia and New Jersey, meanwhile, are just below 1%.

Fourteen states, on the other hand, have no state natural areas at all, and here there does seem to be a geographic correlation as all but two are in the

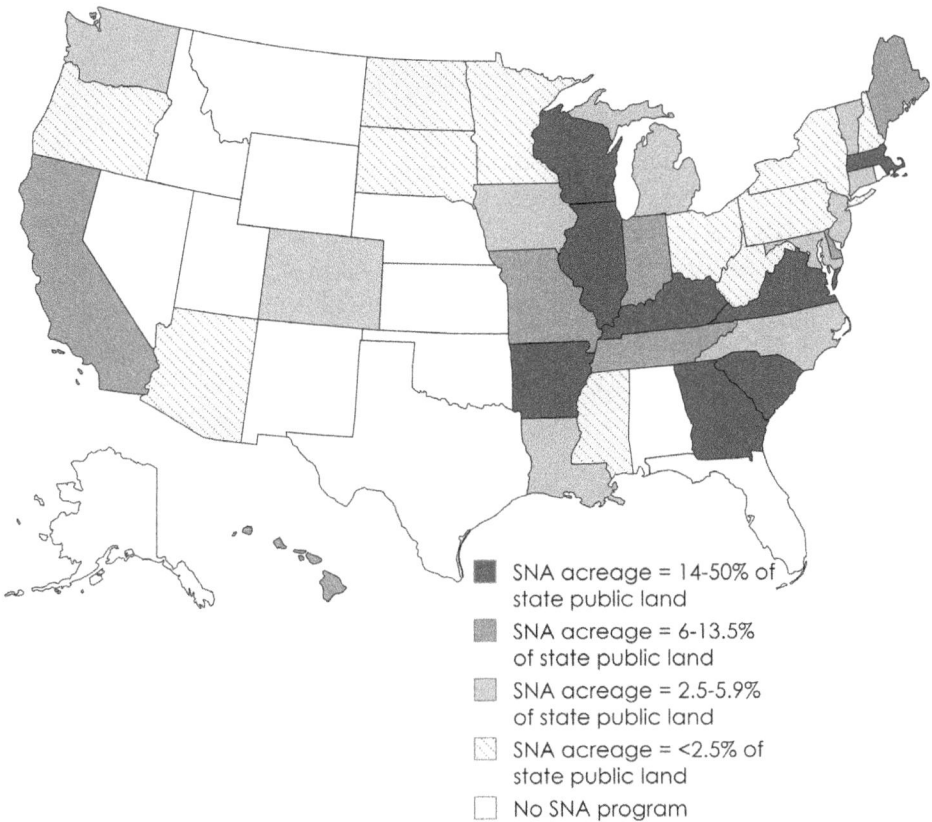

Figure 3.1 State natural areas as percentage of all state public land
(Data sources: See Table 3.1 and appendix.)

West or Great Plains. Florida is one of those two nonwestern states without SNAs, and this might seem surprising given the state's enthusiastic devotion to land acquisition and its preservation-oriented tradition of low-key, underdeveloped state parks. Since Florida does have a vigorous natural heritage inventory system that identifies rare and important native ecosystems for acquisition priority, it seems as if the state has chosen to pursue similar goals to an SNA program without more formally adopting such a program or designation process. Similarly, North Carolina, which has only a modest 33,300-acre formal SNA system, actually applies ecosystem management approaches (like restoration of native habitats and the avoidance of fragmentation and disturbance) to the bulk of its much larger state park system that mirror the ways most other states manage their SNAs.[16] Thus, while SNA programs are vital and the most common way to protect biodiversity and endangered landscapes, a few states do achieve similar goals outside that framework.

Administratively, SNAs are all over the place. In some states, like New York or Tennessee, they are embedded within state park agencies, while in many other states with large centralized natural resource agencies, there exists a subunit that coordinates SNAs across park, forest, and wildlife area jurisdictions. In a few other states, like Illinois, Arkansas, and Kentucky, SNAs are coordinated by independent boards or, in Kentucky's case, a full department-level office. That last administrative category, not surprisingly, tends to enhance and solidify the SNA project within a state.

Managing State Natural Areas

Because the whole idea behind SNAs is to protect biodiversity, rare plant and animal communities, and exceptional examples of native landscapes, they do not have any sort of multiple or dual use mandate; instead, they, along with state wilderness areas, can be considered the only categories of state land managed solely under a preservation mandate. This means, of course, that resource extraction activities are strictly off-limits and recreation, while certainly allowed, is quite muted and restricted to the most passive forms like hiking or birdwatching. In fact, some SNA systems have units that are so fragile they are kept off-limits to the public or require special visitation permits.[17] And even for the majority of sites that are fully accessible, they tend to have limited or even no trail access and no camping or facilities beyond, at most, a gravel parking lot. The message this sends to recreationists is clear: you are welcome, but this place is not designed or intended for your recreation.

In some states that closed their state parks early in the pandemic, this caused problems for natural areas as visitor traffic spilled over into SNAs not built for that level of visitation, and, as a result, sometimes they ended up heavily abused.[18] This was generally true even before the pandemic for SNAs with particularly beautiful or unusual features like a dramatic bluff, waterfall, natural bridge, or gorge. Especially in the age of Instagram photos and super-easy GPS geotagging, such formerly remote and obscure places have often become virally popular and overcrowded without any of the infrastructure, funding, or staffing to handle the crush. As a result, many such delicate sites have been damaged through erosion, soil compaction, trash, and graffiti.[19]

While biologically necessary, restrictive access policies and a lack of any infrastructure do little to win over broad constituencies of users or the support of the elected officials who represent them. And this, in a nutshell, is the political problem of state natural areas; since they require restrictive policies that limit recreational access and do not provide any extractive material resources, they often lack a clear and direct constituency beyond the most ecologically informed citizens. To many state legislators, this may seem like all downside (restrictions on lands "locked up and doing nothing") and no upside (revenue potential, heavy visitation linked to tourism, supply of needed resources), and so, not surprisingly, SNA systems limp along with minuscule budgets and very sparse staffing. In other words, seen from a free market mindset, SNAs are the poster child of public lands that supposedly do not pay their way. Of course, the ecological services framework would suggest that these bastions of ecological integrity are actually spectacularly valuable in proportion to the abundant ecological services their highly protected systems provide. And those who stress intangible values of beauty, solitude, emotional well-being, spiritual inspiration, and the inherent value of nonhuman life also find the public goods on SNAs to be of incalculable value. However, these services and values still go largely unrecognized and unmeasured by policymakers and by markets as currently constituted.

This means that SNA programs, for the most part, occupy this uneasy territory whereby chronic underfunding, understaffing, and lack of political clout create enormous limitations in what can be achieved (in terms of acquisition or active stewardship and restoration projects) and, at least in some places, constant political vulnerability. Working in their favor, however, is the tenacious dedication to mission and focus that talented and motivated field staff (botanists, ecologists, wildlife biologists, etc.) bring to their agencies and the SNAs under their care. Because their corner of state land management tends to be as small, low budget, and inconspicuous as it is, these programs and their staff toil away in an obscurity, which can also have its advantages. This under-the-radar status, despite a chronic lack of resources, also allows for some latitude of action—tremendous experimentation and innovation and creative partnerships with private conservation groups and the building of networks of expertise to share.

While state natural areas vary wildly in terms of size from single-digit acreage to tens of thousands of acres, they mostly tend to be on the small side. For example, the average unit size in Wisconsin's very large SNA system is only 585 acres.[20] In more densely populated eastern states, they are also often not far from human settlement and even suburban or exurban sprawl. These facts make management a great challenge as smaller tracts of protected land that exist almost as islands are much more vulnerable to invasive species and habitat fragmentation than huge tracts of wild back-country. So, unlike the backcountry land manager who might take a hands-off approach to his or her wilderness realm or the state park ranger who manages crowds of visitors all day, the natural areas manager has largely assumed the role of Leopold's active tinkerer—an ecosystem restorationist and land steward whose tools include controlled burns, brush removal, stream rehabilitation, native plantings, seed collection, wildlife monitoring, and, increasingly, efforts to bolster resilience in the face of climate change. Unfortunately, this work is quite time and labor intensive, and despite the incredible ecological service productivity and rich biodiversity that is un-leashed in a healing, well-stewarded natural area, this accrues no credits in the budget writer's mind, only unrecovered costs. Thus, this vital resto-ration work is often, in the words of one natural areas program director, more like "triage" whereby needed work is put on the backburner so that even more desperately needed work can be attended to.[21] Restorationists, therefore, almost always feel like they can never come even close to getting a handle on everything that needs to get done as quality stewardship takes so much care and effort.[22] This catch-as-catch-can approach is made to work as best as possible, but to help move things along, many natural areas managers have become adept at pulling together project-based funding to supplement their allotted budgets, most often from federal grants and non-profits.[23] They can also extend their reach through coordination with staff in other divisions or agencies if their state natural area unit is embedded within larger state parks, forests, or wildlife areas.

The Importance of Volunteers

Perhaps even more importantly, natural areas managers, much like their park superintendent colleagues, have come to rely heavily on volunteers and private conservation organizations like the Nature Conservancy who they often trust enough to authorize to work independently as restoration crews. Illinois and Wisconsin have especially well-developed volunteer networks for their extensive SNA programs.[24] In the latter state, many hundreds of volunteers from 41 community groups worked 7,188 hours for an estimated value of $193,755 in labor in 2021.[25] Not only does this citizen stewardship work vastly extend the reach of limited natural areas staff, but in a more intangible way, it also grows a whole community of biotic citizens, to use Leopold's phrase, who become profoundly bonded to the wild landscapes around them. Unlike emptying garbage cans in state park restrooms (as selfless and public spirited as that is), stewardship volunteerism builds a whole network of committed citizen-scientists with invaluable real-world habitat restoration experience.[26] And perhaps most importantly from a political point of view, this begins to develop a tenacious constituency to defend SNAs from whatever depredations they may face in the future.[27]

Besides these limitations in staffing and operations that SNA managers face, there are also shortfalls in capital budgets for acquisition. This is especially important given SNA programs' mission of inventorying rare and endangered biotic communities and then trying to bring them under protection. By definition, these remnants of native biota are few and far between, and especially if they are on private land, the clock is often ticking as they could be developed or logged or cleared for farming at any moment. This situation is where public managers' partnerships with the Nature Conservancy (TNC) and other land trusts and private conservancies become crucial. These organizations are designed to acquire endangered landscapes with a speed and nimbleness that underfunded bureaucracies cannot match. Using a variety of tools from outright purchase to the use of conservation easements[28] and the purchase of development rights,[29] these groups can move in as quickly as possible to secure an ecologically valuable and threatened site, and for this reason, state agencies have come to depend heavily upon them. An ecologically sensitive TNC-acquired site may then get SNA designation and TNC will continue provide management and stewardship or else it may eventually be transferred to the state.[30]

While privatization advocates often hold up the private conservancy model as a viable alternative to public ownership, such organizations would be the first to reject that idea as only government has the wherewithal to hold and manage so large and diverse a collection of lands as exist in the U.S. Instead of rivals or alternatives, TNC and state governments are true partners working fully in tandem toward the same goal, with both acquiring, managing, and stewarding natural areas, sometimes side by side on the same tracts and sometimes separately, but always in the same direction.

STATE NATURAL AREAS: *Spotlight on Wisconsin*

Not only was Wisconsin the pioneer in establishing the nation's first state natural areas program in 1951, but it also ranks first among the 50 states in total acreage (406,000 acres) as well as number of units (694) protected as SNAs.[1] The story begins in 1945 when the predecessor of the DNR board, the Wisconsin Conservation Commission, at the behest of one of its commissioners, Aldo Leopold, created a Natural Areas Committee to identify and work to protect ecologically unique areas that had been disappearing fast.[2] In 1951, the legislature formalized this somewhat ad hoc structure by creating the State Board for the Preservation of Scientific Areas, which in 1985 was renamed the Natural Areas Preservation Council, while scientific areas were henceforth to be known as state natural areas.[3]

Wisconsin is one of only a few states with SNA programs that designate all types of land ownership. Of the 694 SNA units in the system, 260 (37%) are owned by outside partners. Of those units, 44% are on federal land (mostly national forest), 25% county owned, 19% owned by private conservancies or land trusts, 8% owned by schools (often school forests or university-owned lands), 2% owned by municipalities, and 2% owned by private citizens.[4] These SNAs on non–state government land are typically guided by a memorandum of understanding that lays out roles, responsibilities, and requirements. As for private land, the DNR will only designate SNAs for land on which conservation easements already exist. The other 434 SNA units (over 221,000 acres) are on state-owned land, but even these have distinctions—about a third of them (139) are *stand-alone* units that exist only as a discrete state natural area and are directly managed by the DNR's Bureau of Natural Heritage Conservation (BNHC). The other two-thirds (295) exist as specific acreage embedded within other much larger DNR properties such as state parks, state forests, state wildlife areas, state fisheries, and so on. Much like federal wilderness areas, these SNAs are an *overlay* category of public land and are managed by the relevant bureaus or divisions (parks, wildlife management, or forestry) in coordination with the BNHC.[5]

The 1985 reorganization of the DNR and SNA program also created a distinction between *designated* SNA sites and *dedicated* sites. While designated status (541 sites, or 78%) offers significant protections that can be withdrawn from particular sites only in the rarest circumstances, dedicated SNAs (153 sites, or 22%) have perpetual preservation and ecologically informed stewardship requirements legally attached to the land titles. The DNR has slowly been working to add sites to the list of dedicated SNAs, prioritizing state-owned, stand-alone SNAs and those owned by private conservation organizations.[6]

While SNA units range in size from 3 to 9,612 acres, they tend overall to be fairly small, with a mean size of 585 acres and a median of 239 acres—a fact that might speak to the dire fragmentation of high-quality habitats across the land.[7] But those parcels, however modest, provide rich and invaluable habitat and refuge for imperiled species and, as such, are an irreplaceable asset for ecological preservation. In fact, while SNAs account for just 1.2% of Wisconsin's land mass, 90% of rare plants and 75% of rare animal species are found to be present on SNAs.[8] The bureau's self-stated goals in their management of the SNA program are to stress ecological integrity, ecological representation, and habitat connectivity throughout their decision-making processes and in service of their mission, which is

> to locate, establish, and conserve a system of SNAs that as nearly as possible represents the wealth and variety of Wisconsin's native landscape for education, research, and most importantly, to help secure the long-term protection of Wisconsin's biological diversity for future generations.[9]

This ambitious mission coupled with the physical expansiveness of the Wisconsin SNA system would be a tall order to fulfill for even the most well-resourced state program, but natural areas management in Wisconsin, as in pretty much every other place, subsists on a shoestring. The program's operations budget in 2020 was just $3.09 million, with the bulk of that coming from the BNHC's Endangered Resources Fund (mostly financed through state tax refund check-off boxes and special license plates) and the rest through program agreements, federal wildlife grants, a bit of timber revenue, and donations.[10] This very meager budget can only support a limited staff of 3.5 full time equivalent employees to handle the program's central administration and 9 regional field ecologists and 34 natural areas technicians scattered across the state.[11] Fortunately, this staff must fully manage only 20% of the SNAs (the state-owned stand-alone units), and for the rest, their work is heavily supplemented by the personnel of other state agencies, federal or county managers, and the highly trained staff of NGOs like the Nature Conservancy or various land trusts. Furthermore, Wisconsin is lucky to have one of the nation's densest volunteer steward networks, which in 2021, for example, provided 7,188 hours of labor worth hundreds of thousands of dollars for management and restoration activities on 55 sites.[12] So, by hook or by crook, a complicated patchwork of funds and labor has been pieced together from public and private sources involving numerous state, federal, and local agencies and conservation organizations. What is lacking in budgetary resources is perhaps made up for with dedication, ingenuity, and persistence.

The management of Wisconsin's SNAs is largely a matter of ecological restoration and maintenance efforts that perpetuate natural communities and protect biodiversity. Thus, management on the small, fragmented parcels that typify the SNA inventory must come to mimic natural processes using tools such as controlled burns, invasive control, and occasionally even logging in certain places to restore open savanna habitats or tallgrass prairie or maintain a rare forest community. Most SNAs have unique management plans, and those embedded in other categories of land, like the recreation-intensive state parks or extraction-oriented state forests, must manage the SNA acres embedded within them as "native community management areas," which guarantees their special treatment.

The BNHC has identified some fairly dire threats that the SNA system and biodiversity in general are beginning to face in Wisconsin, including worsening habitat fragmentation, phosphorus-based water pollution, invasives, deer overpopulation, and, of course, climate change.[13] In addition, especially since the pandemic, the SNA system has seen an explosion in visitation and a level and intensity of use that it is ill equipped to handle. Requests are increasingly made to the DNR to allow damaging and incompatible uses such as horseback riding, mountain biking, snowmobiling, or rock climbing. However, SNAs, especially stand-alone units, have little to no infrastructure (many even lack trails) and no on-site staff to regularly patrol and monitor. In previous years, they had mostly seen relatively light visitation and low-impact activities like hiking, photography, fishing, hunting, or birdwatching. But with a resurgence in outdoor recreation and the advent of viral media and geotagging, SNAs have become much more popular destinations. This problem has not gone unnoted by the BNHC:

> Herein lies a program conundrum: heightened public awareness of SNAs may help build allies and advocates for these properties, yet increased visitation also has the potential to degrade these sites. While increased visitation and associated site degradation are not as significant as the statewide environmental challenges detailed later in this document, incompatible or excessive public use is a growing concern.[14]

Given all the many ways that shifting political winds since 2010 have drastically altered Wisconsin's once-famous commitment to public lands and wildlife (including the utter collapse of land acquisition and state park budgets), it is perhaps surprising that the integrity of the state natural areas program has remained largely intact and unaffected by this political onslaught. Part of this might be due to the fact that the legislation that created Wisconsin's state natural areas program notably gave the DNR the full authority to identify, designate, and even acquire sites without legislative approval.[15] By contrast, many other states require legislative consent for each and every designation—a process often bogged down in procedural delay and political interference. Amazingly, even the gold-standard dedicated SNA status with its perpetual stringent protection does not require legislative approval in Wisconsin (but it does require the governor's approval). Thus, Wisconsin's long-standing process of administrative approval controlled by a committed, scientifically informed, and well-established bureau with a tiny but dedicated funding line has, perhaps more than any other factor, contributed to the program's size and durability. That, and perhaps the desire to make Aldo Leopold proud.

NOTES

1. See Table 3.1.
2. Bureau of Natural Heritage Conservation, *State Natural Area Strategy* (Wisconsin DNR Report PUB-NH-401 2021, July 2021), p. 3.
3. *Ibid.*, pp. 3–4.
4. *Ibid.*, p. 6.
5. *Ibid.*, pp. 5–6.
6. *Ibid.*, p. 8.
7. *Ibid.*, p. 5.
8. *Ibid.*, p. iv.
9. *Ibid.*, p. vi.
10. *Ibid.*, p. 7; Natural Resources Foundation of Wisconsin, *A Virtual Tour of State Natural Areas We Know and Love* (PowerPoint Presentation, May 2020), slide 8, available at: https://www.wisconservation.org/wp-content/uploads/2020/05/SNA-Webinar-Presentation.pdf.
11. Bureau of Natural Heritage Conservation, p. 6.
12. Wisconsin Department of Natural Resources, *2021 SNA Volunteer Report* (Report, 2022), p. 3, available at: https://widnr.widen.net/s/bpqnjh97dc/sna_2021_volunteer_report.
13. Bureau of Natural Heritage Conservation, pp. 15–21.
14. *Ibid.*, p. 11.
15. *Ibid.*, p. 4.

State Wilderness Areas

At the federal level, the idea of legally designating large areas of roadless wildland and protecting them from intrusion came to fruition with the creation of the National Wilderness Preservation System in 1964. It eventually grew from its original 9 million acres to 111.7 million acres (or 18% of all federal land) today.[31] By contrast, the scale and reach of state wilderness systems is far more modest, with only eight states having a formal wilderness system and just two of those states (New York and Alaska) having two-thirds of all state wilderness acreage, which currently stands at about 3.7 million acres.

If state natural areas contain the DNA of Aldo Leopold, then the idea of officially designated wilderness areas surely is the offspring of John Muir, who saw wildland as a "window opening into heaven, a mirror reflecting the Creator."[32] Early preservationist thought, which focused on the beauty of untamed nature, began to call for the protection of large primitive tracts of land as a counterpoint to civilization and a realm where any traces of the built environment are absent and solitude and reflection are possible.[33] This notion can be seen in the language of the Federal Wilderness Act of 1964:

> A wilderness, in contrast with those areas where man and his own works dominate the landscape, is hereby recognized as an area where the earth and its community of life are untrammeled by man, where man himself is a visitor who does not remain. An area of wilderness is further defined to mean in this chapter an area of undeveloped Federal land retaining its primeval character and influence, without permanent improvements or human habitation, which is protected and managed so as to preserve its natural conditions and which (1) generally appears to have been affected primarily by the forces of nature, with the imprint of man's work substantially unnoticeable; (2) has outstanding opportunities for solitude or a primitive and unconfined type of recreation.[34]

But as the science of ecology advanced, such arguments were increasingly superseded by biological justifications, though they are by no means mutually exclusive. In fact, the National Wilderness Preservation System, despite all the talk of solitude and primeval character in its enabling legislation, can also be considered one of the pillars of biodiversity preservation (especially for wide-ranging mammals) in the United States, whether or not that was Congress's original intent.[35]

Table 3.2 summarizes wilderness preservation at the state level. Only eight states have some version of an official wilderness system or a close equivalent,[36] although the criteria for the designation of tracts as wilderness varies from state to state. Some of these wilderness systems were created through legislation (California, Maryland, and Michigan, for example), while others, like Wisconsin and Missouri, were set up through administrative rulemaking. The same is true for granting approval for inclusion of specific tracts. Besides the eight states with official programs, another five states (Ohio, Oklahoma, Hawaii, Maine, and South Carolina) have ad hoc individual units that are explicitly managed as wilderness but outside of any larger official system or process.[37] For example, Ohio's Shawnee Wilderness and Oklahoma's McCurtain County Wilderness were created by their respective legislatures as one-off, though permanent, designations.[38] Minnesota's 18,000 acres of ad hoc wilderness are on state trust land inholdings within the much larger federal Boundary Water Canoe Area (BWCA) Wil-

TABLE 3.2 STATE WILDERNESS AREA SYSTEMS

State	Acres of state wilderness areas or equivalent (in thousands)	Acres of state wilderness area (or equivalent) as percentage of all state land	Official wilderness program?	Legislative or administrative designation
New York	1,358.3[1]	31.8%	Yes	Administrative
Alaska	1,133.4	1.1%	Yes	Administrative
California	547.5	18.7%	Yes	Either
Maine	232.5	22.6%	No	Legislative
Pennsylvania	152.9	3.8%	Yes[2]	Administrative
Maryland	66.0	13.2%	Yes	Legislative
Michigan	45.7[3]	1.0%	Yes	Legislative
Hawaii	37.0	2.4%	No	Either
Missouri	25.2	2.6%	Yes	Administrative
Minnesota	18.0[4]	0.2%	No	Legislative
Wisconsin	14.5[5]	0.9%	Yes	Administrative
Oklahoma	14.0	1.3%	No	Legislative
South Carolina	10.9	2.4%	No	Administrative
Ohio	8.0	1.4%	No	Legislative
Total U.S.	3,658.8	1.8%; not including trust lands 6.0%	NA	NA

Data sources: See appendix.

[1] In addition to this, there is, in the Adirondacks and Catskill preserves, another 1,428,209 acres of wild forest, which is a slightly less restrictive designation that allows for motorized conveyance.

[2] Rather than wilderness, Pennsylvania has a designation called wild areas that, in most respects (minimum size, no development or active management), is substantially similar to wilderness.

[3] This figure includes a 4,492-acre proposed wilderness area that must be protected as wilderness until a final decision is made. Otherwise, all the remaining acres are in just one preserve, Michigan's incomparable Porcupine Mountains Wilderness State Park.

[4] This acreage consists of state trust lands embedded as inholdings within the enormous federal Boundary Waters Canoe Area Wilderness. The state had determined to treat this land as wilderness as well. However, it is in the process of exchanging some of these inholdings with the federal government for productive federal timberland elsewhere in the state and selling the rest to a conservation organization who will transfer it to the BWCA. So eventually, Minnesota should have no informal state wilderness areas.

[5] This figure denotes acreage in the official wild resource management area (WRMA) designation, which is Wisconsin's equivalent of a wilderness area. In addition to these WRMA acres, there is also the 2,373-acre Newport State Park that is explicitly managed by the DNR as, in their words, "a wilderness park."

derness and are maintained as wilderness so as to not disrupt the popular BWCA. Miranda Holeton and David Takacs report that the state is currently in the process of selling some of these acres to the U.S. Forest Service and exchanging the rest for federal timberlands elsewhere in the state.[39] When this process is complete, Minnesota should have no remaining state wilderness areas.

Given that wilderness areas are only present in just over a dozen states and account for a relatively small portion of state-owned lands, it is worth pointing out just how uniquely robust wilderness protection is in four states—New York (an astonishing 32% of all state-owned land), Maine (23%), California (19%), and, most surprising of all, dense and heavily urbanized Maryland, with 13% of its public lands protected as roadless "wildlands." New York's wilderness achievements are solely due to the mandates of the "Forever Wild" provision of the state constitution pertaining to the Adirondack and Catskill Parks. Eventually, specific roadless portions of this de facto wilderness (about 45%) were administratively granted official wilderness land use classification by the Adirondack Parks Agency and the New York State Department of Environmental Conservation starting in the 1970s.[40] Similarly, the nearly one-quarter of Maine's public lands that are held as wilderness are mostly due to the stipulations written into the charter of Baxter, its large special status park (see Chapter 2).

As for the three-quarters of states with no wilderness areas, the question arises as to what factors would explain this resistance. Especially for western states, but also those bordering Appalachia, it might be that abundant federal wilderness areas obviate the need to provide state wilderness. In many other states, perhaps it is a lack of qualifying lands that meet some basic wilderness criteria on size and roadlessness. Or perhaps, as the decades-long fight at the federal level over wilderness designation suggests, it is outright ideological hostility for a land use classification that is seen in many quarters as a "lock-up" of productive land that prevents any meaningful amount of revenue from being drawn from it. Proper wilderness management, after all, largely precludes any other nonpassive uses, be they extraction or more intrusive forms of recreation. In fact, Baxter State Park's motto of "wilderness first, recreation second" explicitly spells out these priorities.[41] Perhaps because wilderness preserves are much larger and less remote, their valuable ecosystems are usually less intensively managed than those on the smaller, more fragmented state natural areas. To manage a wilderness area, then, is largely to leave it alone and perhaps patrol its trails.

This chapter has presented two categories of state public land—state natural areas and state wilderness areas—as the places in the state land management realm that are focused, first and foremost, upon the preservation of nature and ecosystem health. While these areas are fairly modest in scale and unevenly distributed geographically, they nevertheless offer quite meaningful protection to some of the best and richest parcels of state land. For this reason, Table 3.3 attempts to create a "preservation orientation score" for the states based upon which states have wilderness and natural areas

TABLE 3.3 STATE LANDS PRESERVATION ORIENTATION SCORE RANKING

Rank	State	Preservation score[1]
1	New York	.60
2	Kentucky	.53
3	Georgia	.51
4	Wisconsin	.50
5	California	.49
6	Maine	.47
7	South Carolina	.44
8	Maryland	.43
9	Hawaii	.40
10	Missouri	.35
10	Illinois	.35
11	Pennsylvania	.32
12	Michigan	.30
13	Massachusetts	.29
14	Tennessee	.25
15	Arkansas	.24
15	Virginia	.24
16	Indiana	.23
17	Minnesota	.22
17	Ohio	.22
18	Delaware	.19
18	New Jersey	.19
19	Oregon	.18
19	Vermont	.18
19	Colorado	.18
20	Washington	.17
20	Louisiana	.17
21	North Carolina	.16[2]
22	Iowa	.15
23	Alaska	.14
24	West Virginia	.13
24	Arizona	.13
25	Connecticut	.09
26	New Hampshire	.07
26	Oklahoma	.07
27	South Dakota	.02

(Table 3.3 continued at top of next page)

TABLE 3.3 STATE LANDS PRESERVATION ORIENTATION SCORE RANKING *(continued)*		
Rank	State	Preservation score
28	Mississippi	.01
28	North Dakota	.01
29	Texas	.00
29	Montana	.00
29	Utah	.00
29	Wyoming	.00
29	New Mexico	.00
29	Rhode Island	.00
29	Florida	.00
29	Idaho	.00
29	Alabama	.00
29	Kansas	.00
29	Nebraska	.00
29	Nevada	.00

Data sources: See appendix.

[1] This score is a 0–1 scale calculated from: 1) percentage of all state-owned land protected as state natural area (or equivalent designation), 2) percentage of all land in state protected as state natural area (or equivalent designation), 3) status of state natural area program (official, informal, or nonexistent), 4) percentage of state-owned land protected as wilderness area (or equivalent designation), 5) percentage of all land in state protected as wilderness area (or equivalent designation), and 6) status of wilderness program (official, informal, or nonexistent).

[2] This relatively low score is perhaps undeserved in that North Carolina, while having a relatively small natural areas program, overtly manages the bulk of its state park system in a way that closely resembles how SNAs are managed, a fact that is not picked up in this scale's methodology.

programs and/or tracts and in what quantities. Keep in mind, however, that such a measure is imperfect as it misses those efforts at good preservation-oriented management (in places like North Carolina and Florida) that take place outside formal state natural area and wilderness programs. This measure, instead, tries to gauge a state's orientation to the broad purpose of preservation based primarily on how its land use classifications and the laws and programs that undergird them are arranged and applied.

New York, Kentucky, Georgia, Wisconsin, and California are the states with the highest preservation orientation scores. While there is not much of a geographic pattern in the highest-scoring states (with the South, Northeast, Pacific, and Great Lakes states all represented), no states in the interior West are in the top 20 states, and all Great Plains states are clustered in the bottom third. It is important to note here that these scores reflect the orientation of the lands that a state possesses and whether there is an accompanying legal and programmatic framework to signify commitment to the preservation goal. It is therefore possible, though also quite interesting, that Kentucky, ranked fourth from the bottom in overall state land (1%), is nonetheless ranked second behind New York on its orientation to preservation goals. It is probably also worth noting that those states, largely western, with huge trust land holdings that by mandate preclude preservation-oriented management are probably doomed in this measure to have very low scores as their trust lands overwhelmingly dilute all their other holdings.

Pikes Peak State Park, Iowa (Photo by author)

4

Land of Many Uses, State Edition

State Forests and Multiple Use Lands

> "Multiple use" means the harmonious and coordinated management
> of timber, recreation, conservation of fish and wildlife, forage,
> archaeological and historic sites, habitat and other biological resources,
> or water resources so that they are utilized in the combination that will
> best serve the people of the state, making the most judicious use of the
> land for some or all of these resources and giving consideration to the
> relative values of the various resources.
>
> —Florida Statute § 253.034 (2)

With 21.4 million acres, state forest systems in the U.S. are about double
the size of state park systems but with far less visibility and attention. This
is the category of land use most explicitly dedicated to multiple use principles, whereby land is supposed to be managed in a way that balances all
three broad purposes of public land—recreation, preservation, and resource
extraction. Indiana's multiple use mandate, for example, is "to protect and
conserve the timber, water resources, wildlife, and topsoil in the forests
owned and operated by the division of forestry for the equal enjoyment and
guaranteed use of future generations."[1] In the field, however, the concept
of multiple use is unavoidably vague and hard to apply. Critics argue that
its ambiguity allows managers to justify essentially any course of action,[2]
and thus, of the three broad uses of public land, resource extraction usually
gets elevated to "first among equals." State managers are generally quite
unapologetic about this focus on using state multiple use land to produce
commodities such as timber or energy. This is clear, for example, in the way
Alaska interprets its multiple use mandate:

> The primary purpose is timber management that provides for the
> production and utilization of timber resources while allowing oth-
> er beneficial uses of public land and resources. State Forests provide
> fish and wildlife habitat, clean water, opportunities for recreation
> and tourism, and minerals.[3]

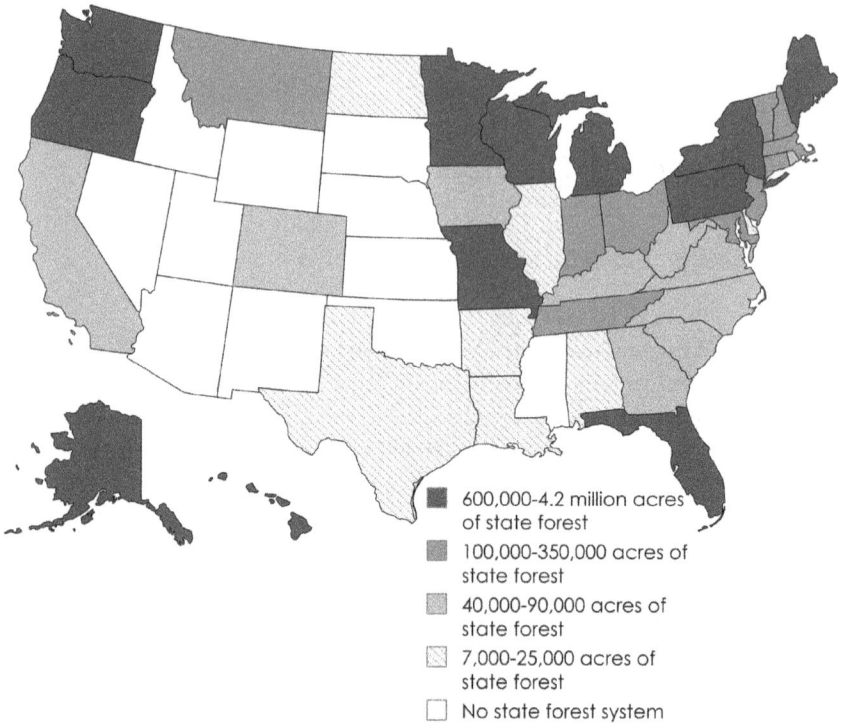

Figure 4.1 State forest systems by acreage (Data sources: See Table 4.1 and appendix.)

While state forests certainly provide opportunities for recreation, such recreation tends to be much more restrained and low-key than what is typically found in state parks. The campgrounds are fewer and more primitive, the trail systems a bit less developed and extensive, and infrastructural amenities like lodges or sports facilities generally nonexistent. This varies, of course, by state, with some state forest systems more akin to working forest plantations and others, like Florida's, much more geared to recreation. The same is true regarding the extent to which explicit preservation as a multiple use gets practiced, with some states, like Massachusetts, Maine, Pennsylvania, and Maryland, carving out significant swaths of their state forest lands for natural areas, wildlands preservation, and forest reserves while other states, like Michigan, setting aside very little of their state forests for strictly preservation-oriented management goals.

All but nine states have state forest systems or their multiple use equivalents, and while there is a tier of states—Minnesota, Michigan, Pennsylvania, Alaska, and Florida—with massive state forest systems with over a million acres, many more have relatively modest systems with just tens of thousands of acres, as Table 4.1 shows. Missouri also has a million-acre

TABLE 4.1 STATE FOREST AND OTHER MULTIPLE USE LAND

State	Acres of state forest land and equivalent multiple use land (MUL) (in thousands)	State forests/MUL as percentage of all state public lands	State forests/MUL as percentage of total land in state	Administered by independent agency/ commission
Minnesota	4,200.0[1]	50.0%	8.2%	
Michigan	3,859.8	84.0%	10.6%	
Pennsylvania	2,200.0	55.0%	7.7%	
Alaska	2,134.9	2.1%	0.6%	
Florida	1,164.6	21.9%	3.4%	X
Missouri	1,019.2[2]	83.6%[3]	2.3%	X
New York	784.5	18.4%	2.6%	
Oregon	745.2[4]	43.1%	1.2%	X
Hawaii	684.0	45.0%	16.6%	
Wisconsin	667.2[5]	42.1%	1.9%	
Maine	662.0[6]	64.4%	3.4%	
Washington	626.0[7]	16.2%	1.5%	
Massachusetts	333.3[8]	57.0%	6.6%	
New Jersey	233.8[9]	27.9%	4.9%	
Maryland	228.7	45.7%	3.6%	
Montana	203.0[10]	3.6%	0.2%	
Ohio	200.0	33.9%	0.8%	
Tennessee	166.9	17.4%	0.6%	X
Vermont	165.2	47.2%	2.8%	
Connecticut	160.8	66.1%	5.2%	
Indiana	160.8	39.8%	0.7%	
New Hampshire	100.4	43.1%	1.7%	
South Carolina	92.6	20.0%	0.5%	X
West Virginia	72.7	13.1%	0.5%	
California	72.0	2.5%	< 0.1%	X
Virginia	72.0	16.7%	0.3%	X
Colorado	71.0[11]	2.1%	0.1%	
North Carolina	59.3	6.4%	0.2%	X
Rhode Island	59.2[12]	84.6%[13]	8.9%	
Georgia	58.5[14]	8.2%	0.2%	X
Kentucky	48.8	20.0%	0.2%	X
Iowa	43.7	11.2%	0.1%	
Arkansas	23.5	4.6%	< 0.1%	X
Illinois	21.4	5.4%	< 0.1%	
Delaware	20.0	17.5%	1.6%	X
Alabama	14.0	2.6%	< 0.1%	
North Dakota	13.9	1.7%	< 0.1%	X
Louisiana	8.0	0.6%	< 0.1%	
Texas	7.3	0.4%	< 0.1%	X
Total U.S.	21,365.2	10.7%	0.9%	

(Table 4.1 notes appear at top of next page)

Data sources: See appendix.

Note: Mississippi, Nebraska, Arizona, New Mexico, Oklahoma, Idaho, South Dakota, Wyoming, Nevada, Kansas, and Utah have no state forest systems.

[1] Minnesota state forests are totally integrated with the state's school trust lands.

[2] At some point several decades ago, Missouri transformed all its state forests and wildlife management areas into what they now call conservation areas. These lands are essentially multiple use tracts. Of this total, 815,006 acres are owned by the state and 204,169 are leased.

[3] This figure is calculated only from the 815,000 acres of conservation areas that are owned by the state, not leased. Additionally, please note that this category of state land in Missouri is double counted under wildlife management areas as well since it is a hybrid of the two.

[4] Of this total, 32,598 is on state trust land.

[5] This total consists of 536,986 acres of state forest and 130,263 acres of scenic water areas (also called flowages) and state rivers and riverways, much of which is open to forest management.

[6] In Maine, the functional equivalent of state forests is called public reserved lands. In addition to 632,500 acres of public reserved lands, 29,537 acres of Baxter State Park, which is a special status state park governed by a separate authority, are held as a scientific forest management area that authorizes timber production, thereby acting much as a state forest and thus included in this figure.

[7] The Washington state forest system is wholly made up of forested tracts of state trust land.

[8] Of this figure, 233,335 acres are state forest and 100,000 acres are watershed management lands where forest management is practiced. Of the state forests, nearly half (111,227 acres) are reserves off-limits to logging, while the rest (122,108 acres) are regular managed woodlands.

[9] Includes 2,039 acres of New Jersey Water Authority watershed lands.

[10] Montana's state forest system consists entirely of state trust land.

[11] Colorado State Forest is a single unit of state trust land run by Colorado state parks.

[12] Rhode Island maintains management areas, which are a hybrid of state forest and wildlife management area. Of this figure, 47,182 acres are state owned and 12,018 acres are leased. These acres are also counted in Table 5.1 for wildlife areas.

[13] This figure is calculated only from the 47,182 acres of management areas that are owned by the state and not leased. Additionally, please note that this category of state land in Rhode Island is double counted under wildlife management areas as well since it exists as a hybrid of the two.

[14] Some of these tracts are owned by local governments but managed by the state within the state forest system.

system, but its conservation areas, along with Rhode Island's management areas, are not technically state forests but perhaps the truest sort of multiple use lands, fusing forests and state wildlife areas into a hybrid type of unit. In both states, these hybrid multiple use lands make up at least five-sixths of all their state-owned lands. Other states with half or more of their public land base as state forest include Connecticut, Michigan, Minnesota, Pennsylvania, Maine, and Massachusetts. In terms of what percentage of a state's entire landmass consists of state forest land, Figure 4.1 shows that Hawaii and Michigan are the champions at nearly 17% and 11% respectively, while Minnesota, Pennsylvania, Massachusetts, Rhode Island, and Connecticut are all made up of between 5% and 10% state forest land. Except for Mississippi, all the states without state forest systems are in the Great Plains or the Mountain West.[4]

A Very Brief History of State Forests

The big state forest systems of the Upper Midwest (Minnesota, Michigan, and Wisconsin) along with Pennsylvania and New York may not have come to exist if those states' forestlands were not laid to waste in a few decades' time during the 19th century. The rampage of unsustainable timber harvesting had liquidated much of the forest in these states by the turn of the century.[5] Ruinous fires repeatedly swept the stump fields filled with dry and resinous logging debris, and this sterilized the soil in many places. In other places, the thin, rocky soil overlying the Canadian Shield was never suited for farming, and so the farms that replaced much of the logged areas never prospered. The result was that by the 1920s and 1930s, millions of acres of once-towering forests were now failed farms or abandoned and tax-delinquent tracts of brushy wasteland.[6] In most places, the law stipulated that when taxes went unpaid for a period, the land would eventually be forfeited to the county.

This period was the tail end of the Progressive Era, and the Northeast and Upper Midwest were the geographic epicenters of this political movement. So, it should be no surprise that the solution to this debacle caused by avaricious, unregulated markets came to be seen as public control. States quickly passed laws to allow governments to hold rather than resell the forfeited lands and manage them in the public interest in order to make them healthy and productive once more. Since counties were generally in no position to own and manage this land, they generally transferred it to state governments in exchange for a cut of the revenue from eventual timber production.[7] On the West Coast, Oregon largely followed this same pattern in acquiring its state forest land.[8] While Minnesota likewise acquired much state forest land through tax forfeiture, it was also the only eastern state that retained the bulk of its school lands granted at statehood in 1858, and much of this land was also put into the state forest system.[9] Similarly, Washington state forests retain a mix of tax-forfeited acquisitions alongside school trust grants, while Montana's system is wholly composed of trust lands granted at statehood. The extent to which these three states mix and merge their regular land management classifications (state forests) and their trust lands is somewhat unusual as most states with extensive trust holdings manage them in a strictly segregated way. This segregation is due to the built-in fiduciary duties and revenue maximization obligations that most trust arrangements require and that seem to preclude true multiple use management. These issues are discussed much more fully in Chapter 6.

While the tax-forfeited land was essentially "free" to the states, much of the adjacent cutover land and failing farmsteads that were not tax delinquent were, nevertheless, for sale at deeply depressed prices. The same states, then, bolstered their growing state forest systems with such purchases.[10] The federal government, meanwhile, did the very same thing after the passage of the Weeks Act in 1911 and the Clarke-McNary Act of 1924, which allowed the U.S. Forest Service (USFS) to purchase forestlands east of the Mississippi in order to establish national forests in those states.[11] That is why state and national forests in Minnesota, Michigan, Ohio, Wisconsin, Pennsylvania, Vermont, and New Hampshire tend to be immediately adjacent and even intertwined in places.

Maine's 600,000-acre state forest equivalents—public reserved lands—have very interesting and much earlier origins. From the beginning of statehood when Maine separated from Massachusetts in 1820, the new state had a unique system whereby all private land sales throughout the state had to set aside a small portion as a public trust (similar in spirit but not the same as the school trust lands).[12] These lands accumulated over the years but were largely ignored and forgotten and exploited by the timber companies who owned adjacent lands and acted as if these public tracts were their own. By the 1970s, however, the state began to take back full control, and these scattered parcels were consolidated as best as possible through land exchanges into more cohesive units and managed as state forests.[13] Meanwhile, Hawaii, with the largest state forest system in the U.S. proportionate to state size, largely carved its system out of the extensive crown lands that the U.S. kept intact after annexation in 1898 and then granted to Hawaii upon statehood in 1959.[14] That same year, Alaska was granted 105 million acres at statehood and put aside 2.1 million of those acres as state forest.[15] Other states largely pieced their systems together after World War 2 through routine processes of state land acquisition, especially after Land and Water Conservation Funds became available in the 1960s and other monies were made available through various bond-authorizing referenda. Florida's very large state forest system was largely built this way, mostly after 1970.[16]

Resource Extraction on State Forests

Timber

As explicit multiple use land, it is not particularly controversial that state forests have ongoing programs of timber harvesting. The political conflict, just as with the national forests, arises from the details—that is, the volume, the methods, or the precise location of the logging. This political conflict over logging at the state level is far less intense and pervasive than what occurs in the national forests for all sorts of important reasons that are addressed further on in this chapter. However, where it occurs, it reveals much about the political contours of state land management.

When the big state forest systems were established on cutover land in the early 20th century, there was practically no logging going on for many decades as the replanted forests were growing back. However, by the turn of the next century, 80 or so years later, many of these tracts had matured to the point where they were eligible to be harvested, and this led to a large increase in the annual harvest on most state forests. According to critics, however, this is not the whole story as this time period also coincided with the intense state budget crises discussed in Chapter 2 and the same accompanying scramble in many states for increased revenue to counteract shrinking general fund budgets.[17] As such, some state forest systems have come to depend on revenue generated from timber sales and energy leases to pay for a significant portion of land management costs (for example, 67% in Michigan in 2013).[18] And at least according to the critics, the desire for greater revenue has driven timber management decisions to at least some extent.

In the late 1990s and early 2000s, around the same time that state forest harvests were increasing, there was a rapid decline in national forest harvests, going from a peak of more than 12 billion board feet in 1990 to about 2.8 billion in 2021.[19] This decline was largely due to a series of successful lawsuits by environmentalist groups invoking the endangered status of the spotted owl that lived in the remaining old-growth forests of the Pacific Northwest. *Old growth* most often refers to forests that existed in America before European settlement and are generally older than 200 years.[20] In 1991, (federal) District Judge William Dwyer enjoined all timber sales in the national forests of the Pacific Northwest until a timber management plan that did not endanger the owls could be designed and adopted. The result was a new federal policy for preserving significant remnants of old growth and adopting an *ecosystem management* approach across the national forest system.[21] This approach essentially elevated concern about biodiversity and ecosystem-level function and became a new framework by which to make multiple-use decisions. Incidentally, eastern national forests largely assembled, like state forests, from cutover lands did not see much of the sharp reduction in harvest volumes as did the older forests on the West Coast.

Table 4.2 shows that the proportional volume of annual harvests in state forests around the country now greatly exceeds that of the national forest system. The selected state forest systems mostly have between 2 and 10 times greater a rate of timber production per 1,000 acres. Washington's figure (at 56 times more production per 1,000 acres) is an outlier due to the presence of older forests in its trust lands, with extremely high levels of biomass (and subject to far fewer old-growth logging restrictions than on federal lands). To compare ecologically identical forests with similar biomass and growth rates, Table 4.3 examines timber production on adjacent state and national forests within the *same* states. In both Wisconsin and Minnesota, state forests produce about double the volume of timber per acre than the national forests. This is very much in line with Koontz's four-state comparison to the federal logging program.[22] One reason timber output on Minnesota's national forests is so relatively low probably has to do with the fact that the million-acre Boundary Waters Canoe Area Wilderness takes 27% of the state's federal forestland out of production. Table 4.4, meanwhile, also looks within states to compare state and federal timber production as a percentage of overall production. In Minnesota, the similarly sized federal and state forest systems make up 21% and 23% of the state's timberlands respectively, but federal land contributes only 5% to the state's overall output as compared to 16% for state land. Even more dramatically, in Oregon, national forests make up almost half of the forest acreage in the state but only 14% of the state's timber output, while state and local forests make up 4% but contribute 10% of the output.[23]

Longtime critics of the USFS, such as Robert Nelson and Holly Fretwell and Shawn Regan, not only bemoan what they consider a "lock-up" of wilderness lands but also argue that the agency's supposedly sclerotic bureaucracy and its overly subjective ecosystem management approach are to blame for the collapse in federal production.[24] In contrast, Nelson lauds the states as the true practitioners of traditional forestry in the efficiently utilitarian model of Gifford Pinchot, the first director of the USFS.[25] Perhaps the biggest debates around public forest management involve the extent to which mature and old-growth forests (the latter of which are vanishingly rare on state forest land) are seen to be valuable and desirable natural assets.[26] In the mindset of traditional forestry, old-growth or mature forests are just "overripe" places with wasted and declining timber and sparse wildlife, whereas young forests are vigorous and healthy.[27] From a true ecosystem management perspective, however, mature forests are understood as especially rich in biodiversity, capable of tremendous amounts of carbon storage and other ecological services, and especially important for conservative niche species like fishers, spotted owls, and salamanders, to name a few.[28] And because mature and old-growth forests are relatively rare on state lands

TABLE 4.2 SELECTED STATE AND FEDERAL FOREST SYSTEM TIMBER HARVESTS

Jurisdiction	Annual state forest timber production (mmbf[1]) and data year	Production (mmbf) per 1,000 acres of public forestland
Indiana	11.1 (2009–2019 average)	0.069
Ohio	9.8 (2018)	0.049
Washington	529.2 (2016)	0.845
New York	24.1 (2002–2013 average)	0.031
Michigan	500.0 (2015)	0.130
Pennsylvania	63.2 (2016)	0.029
Maine	62.0 (2011–2021 average)	0.094
U.S.	2,800.0 (national forests, 2021)	0.015

Data sources: Indiana Department of Natural Resources, 2019 Division of Forestry Annual Report, p. 4 available at: https://www.in.gov/dnr/forestry/files/fo-dnr-dof-2019-annual-report.pdf; Ohio Department of Natural Resources, Division of Forestry FY 2018 Annual Report, p. 16, available at: https://ohiodnr.gov/static/documents/forestry/reports/AnnualReport_FY2018.pdf; Washington Department of Natural Resources, *2017 Washington Timber Harvest Report*, p. v, available at: em _obe_wa_timber_harvest_2017_final3.pdf; for New York, Pennsylvania, and Michigan, see, Robert Nelson, *State-Owned Lands in the Eastern United States* (PERC Public Lands Report, March 2018), pp. 14, 20, 27; Maine Department of Agriculture, Conservation, and Forestry, Bureau of Public Lands, *Fiscal Year 2021 Annual Report* (March 1, 2022), p. 20, available at: https://www .maine.gov/dacf/parks/publications_maps/docs/2021BPL-AnnualReport.pdf; Anne Riddle, *Timber Harvesting on Federal Lands* (Congressional Research Service Report R45688, October 25, 2022), p. 8, available at: https://sgp.fas.org/crs/misc/R45688.pdf.

[1] Mmbf refers to millions of board feet.

TABLE 4.3 COMPARATIVE FEDERAL-STATE TIMBER HARVEST VOLUMES WITHIN SAME STATES

Jurisdiction	Annual timber harvest (in thousands of cords) and year	Total acres in system (in thousands)	Cords harvested per acre in system
Wisconsin state multiple use lands	256.4 (2016)	979.1	0.26
Minnesota state multiple use lands	812.0 (average 2012–2016)	4,898.7	0.16
National forests in Wisconsin	207.3 (2016)	1,530.6	0.13
National forests in Minnesota	258.0 (2016)	3,666.0	0.07

Data sources: Minnesota Department of Natural Resources, *Sustainable Timber Harvest Determination* (March 1, 2018), p. 3, available at: https://files.dnr.state.mn.us/forestry/subsection/harvest -analysis/stha-determination-report.pdf; Wisconsin Department of Natural Resources, *Timber Harvest in Wisconsin* (May 2017), p. 5, available at: https://dnr.wisconsin.gov/sites/default/files/topic /ForestBusinesses/TimberHarvestWisconsin.pdf; Minnesota Department of Natural Resources, *Minnesota's Forest Resources 2017* (May 2019), p. 24, available at: https://www.leg.mn.gov/docs /2019/other/190834.pdf.

TABLE 4.4 COMPARATIVE FEDERAL-STATE TIMBER SALES IN OREGON AND MINNESOTA AS PERCENTAGE OF TOTAL ACREAGE AND SALES

Jurisdiction	Percentage of total forest acreage in state	Percentage of all timber sold in state
Oregon state/local forests	4%	10%
Oregon national forests	48%	14%
Minnesota state multiple use lands	23%	16%
Minnesota national forests	21%	5%

Data sources: Oregon Forests Resources Institute, *Oregon Forest Facts 2021–2022 Edition* (2021), p. 3, available at: https://oregonforests.org/sites/default/files/2021-01/OFRI_2021ForestFacts_WEB3 .pdf; Steven Davis, "The Forests Nobody Wanted: The Politics of Land Management in the County Forests of the Upper Midwest" in *Journal of Land Use and Environmental Law* (Vol. 28, No. 2, Spring 2013), p. 207.

and have such profound biological value and aesthetic appeal, there is much pressure to preserve them as an integral part of any balanced multiple use–oriented system.

Since the 1990s at least, it is federal land managers, rather than state ones, that have operated more in line with an ecosystem management framework and thus proven more willing, in multiple-use settings, to restrain the most aggressive commodity-production scenarios. To use another state-federal comparison from neighboring units within the same state, Wisconsin's state forests reserve about 13.7% of forested acreage for nontimber management (as state natural areas, for example) while Wisconsin's national forest, the Chequamegon-Nicolet, has 22% of its forested acreage in special, more ecologically protective categories,[29] despite being one of the most heavily logged national forests in the entire system.[30] Far more dramatically, Tomas Koontz, in his comparison of state and federal forests in Oregon, finds the old-growth-heavy Siuslaw National Forest to be 81% off-limits to logging as compared with only 2% of the land base of the state forests.[31]

A related debate concerns logging methods. State foresters employ a variety of methods, but even-age management (or clear-cutting), where all the trees are removed at once from a timber sale tract, remains most heavily relied upon. It is without a doubt the most cost effective, taking the least time and labor for the volume of trees removed, and foresters also claim that it beneficially opens the land to fast-growing replantings and wildlife browse.[32] However, it has maximum disruptive effects, especially on water and soil;[33] is aesthetically quite jarring; and has a fairly bad reputation from a public relations standpoint. In the Upper Midwest, it is also common to use clear-cutting on short 30- or 40-year rotations to keep artificially large tracts growing in aspen and birch, which are two short-lived pioneer species favored for pulp production and game species like deer and grouse.[34] The forests of Michigan, for example, went from consisting of an estimated 0.8% aspen/birch in presettlement times (1800) to 16.5% today, an increase of 982%.[35] Selective logging and thinning operations are generally less ecologically disruptive but far more expensive. As a result, logging methods that enhance forest health and reduce negative impacts are seen by many foresters as more akin to restoration than any kind of profitable timber operation.

A few states take ecosystem management and concerns over old-growth forests and biodiversity more seriously than is typical. As previously mentioned, Massachusetts, Maine, Pennsylvania, Maryland, New York, and a few others have taken significant state forest acreage out of production to create ecological reserves, natural areas, or designated wildlands. Oregon, a traditionally high-volume timber producer, has also moved recently in the direction of an ecosystem management approach as it has identified critical habitat conservation areas within its state forests to set aside from logging for at least the next 70 years. It also decided to stop using timber sales revenue as a tool to plug state budget holes.[36] Angry timber producers and counties dependent on a share of logging revenue sued in state court and in 2019 won a $1.1 billion judgment that was overturned on appeal.[37] The case revolved around the meaning of the legal mandate for the state to manage the forests for the "greatest permanent value," which the counties interpreted as timber production and the state thought of as overall forest health.[38]

Other states, meanwhile, have moved in the other direction in terms of policy. Washington State, for example, which already has the highest state forest timber output per acre in the nation, has recently moved to modestly reduce overall harvests but allow logging on 38,000 acres of mature state forest that is currently designated as habitat for the endangered marbled murrelet.[39] Montana, meanwhile, passed legislation in 2021 explicitly prohibiting the preservation of state forests (what the law calls *nonuse*) for old growth or any purpose.[40] Other states have opted to increase logging for budgetary reasons. In 2017, for example, Governor Mark Dayton of Minnesota asked the DNR to boost annual timber harvests from their long-standing level of 800,000 cords to a million; however, an independent third-party auditor determined that this was a level beyond what the state forests could sustain, and the target was reduced to 870,000 cords.[41] In Wisconsin, it was the legislature in 2015 that rather arbitrarily ordered that the DNR allow logging on 75% of all state land rather than the previously eligible 67%.[42] To meet these new goals, the agency has had to get much more aggressive in their timber program, cutting into previously off-limits older mature stands and cutting so perilously close to lakeshores that citizen groups filed complaints accusing the agency of violating its own field manual regarding lake buffers. These charges were seen as credible enough that third-party auditors were called in to investigate.[43]

Energy Production

Although timber is obviously the most common resource extracted from state forest lands, energy production is also a major source of revenue and extraction activity, depending on the state and its geology. As an extractive use, energy production tends to be more controversial than even the most aggressive logging program because mining or establishing the infrastructure of roads, floodlights, well pads, and pumpjacks necessary for fracking or oil production requires an intense and, by definition, unsustainable level of development on public conservation lands that often precludes any other multiple use, at least in the immediate production zone. However, it also produces substantial revenue for generally underfunded agencies. In Michigan, for example, oil and gas leasing revenues brought in $750 million from 1998 to 2008.[44] As with logging programs, state forest energy production tends to exceed federal production on neighboring national forests. While oil and gas revenue from Michigan state forests was $43.6 million in 2012, Michigan's adjacent national forests (which are fairly close in size and geographic proximity to the state system) produced just $1.4 million that same year.[45] "The Forest Service," Nelson claims, "could learn some lessons from Michigan in the management arts of making active, productive use of public forests."[46]

For states, the lucrative benefits of energy production seem to clearly outweigh the profound impacts of such activity on the resource base. By the height of the fracking boom, Pennsylvania had leased 700,000 acres of state forest land, or roughly a third of the system, for gas leasing. Before long, well pads and roads and outbuildings began to fragment and industrialize previously solid blocks of wild forestland, and alarm rose not only among environmentalists but also the forest products industry, who began to feel that their "multiple use" was starting to be crowded out by another one. In 2010, then Governor Ed Rendell announced a moratorium (cancelled and then reauthorized by his two successors in subsequent years) on all new leases on state forest land.[47] The already-leased parcels, however, have the potential of adding 1,000 additional well pads and up to 10,000 more wells in the next several decades.[48] Even Florida, known for its relatively well-protected state forests, felt the urge to get in on the energy boom, with the legislature in 2012 and 2016 attempting (unsuccessfully) to authorize fracking on state land—specifically Blackwater State Forest.[49] Ohio, meanwhile, has gone so far as to allow strip mining, perhaps the most ecologically impactful form of extraction, to remove coal from Perry State Forest. This proposal too was withdrawn after strong public opposition.[50]

State Forest Carbon Offsets— Financial Salvation, Fraud, or Both?

In addition to the traditional resources, like timber, energy, and minerals, that are extracted from state forests, a newer trend has been for some state (and county) forests to leverage their substantial forest resources by selling credits to carbon trading firms who then market them to corporations looking to offset their carbon emissions. Michigan and Wisconsin were the first states to sign offset contracts, but at least a half dozen other states, including Alaska and Washington, are moving forward as well.[51] At first glance, the idea seems sound as states protect vast tracts of forestlands that store tremendous amounts of carbon. Selling offsets, then, would seem to be a win–win situation—a way to cash in on this important ecological service and serve as an important new revenue source for state land agencies while reducing carbon in the atmosphere. The nation's first state forest carbon contract involved Michigan's 105,000-acre Pigeon River State Forest and earned the DNR $10 million. Annual revenue from a similar carbon project on county forest land in Iron County, Wisconsin, meanwhile, might end up being equal to 10% of the county's total budget.[52]

Upon closer inspection, however, it becomes quite evident that the carbon reduction claims of proponents of public forest carbon offsets are somewhat spurious. The reason for this has to do with the principle of *additionality*—that is, a true offset has to create a real additional amount of carbon reduction in the atmosphere. For this to be true for offset credits on forests, they would need to do one of three things: 1) prevent the imminent destruction of a particular forest (as is often the case in tropical rainforests), 2) replant a new forest where one had been cleared with no prior plans for replanting, or 3) significantly lengthen logging rotations on managed forests to allow the trees to get much larger and store more carbon than they otherwise would. The state and county forest carbon offset deals signed thus far achieve none of these three requirements for actual carbon reduction. These forests have been protected in the public domain for three-quarters of a century or longer and are secure into the future. State regulations already require clear-cuts to be reforested, and no changes to logging rotations or methods have been asked of state or county managers. When challenged with these facts, public and company officials vaguely suggest that massive possible increases in future logging will have been headed off. But this is almost certainly untrue, as state and county forest harvest volumes are determined by large-range plans and state laws. Many of the forests in question are also third-party certified by the Forest Stewardship Council, which has strict protocols against overharvesting. Even some foresters admit that these offsets actually do nothing except provide revenue. According to one Wisconsin county official, "It's a little asinine to pay us to do something that was already going to happen, which could allow someone to pollute somewhere else. I'm not sure this is an environmental salvation."[53] Despite their dubious efficacy, state forest carbon offset credits involve a lot of money, which hints at both why these deals are being so vigorously pursued and the incentives that are structured into such deals. Large energy-intensive corporations, like airlines and utilities, badly want or need to reduce their carbon liabilities, and as such, public forest carbon offsets provide a ready market for the companies who arrange carbon deals. For these middlemen, who typically take a 10%–33% cut of the deals they strike,[54] carbon offsets on state forests have the massive advantage of low monitoring and compliance costs since these forests are reputable, publicly managed, and externally certified entities. Compare that to the costs and headaches of keeping tabs on projects to save a patch of Amazon from itinerant cattle ranchers or replanting forests in Indonesia. The fact that state forest carbon offset projects thus far have probably not reduced carbon emissions at all seems to be of no particular concern when so much money is at stake. Perhaps if the growing criticism of these deals gives pause to public officials or consumers of offsets in the future, then they might be restructured to actually change forest management to lengthen rotations or even preserve old growth. If the price of carbon credits rises high enough, this might actually be one of the most lucrative uses of state forests going forward.

STATE FORESTS: *Spotlight on Michigan*

With 3.9 million acres, Michigan has the nation's second-largest state forest system, just under Minnesota's 4.2 million acres. However, if one were to randomly pick any acre of state land in Michigan, the odds would heavily favor that acre being part of a state forest, as they dominate state lands in Michigan, making up five out of every six acres. This massive system alone encompasses 10.6% of the state's entire land base. Michigan's state forests owe their existence almost entirely to the mass tax forfeitures that followed the 60-year rampage of destructive and unrestrained clear-cutting that marked the logging era. No state east of the Rockies, except perhaps neighboring Wisconsin, had such bountiful and commercially valuable timber resources that, according to forest historians, were "massed in vast stands" usually adjacent to waterways for easy transport to mills.[1] Built into this model was a literal "cut and run" strategy whereby once the valuable virgin timber was stripped, the logging companies would abandon the tract without paying further property taxes and move on. As a result, in the early 20th century, Michigan largely stood as a cut-over wasteland, fire prone and forsaken. Indeed, in 1871, the droughty year of the Great Chicago Fire, cutover logging debris ignited fires that consumed 2.5 million acres, with another 1 million acres burning in the Lower Peninsula's "Thumb" region in 1881 and a further 2 million acres in 1908.[2] Meanwhile, the farms that replaced the forests in the northern half of the state largely failed in the unsuitable soil and climate.

Eventually, the legislature came to realize that, moving forward, at least some forestland would need to come under public ownership, and so, in 1899, the State Forestry Commission was established. In 1903, 34,000 acres of tax forfeitures were transferred to the state to be held as public forest, and within six years, a state forest reserve system had been formally established under Public Law 289.[3] In the ensuing decades, the state forest system grew rapidly to its present size of 3.9 million acres, divided into six state forests, with each further subdivided into between two or three large forest management units.[4] In 1965, conservation agencies in Michigan were reorganized into a centralized DNR housing a Forestry Division that oversees the state forest system. In FY 2024, the Forestry Division's budget was $69.6 million, $11.4 million of which were general funds, with the rest largely from revenues generated from resource production.[5] This division has 300 employees who oversee not only the forest acreage but over 3,000 campsites, 880 miles of trails, and 13,000 miles of access roads.[6]

Like most state forest systems, Michigan's operates under a multiple use principle that places production of useful resources front and center while still recog-

nizing the importance of ecological limits. Specifically, it seeks to do the following:

> Encourage the efficient use of the forest's multiple products and services
> to ensure economic viability and a wide range of environmental and so-
> cial benefits, while taking into account environmental, social, and oper-
> ational costs of production, and ensuring the investments necessary to
> maintain the ecological productivity of the forest. . . . Encourage multiple
> uses of forests and, where economically competitive, local processing of
> forest products, in line with efficient and ecologically-sound manage-
> ment and in collaboration with partners, forest policy, and procedures.[7]

Toward that end, Michigan produces a lot of timber; about 913,000 cords in FY
2023 (which is close to Minnesota's similarly sized state forest system).[8] This
accounts for about 18% of all timber produced in the state of Michigan,[9] and
per acre, it is far above the harvest volumes produced on Michigan's 2.9 million
acres of adjacent national forests.[10]

Michigan also produces a lot of oil, gas, and mined substances on its state-
owned land. As of 2022, the state had leased nearly 576,000 acres, a fair
amount of it on state forest land (though many of those leases will never actually
be developed).[11] Oil and gas revenues alone have generated more than a quar-
ter-billion dollars in revenue over the last seven years, which is constitutionally
required to go into a trust fund that generates endowments for parks, wildlife,
and land acquisition.[12] Michigan has also been a leader in selling carbon credits
on state forest lands (as discussed earlier in this chapter), despite the controversy of whether this actually reduces carbon, as it does not seem to require anything of the DNR that they were not already doing in terms of forest management.

In most states with multiple use lands, the key political flashpoint is how to
balance the goals of production and preservation. In other words, what are policymakers and forest managers actually willing to do and forego in order to protect
biodiversity and not just pay it lip service? The Michigan state forest system was
created to restore and heal and protect what had been ravaged; in fact, it was not
until 1935 that the law authorized the cutting down of live timber on state forests.[13] Although the land still bears the worst scars of the logging era in spots,
such as the barrens around the Upper Peninsula's Kingston Plains, the establish-
ment of state forests largely did as intended and allowed lush and productive
forests to regrow. By the late 20th century, some of these forests were nearing
the age when they could provide a commercially valuable timber harvest, and it
was at this point that logging on state forest lands began to accelerate.

Political battles over forests and multiple use often have a pendular quality, and Michigan has been no exception. In 1992, concerns over the increasing volume of logging gave rise to the passage of the Biological Conservation Diversity Act, which raised biodiversity as a top-level management priority and required the DNR to identify and protect unique ecosystems within state forests as biodiversity steward-ship areas as well as identify which forests had any old-growth characteristics (even as insipient old growth, given how thoroughly logged the state previously was).[14] Furthermore, the state passed the Sustainable Forests Act in 2004, which required the state forest system to operate with third-party sustainable forestry certification, which it does through two accreditation programs, the Sustainable Forestry Initia-tive and the Forest Stewardship Council. Part of this certification requires the iden-tification and protection of what is called high conservation value forest (HCVF).[15]

As a result of these biodiversity requirements, the Michigan DNR has created a rather complicated alphabet soup of HCVF land management categories (in-cluding critical dunes, coastal environmental areas, dedicated management ar-eas, ecological reference areas, biodiversity stewardship areas, dedicated habitat areas, state natural areas, and natural rivers) that, by their own admission, are somewhat interchangeable and overlapping, making it rather difficult to pinpoint an exact number of acres pulled out of timber production.[16] That said, there seems to be around 120,000 acres of protected state forest.[17] While this might seem like a big chunk of land, in the context of a four-million-acre state forest system, it accounts for only about 3%, which compares quite unfavorably to other states' systems, like Wisconsin (at 14% set aside), Pennsylvania (at 10%, with another 22% considered "limited" due to topology and hydrology), and Maryland (at 13.8%).[18] In its 2008 State Forest Management Plan, Michigan is quite forthright in refuting the notion that any significant portion of its massive state forest base should be managed to reach a mature and biodiverse climax state, as it makes clear in its management plan:

> With the exception of some rare community types . . . social and cultur-al values preclude the restoration of our remaining forests to circa 1800 conditions. Such restoration would necessitate dramatic changes in tim-ber production, wildlife management and many forms of recreation.[19]

Still, as political winds shifted toward greater biodiversity protection, the Michigan DNR was not entirely indifferent and, in fact, in 2012 proposed more than 678,000 acres of state forest be designated as biodiversity stewardship areas, as instructed in the 1992 law.[20] While this would not necessarily preclude all timber management, such areas would be managed with a much lighter hand, with the goals of protecting biodiversity and maintaining mature forest structure. Unfortunately for the agency, they had missed their window of opportunity, as the 2010 elections had brought in strong GOP control of state government and such a proposal became a nonstarter in this new political environment. "The state has swung too far toward environmental protection," complained a key Republican senator in 2012.[21] In fact, the forestry division was instructed in the 2012 budget to increase state forest logging by 50% from 0.8 to 1.2 million cords.[22] The next year, this backlash intensified as the legislature passed SB 78, which would remove "the conservation of biodiversity" from the wording and legally binding authorization of the law under which the DNR manages forests. So extreme was this bill that it proved too much even for Governor Rick Snyder, who vetoed his own party's bill in January 2015.[23] Within three years, however, the political pendulum swung back in Michigan with Governor Gretchen Whitmer's election in 2018 and full Democratic control of the legislature in 2022. As a result, the timber wars have quieted for a period as Michigan state forest officials are back to working to identify ecologically sensitive areas and manage them accordingly while simultaneously producing large volumes of timber.

NOTES

1. USDA Forest Service, *National Forests in Michigan* (Washington GPO, 1941), p. 2. In all, it is estimated that approximately 160 billion board feet of timber had been removed from Michigan by 1897. For comparison, there are only about 70 billion board feet standing on all Michigan forests today. Michigan State University Extension, *Forest Basics: Michigan Forest History* (Teacher's Guide, undated), pp. 4-5, available at: https://mff.forest.mtu.edu/PDF/1-Tree Basics/3-History.pdf.

2. Michigan State University, p. 5.

3. *Ibid.*, p. 8.

4. These forest management units (FMU), which have the same sort of names that state forests do, are so large and often geographically apart from other units that they themselves are often referred to as state forests. For example, the 115,000-acre Pigeon River State Forest, which shows up as such on Google Maps and even in some DNR literature, is technically the Pigeon River FMU of the larger Mackinaw State Forest.

5. Erik Eklund, *Budget Update* (Michigan DNR Report, August 10, 2023), pp. 3–4, available at: https://www.michigan.gov/dnr/-/media/Project/Websites/dnr/Documents/Boards/NRC/2023/August-2023/Budget.pdf.

6. Michigan Department of Natural Resources, *Growth Rings: Rooted in the Past, Growing Toward the Future--Strategic Plan 2019–2023* (Report, 2019), p. 4, available at: https://www.michigan.gov/-/media/Project/Websites/dnr/Documents/FRD/General-FRD/StrategicPlan.pdf?rev=bf301831afb54884a1016e656f41d0f2.

7. Michigan Department of Natural Resources, *Michigan State Forest Management Plan* (Report, April 10, 2008), p. 155.

8. Michigan Department of Natural Resources, *1994 Public Act 451, Section 52506 Report Fiscal Year 2022-23* (Report, December 28, 2023), p. 1, available at: https://www.michigan.gov/dnr/-/media/Project/Websites/dnr/Documents/Executive/Legislative-Reports/FY-2024/Sec-52506-PA-451-of-1994---2023-Annual-Forestry-Report.pdf?rev=0e4f6f2186594e15be772b05ee1a9a93&hash=DD6900BC3754A7978C0F34FDC8635CE7.

9. Michigan Department of Natural Resources, *Growth Rings*, p. 8.

10. Michigan's three national forests produce about a third of what Michigan state forests do on about three-quarters of the land. USDA Forest Service, Hiawatha National Forest, *Your Great Lakes National Forest* (Webpage, undated), available at: https://www.fs.usda.gov/detail/hiawatha/about -forest/?cid=STELPRD3808864; USDA Forest Service, Ottawa National Forest, *Fiscal Year 2010 Monitoring and Evaluation Report* (Report, May 2011), p. 5; USDA Forest Service, Huron-Manistee National Forest, *2009 Monitoring and Evaluation Report* (Report, August 2010), p. 41.

11. Michigan Department of Natural Resources, *FY 2025 Capital Outlay Five-Year Plan* (Report, October 24, 2023), p. 28. Almost all oil and gas production occurs in the Lower Peninsula, while mining is more prevalent in the Upper Peninsula. Michigan Department of Natural Resources, *Michigan State Forest Management Plan*, p. 65.

12. Michigan Department of Natural Resources, *Oil and Gas Leasing FAQs* (Webpage, 2023), available at: https://www.michigan.gov/dnr/faqs/minerals/oil-and-gas-leasing.

13. Michigan State University, p. 22.

14. Jeff Alexander, "Policy Winds Blow through Mich. Forests" in *Bridge Michigan* (February 16, 2012).

15. Sierra Club Michigan Chapter, *State Forests, Public Lands, and Biodiversity Stewardship Areas* (Webpage, undated), available at: https://www.sierraclub.org/michigan/state-forests.

16. Michigan Department of Natural Resources, *Michigan State Forest Management Plan*, pp. 160–187.

17. Rae Schnapp, *How Much Forest Do Other States Set Aside from Logging?* (Indiana Forest Alliance Webpage, February 17, 2017), available at: https://indianaforestalliance.org/2017/02 /17/how-much-forest-do-other-states-set-aside-from-logging/.

18. *Ibid.*

19. Michigan Department of Natural Resources, *Michigan State Forest Management Plan*, p. 29.

20. Alexander.

21. *Ibid.*

22. *Ibid.*

23. Jim Lynch, "Snyder Vetoes Biodiversity-Restricting Bill" in *Detroit News* (January 15, 2015).

How State and Federal Agencies Differ

By this point, the data should make it clear that there exist some fundamental differences between state and federal land management in terms of how multiple use principles on public forests are interpreted and implemented. However, this divergence in agency policy outputs and management styles is a relatively recent phenomenon that Koontz traces back to the landmark federal environmental legislation of the 1960s and 1970s, which, in turn, forced a notable evolution in the organizational culture of the USFS.[55] Prior to that point, state foresters and USFS rangers were largely cut from the same utilitarian cloth first laid out by modern forestry's patron saint, Gifford Pinchot.

Legislative and Regulatory Mandates

At the heart of this state-federal divergence is the suite of federal environmental laws that completely transformed federal land management many decades ago. These include the Wilderness Act of 1964, the National Environmental Policy Act of 1969 (NEPA), the Endangered Species Act of 1972 (ESA), and the National Forest Management Act of 1976 (NFMA).[56] What this body of legislation has managed to do is provide a baseline of environmental protection and procedural requirements that simply do not exist in any similar form at the state level. NEPA, most importantly, creates what Uma Outka calls a "uniform template for comprehensive analysis" through its process for environmental impact statements for significant federal actions.[57] While 15 states have some state version of NEPA, only 5, Connecticut, Montana, Minnesota, Washington, and California, are comparable in any meaningful way.[58]

Similarly, while many states maintain their own endangered species lists, and some have explicit protection laws, none come close to the reach of the ESA, and none require, as the ESA does, that peer agencies across government consult before taking action. Likewise, NFMA offers much more prescribed constraints on harvest volumes than what states are typically bound to follow.[59] It also offers the USFS some very explicit instructions as to how to balance multiple uses; for example, all species must be maintained in "viable populations."[60] Furthermore, NFMA has extensive regulations on riparian areas, logging methods, and biodiversity. Koontz confirms this greater federal restrictiveness regarding logging rules in his case study comparison of the USFS to state forest agencies in Ohio, Indiana, Oregon, and Washington.[61]

NFMA also mandates extensive forest planning around major actions as well as broader 10-year plans, all of which are built around NEPA's environmental impact process. Finally, these federal planning processes all require robust public participation and input at numerous stages. This includes extensive comment periods, local question-and-answer sessions, open forums, and sometimes even more interactive policy workshops involving varied external stakeholders and citizen advisory boards. Perhaps most significantly, these laws provide a pathway for external actors to administratively appeal decisions and ultimately a basis for legal challenges in the judicial branch. Indeed, Judge Dwyer's dramatic and historic ruling in 1991 followed exactly this scenario.

States, on the other hand, have a far less developed regulatory infrastructure as they have historically tended to stress economic development over environmental protection, especially given the competition between them to snag investment and capital.[62] A 1999 Defenders of Wildlife Report found that while 36 states had forestry laws, only 20 had legislation specifically pertaining to public forest management practices.[63] Koontz's survey of 48 state forest directors reports that only 26 states had any kind of legally binding multiple use mandate,[64] though this was generally still the guiding management philosophy for those without legal mandates. However, he finds that whether they had a formal multiple use mandate or not, most states do not tend to treat uses equally and instead explicitly prioritize timber production.[65] Conversely, the federal Multiple-Use Sustained-Yield Act specifically calls for "consideration being given to the relative values of the various resources, and not necessarily the combination of uses that will give the greatest dollar return or the greatest unit output."[66] Finally, Koontz notes that only seven states require public input at any stage of state forest planning and that these requirements all tend to be minimal compared to those of their federal counterparts.[67]

The result of this mostly weak to nonexistent state architecture of environmental laws, regulations, and participation requirements is that state timber programs face fewer procedural constraints and obstacles and thus produce more timber volume per acre for higher net profits. This is something critics of the USFS take notice of as they applaud the states and contrast them to a federal agency floundering in a "costly procedural quagmire."[68] Fairfax approvingly compares the clear goals of state agencies to "the rather mushy commands and Byzantine procedural requirements that afflict the federal land management agencies."[69] On the other hand, observers interested in more balanced management, binding commitment to biodiversity, or a more democratic and participatory decision-making process might come away with a wholly different opinion.

The Role of the Courts

Without clear, enforceable mandates that require environmental impact assessments or guaranteed avenues for citizens to appeal, legal challenges to state land management decisions are exceedingly rare; there are simply no legal footholds or fertile grounds for litigation by opponents to state decisions. In the federal realm, by contrast, there are footholds galore, both procedural and substantive, in a context designed for maximum access to judicial oversight. And this oversight, in turn, has seriously dented the USFS's historical autonomy. Much like state forestry departments today, USFS managers were previously the experts in their realm, using forestry science and their professional judgment to guide their decision-making in a rather closed model. But with the passage of the landmark environmental laws in the 1960 and 1970s, along with the expansion of who had standing to sue in court,[70] the judicial branch became the third-party arbiter of which legally binding environmental obligations were and were not being met by the agency. This new reality of statutorily imposed requirements and legal oversight has created for the USFS an incredibly complex and challenging environment that state agencies largely do not face. In his survey, Koontz finds that when state foresters were asked to rate how influential various factors were on their decision-making, the score for "administrative or court challenges" rated among the very lowest out of 33 factors.[71]

The federal realm, however, is a whole different world in this respect. Many federal timber sales are appealed administratively, and still more are challenged in the courts. For example, a USFS-sponsored report in 2015 found that in the 2012/2013 fiscal year, 54% of all timber sale volume was tied up in litigation in the USFS Northern Region, which covers Montana and part of Idaho.[72] Percentages across all the USFS regions are probably not too different. The U.S. Government Accountability Office (GAO) reports that such litigation typically adds between four months to four years onto the sales process.[73] Critics decry this as nothing more than wasteful obstructionism, but the data from an exhaustive 2014 review of 1,125 lawsuits from 1989 to 2008 involving the USFS shows that these cases were not just intended as delaying tactics or nuisances. In the roughly four-fifths of all the cases that were asking for *less* resource use (in other words, the environmentalists' lawsuits), the USFS won only 49% of these cases and lost or settled 51%.[74] Furthermore, in cases specifically involving both the ESA and NFMA, the agency lost 53.7% of the time and won only 46.7%. Conversely, the agency won nearly 70% of the time in cases brought by commodity producers asking for more extraction.[75] So, yes, it is true that environmentalists, because they have been so empowered by federal law, have been extraordinarily litigious, but it is also because the USFS frequently violates federal environmental statutes and only lawsuits force them back toward meeting the obligations of the law. Whether one loves or hates litigation challenging timber sales, there is no denying their importance in pushing federal management into more ecologically friendly territory, as Amanda Miner, Robert Malmsheimer, and Denise Keele, the authors of the lawsuit study, point out:

> The significant and widespread changes in uses of national forests during the past 20 years, many of which were initiated or hastened by litigation, suggests that the legal environment continues to be an important factor in deciding how these forests are managed.[76]

Again, the spotted owl legal wars of the 1980s and 1990s and the resulting advent of the ecosystem management framework are Exhibit A of this phenomenon. And this is a phenomenon almost entirely absent at the state level.

Costs and Revenues

There is no denying that federal timber programs cost more to run and earn less revenue and even fewer profits. Koontz's four-state sample found USFS profit per board foot of timber to range from -0.05 to $0.19, with three of the four national forests losing money, while all the state timber operations made money, ranging from $0.25 to $0.45.[77] In addition to the costs of litigation mentioned previously, there are a few other reasons for this. First, according to Koontz, the USFS spends a good deal of money monitoring ecosystem health and wildlife populations as necessitated by the mandates they operate under. In his 2007 survey, he found that 65% of state forest work units had only foresters—zero botanists, wildlife biologists, hydrologists, or ecologists on staff.[78] Thus, the only inventorying that was done at the state level was simple timber cruising—nothing for wildlife or fish populations or rare plants. Koontz finds that the USFS spent a total of $4 million on monitoring in 1995 in the four-state sample of national forest units while the four states themselves spent no money on this.[79] Another reason for the greater profitability of state timber programs is that because federal regulations are much more protective, there are stricter requirements embedded within federal sales regarding things like roadbuilding standards or soil compaction and erosion control, and this often leads buyers to offer lower bids because they must absorb some of the increased costs.[80] It is clear, then, that the USFS management program takes a more comprehensive approach and thus is not just a timber program—the costs of ecological assessment and monitoring and stricter protections make it appear that the agency is "losing" money rather than actually protecting valuable ecological service function.

In a 1996 report on the differences between state and federal timber programs in the Northwest, the GAO notes how the two sets of actors have totally different incentive structures.[81] As already noted, many state programs must raise plentiful revenue to cover a good portion of their own organizational budgets, and actually losing money on sales would be understood as a complete disaster. Furthermore, in a few states (Minnesota, Montana, Washington, and Oregon), state forest units are partly or wholly drawn from trust lands, which have a separate beneficiary-focused reve-nue-generation mandate. The USFS, on the other hand, is under no such pressure to use timber receipts to cover the costs of their programs; instead, the pressure is to follow the federal environmental and procedural mandates to avoid getting sued. Under such divergent incentive structures, state and federal managers focus their innovative energies in equally divergent ways. State foresters are generally focused on improving timber production effi-ciencies and enhancing revenues while USFS personnel tend to steer their innovations toward better ecosystem monitoring, valuation, and stakehold-er participation formats in order to meet the requirements of their mandates more easily.[82]

Differences in Organizational Cultures and the Role of Outside Interests

These diverging incentive structures point to an even more significant di-vergence in state and federal forest agencies: that of their organizational cultures. In his 1960 public administration classic, *The Forest Ranger*, Her-bert Kaufman profiled the USFS and found an agency that maintained great discipline and esprit de corps despite its incredibly far-flung decentralization (154 units across 40 states and one territory) due to an organizational con-formity that came from shared and strongly inculcated professional values within a rather insular and closed system.[83] This strongly reflected the Pro-gressive Era roots of this agency and the expectation that agencies be guid-ed by scientific expertise and closed off to the corrupting influences of the external political world. Many studies have used this classic as a benchmark to revisit the agency and measure the extent to which it has changed. And the consensus seems to be that the massive shifts in the legislative and legal landscape since the 1960s and 1970s, and the litigation and public partici-pation this unleashed, have served as a sort of crowbar to pry open the agen-cy and subject it to profound organizational changes. State forestry depart-ments, on the other hand, facing no such headwinds, remain much closer to the 1960 *Forest Ranger* ideal.[84]

The changes in the federal political landscape regarding environmental management have combined to create a feedback loop of sorts that further pressures the USFS to adapt and diversify. For example, to comply with wild-life protection, biodiversity, or water quality requirements added since 1960, the agency has had to supplement its engineers and forestry professionals with hydrologists, ecologists, soil scientists, wildlife biologists, and other specialists. And in moving from unquestioned expert to facilitator, conflict manager, and honest broker of polarized stakeholders, the agency has also had to hire social scientists and communications specialists. Furthermore, tremendous numbers of fire management personnel have been hired to deal with an increasingly dire fire situation in an era of climate change.[85] And to comply with the affirmative action initiatives of the 1970s and 1980s and the growing demands for diversity, the agency began to hire more women and non-white staff. As a result of all these changes, USFS staff in 2017 was 34% female and 17% non-white,[86] while forestry and engineering-related positions went from 90% of staff in 1960 to just 36% in 2018.[87] In contrast, Koontz's survey of 373 state forest staff with line authority finds much less diversity—95% were male, 99% were non-Hispanic white, and 84% were foresters with the rest identifying as administrative or fire specialists.[88] Meanwhile, broader 2020 data of all nonseasonal state forest agency employees (and not just those with line authority) finds that foresters make up 47.4% of total staff.[89]

The increased diversity of people and professions in the USFS has brought with it a broader range of thought on how to best manage natural resources and a subsequent change in organizational values. For example, a staff ecologist cannot help but think differently about the nature of a forest community than a forester, just as a soil scientist specializing in mycorrhizal fungi and root networks will view what is going on below the ground differently than a forest road engineer. Thus, legal requirements and lawsuits may have initially forced the reluctant adoption of the ecosystem management framework at the USFS and the hiring of specialists from new professions needed to properly administer it, but as those people joined the agency, the whole paradigm began to change into one more fully invested in and committed to these ideas.

The results of this federal-state divergence in forest management, then, are clear: while state forestry agencies still largely reflect the Pinchot-influenced ideal described by Kaufman, the USFS has been forced by laws and lawsuits to evolve into a more complex and heterogenous agency unavoidably thrust into a mediator/facilitator role in a fraught political context. In contrast, state forestry staff largely toil away in unperturbed obscurity, unhampered to any great degree by those same political gales. As Koontz summarizes it:

> Compared to federal public forest administrators, state public forest administrators exhibit a higher degree of professional discretion, workforce homogeneity, traditional interactions with citizens (forester as expert, communicating privately with timber interests) and unity of views about appropriate forest management.[90]

Indeed, when asked to rank priorities, 54% of Koontz's state forestry respondents chose the statement "using forests to produce goods and services" while only 27% prioritized "ecological integrity" and 19% professed neutrality. When asked whether state forest management should emphasize commodity or noncommodity (such as recreation and wildlife) production, 48% preferred the former, 17% the latter, and 36% claimed to be neutral.[91] By contrast, Greg Brown and Charles Harris's 1990 survey of USFS rangers finds an average score of 3.91 on a 5-point scale (5 being most unfavorable and 1 being most favorable) regarding the question of whether there should be "increased production of wood from National Forest System lands." On the question of whether to stress greater recreation on national forests, the score was 1.77.[92]

Just as there is a dearth of litigation at the state level, so too is there a notable lack of public input and the political pressure such participation often brings. As discussed, state foresters largely remain aloof from and above the political fray, whereas federal managers have had to gravitate into much more facilitative conflict management roles due to the abundant participation mandates that are written into federal law. "State forest administrators," Koontz claims, "enjoy substantial insulation from stakeholder demands, drawing largely on their professional experience."[93] This means that state forest managers' communications tend to be much more unidirectional, rather than interactive or collaborative. In Koontz's survey, when asked for reasons why they communicate with the public, state administrators chose the answer "gain acceptance and support for our actions" more frequently than "learn how the public wants us to manage the forest."[94] One study of county forest administrators in Wisconsin's huge 2.9-million-acre county forest system finds this insulation at the more local, substate level to be even more pronounced.[95] The great irony, then, is that the closer and more intimate the level of government, the fewer avenues for democratic access and structured input. At least regarding forest management, the citizen finds the greatest opportunity to influence decision-making and partake in the most sophisticated and deliberative collaborations like workshops and advisory boards at the federal level.

Where structured, formal venues for participation and input are rare or nonexistent, administrators tend to hear from external actors only in a more informal manner and from a narrower range of interests who might already have established lines of access. In the world of forest management, this would likely be timber interests, other commodity users, and chamber-of-commerce types. Essentially, what federal guarantees of public participation achieved was to open the doors to other interest sectors more concerned about the environment. State forest managers, on the other hand, still occupy that world of informal access, informally granted. Koontz's questionnaire tallies who state foresters communicate with more than three times a month, and 54% mentioned timber interests as compared to 14% mentioning environmental activists,[96] a ratio that would likely be quite unfamiliar to a contemporary USFS official.

Along with the absence of litigation opportunities, this lack of formalized input and access tends to create a feedback loop whereby environmental activists shift their limited attention and resources to where they have the best chance at gaining the greatest policy influence—that is, the national forests. Even when state forest management gets contested, the opposition is usually from a much smaller state, local, or regional environmental groups with far less resources and organizational wherewithal than the big national groups, who focus almost entirely on national forests. And political success, like the Dwyer ruling, begets more attention and political pressure using the same playbook, while state forests remain a political backwater. The same is true for public perceptions as well; national parks and forests have much more salience and visibility than state parks and forests. Koontz cites a 2003 study in Columbus, Ohio, that found the public much more familiar with Wayne National Forest than much-closer Ohio state forests.[97] People will care more about the things they know more about.

So, what are the prospects for there to be a similar evolution in state forest departments as there was in the USFS? After all, state and federal forest agencies were essentially twins until the late 20th century. What changed the USFS was legislation imposed upon them by Congress. Something similar coming out of state legislatures might be the surest avenue toward enduring changes in organizational cultures in state forest agencies. The prospects for this are as mixed and varied as the 50 states.

Horicon State Wildlife Area, Wisconsin (Photo by author)

5

State Wildlife Areas

Values and Priorities in Conflict

> The elegant simplicity of wildlife conservation in North America is that citizens of states own the wildlife. This concept, known as the public trust doctrine, underpins the North American Model of Wildlife Conservation. Its roots are in common law and it invests authority and trust responsibility for wildlife to the states, rather than to a national entity disconnected from local issues.
>
> —**Association of Fish and Wildlife Agencies**, *The State Conservation Machine*

The Origins of State Wildlife Management

Except for endangered species, migratory birds, and marine mammals (which are all federally managed), states are generally seen as having primary jurisdiction over most fish and wildlife,[1] and for this reason, state lands set aside specifically for wildlife occupy an especially important niche in state public lands systems. State fish and game agencies largely began to spring up in the late 19th and early 20th centuries due to the same progressive conservationist impulses that were animating the push for forest conservation as well as the state park movement.[2] Until that point, wildlife in America was subject to chaotic and unregulated slaughter, and by the turn of the century, populations of many important species, including bison, waterfowl, beaver, elk, white-tailed deer, and most predators, were in free fall. In *Greer vs. Connecticut* in 1896, the Supreme Court laid out a public trust doctrine regarding wildlife, finding that "the power or control lodged in the State, resulting from this common ownership, is to be exercised . . . as a trust for the benefit of the people."[3]

In keeping with progressivism's emphasis on expert technocratic government, these early wildlife agencies tended to be modeled after federal regulatory commissions with fairly extensive independence from both legislative and executive branches.[4] Over time, some of these agencies remained as commissions, while many others evolved into integrated divisions of cabinet-level departments. Meanwhile, many state agencies were finding that their newfound power to manage wildlife populations only went so far without better habitat conservation, and so, by the early 20th century, state legislatures began to authorize their game commissions to acquire wildlife refuges, often using specially earmarked funds from hunting and fishing fees. And so, at differing paces and with variable levels of assertiveness, the 50 states began piecing together their extensive wildlife management area (WMA) systems. By the 2000s, WMAs were, according to Robert Nelson, the "rapid growth" area in an otherwise moribund state land acquisition scene.[5] This might be due, perhaps, to the relative autonomy, both administrative and financial, of some state wildlife agencies as compared to, say, state parks, and this has allowed them to more quietly amass WMA systems in a somewhat under-the-radar way without the interference or second-guessing from legislatures or governors that often accompanies other land acquisitions.

State WMA Systems

As Table 5.1 shows, state wildlife lands,[6] which total 37.7 million acres (20.8 million owned fee simple) and are present in all 50 states, are the largest category of state land apart from the separate trust land system. In absolute acreage, Alaska, Florida, Minnesota, Louisiana, and Missouri have the largest state-owned WMA systems, each with between 800,000 and 4.2 million acres of land. However, if one looks instead at the extent to which a state's wildlife lands dominate their holdings overall, Kansas, Rhode Island, Missouri, Georgia, Arkansas, and West Virginia all have over 70% of their state-owned holdings as wildlife lands. Figure 5.1, meanwhile, shows how extensive state-owned wildlife lands are relative to the size of a given state.

State wildlife lands are incredibly diverse and run the gamut from priceless to quite lackluster. They can range, on one hand, from some of the most biodiverse and ecologically sensitive lands in some states' entire inventory and include storied landscapes like South Carolina's Jocassee Gorges, Wisconsin's Horicon Marsh, Oklahoma's McCurtain County Wilderness Area, and Tennessee's Bridgestone-Firestone Centennial Wilderness. In fact, a large percentage of state-designated natural areas (see Chapter 3) can be found on WMAs, and as previously pointed out, California even has a special category of wildlife lands, called ecological reserves, managed strictly as natural areas. However, at the other end of the spectrum, WMAs can often consist of little more than brushy fields of non-native grasses and shrubs, reclaimed coalfields, or even croplands with the purpose of providing cover and forage for just a few popular game species.

TABLE 5.1 STATE WILDLIFE MANAGEMENT AREAS

State	Acres of state-owned WMAs (in thousands)	Total acres of state-managed WMAs—leased and owned (in thousands)	State-owned WMAs as percentage of all state public land	State-owned WMAs as percentage of all land in state	Wildlife agency as division of larger department or stand-alone
Alaska	4,200.0[1]	4,200.0	4.2%	1.2%	Stand-alone
Florida	1,552.8[2]	6,131.8[3]	29.2%	4.5%	Stand-alone
Minnesota	1,213.7[4]	1,300.0	14.4%	2.4%	Division
Louisiana	826.2	1,600.0	57.7%	3.0%	Stand-alone
Missouri	815.0[5]	1,019.2	83.6%	1.8%	Stand-alone[6]
California	701.5[7]	1,185.2	23.9%	0.7%	Stand-alone
Wisconsin	649.4[8]	685.7	40.9%	1.9%	Division
Washington	614.3	1,000.0	15.9%	1.4%	Stand-alone
Georgia	571.1	1,200.0	79.9%	1.5%	Division
North Carolina	534.0	2,000.0	58.0%	1.7%	Stand-alone
Tennessee	512.8	1,640.0	53.3%	1.9%	Stand-alone
Pennsylvania	500.0	500.0	12.5%	1.7%	Stand-alone
Utah	458.1	500.0	8.4%	0.9%	Division
West Virginia	392.6	1,400.0	70.5%	2.5%	Division
Montana	387.0	451.0	6.9%	0.4%	Division[9]
Colorado	386.6	890.9	11.3%	0.6%	Division
Hawaii	375.3[10]	375.3	24.7%	9.1%	Division
Alabama	366.7	750.0	69.3%	1.1%	Division
Arkansas	365.5	2,976.1	71.6%	1.1%	Stand-alone
Texas	361.8	746.5	21.1%	0.2%	Division
Michigan	364.2	397.2	7.9%	1.0%	Division
New Jersey	357.7	360.5	42.7%	7.5%	Division
Oklahoma	354.8	1,392.9	32.1%	0.8%	Stand-alone
South Dakota	286.6[11]	286.6	25.1%	0.6%	Division
South Carolina	250.0	1,000.0	54.0%	1.3%	Division
New York	247.4	249.9	6.0%	0.8%	Division
Iowa	239.7	390.0	61.3%	0.7%	Division
Idaho	228.3[12]	372.8	8.5%	0.4%	Stand-alone
Virginia	216.0	216.0	50.1%	0.9%	Stand-alone
New Mexico	199.7	199.7	2.1%	0.3%	Stand-alone
Wyoming	178.9	486.3	4.6%	0.3%	Stand-alone
Massachusetts	173.6	228.8	29.7%	3.5%	Stand-alone
Nevada	160.0	160.0	49.1%	0.2%	Stand-alone

(Table 5.1 continues at top of next page)

State	Acres of state-owned WMAs (in thousands)	Total acres of state-managed WMAs—leased and owned (in thousands)	State-owned WMAs as percentage of all state public land	State-owned WMAs as percentage of all land in state	Wildlife agency as division of larger department or stand-alone
Indiana	150.3[13]	163.2	36.4%	0.7%	Division
Oregon	149.1[14]	194.4	8.6%	0.2%	Stand-alone
Kansas	141.5	437.2	97.6%	0.3%	Division
Ohio	135.0	400.0	22.9%	0.5%	Division
Mississippi	133.0	685.6	12.3%	0.4%	Division[15]
Vermont	130.0	130.0	37.1%	2.3%	Division
Maryland	127.1	127.1	25.4%	2.0%	Division
Kentucky	126.5	525.0	52.0%	0.5%	Stand-alone
Nebraska	110.5	184.4	7.2%	0.2%	Division
Illinois	102.3	176.3	25.7%	0.3%	Division
Maine	100.0	100.0	9.7%	0.5%	Stand-alone
North Dakota	94.6	119.6	11.5%	0.2%	Stand-alone
Delaware	68.0	68.0	59.3%	5.4%	Division
New Hampshire	60.0	60.0	25.7%	1.0%	Stand-alone
Rhode Island	48.2[16]	59.2	86.4%	7.2%	Division
Connecticut	32.0[17]	34.2	13.2%	1.0%	Division
Arizona	25.4	34.4	0.3%	0.03%	Stand-alone
Total U.S.	20,774.8	39,786.7	10.4%; not including trust lands 34.2%	0.9%	NA

Data sources: See appendix.

[1] Includes game refuges, wildlife sanctuaries, and critical habitat areas.

[2] This figure does not refer to state-owned land generically but rather to just those WMAs under the full control and management of the Florida Fish and Wildlife Conservation Commission.

[3] These 4.58 million extra acres of WMAs in this figure are those whose management responsibilities are shared between the Florida Fish and Wildlife Conservation Commission and another agency or partner. Specifically, 2.47 million acres are on federal land, 2.06 million acres are state owned but on other jurisdictions (mostly state forests and water management district lands), and only 46,785 acres are on private land.

[4] Of this total, 230,000 acres are also technically state forests.

[5] These acres are referred to as conservation areas and are managed as general multiple use land for wildlife and forestry. As such, these same acres are listed for Missouri in the state forests table.

[6] Technically, the agency that handles fish and wildlife is the Missouri Department of Conservation, which oversees a system of conservation areas, which are an amalgam of WMAs and state forest–like multiple use lands. The other state lands agency is the Missouri DNR, which oversees state parks and natural areas.

[7] Includes 237,085 acres of ecological reserves, which are wildlife lands with added natural area status.

[8] Includes wildlife areas and fishery areas.

[9] Unlike most states with the division model for state fish and wildlife agencies under a DNR-like parent agency, in Montana, the parent agency is the Department of Fish, Wildlife, and Parks, with the parks division being rather small and insignificant. The Montana DNR, meanwhile, oversees state forests, trust lands, and other environmental regulation.

[10] These include game management areas and wildlife sanctuaries.

[11] WMAs are referred to in South Dakota as game production areas.

[12] Includes 2,799 acres of wildlife habitat areas.

[13] This figure includes 27,321 acres of conservation areas managed by the Indiana DNR Division of Fish and Wildlife.

[14] Includes 3,490 acres of state trust land.

[15] While Mississippi has a Department of Wildlife, Fisheries, and Parks, the Mississippi park system is quite small, and the fish and wildlife aspects of the department are clearly dominant.

[16] These acres are so-called *management areas*, which are multiple use lands used for both wildlife conservation and forestry. They are counted as well in the state forests table.

[17] Includes refuges and conservation areas.

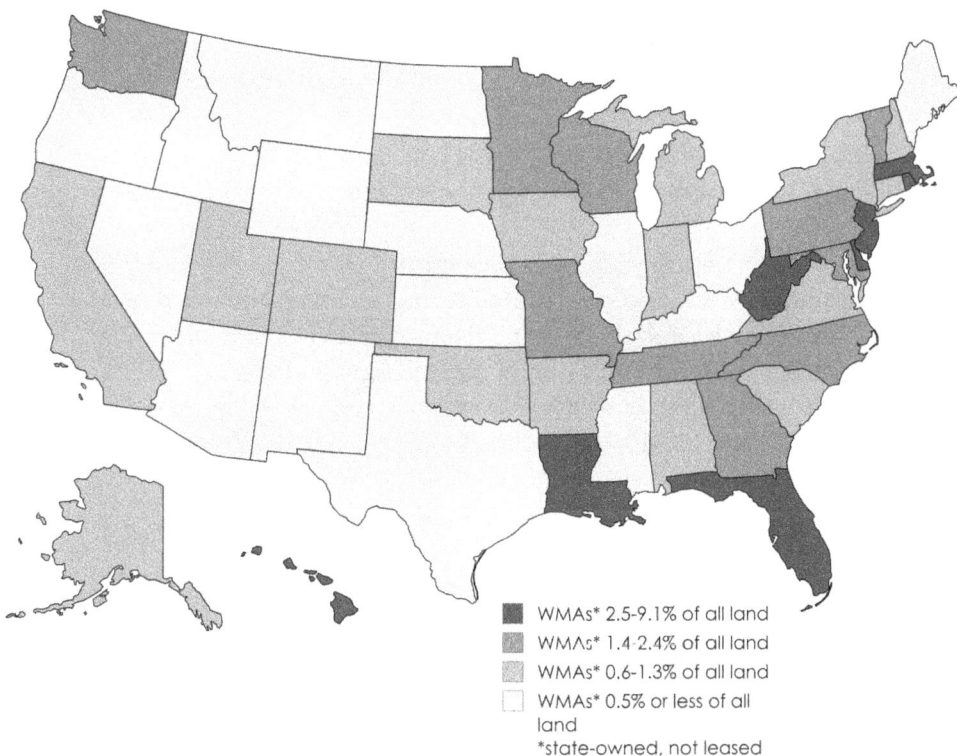

Figure 5.1 Wildlife management area systems by percentage of all land in state
(Data sources: See Table 5.1 and appendix.)

WMAs are also the state land category most likely to include leased land or conservation easements. In fact, leased land makes up nearly 45% of the system (though this figure is a moving target as leases for wildlife habitat are often quite transient). The most common arrangement, especially in the West and the South, is for large areas of federal land (often land around dams and reservoirs but also Bureau of Land Management and national forest lands) to be leased by a state fish and game agency for a set period. In some western states, it is also occasionally state trust land that is leased for WMAs. In other states, it is more often private land, often owned by power or paper companies or agribusiness, that is leased. Measuring state wildlife lands becomes even murkier when agencies make claims that reference all the land on which they in some way manage wildlife—a figure can often amount to additional millions of acres of private land in a given state subject to any sort of loose cooperative arrangement. For our purposes, however, the concept of wildlife lands will be limited strictly to land owned or leased by state agencies explicitly for use as an official state WMA. Since leased areas are much more ephemeral than WMAs owned outright, land managers are often more reluctant to invest resources in restoration, native plantings, or other long-term habitat-improvement projects. Given their perpetually inadequate budgets, they would naturally prefer to invest more heavily in preserves that they own and directly control.[7]

In terms of the preservation-extraction-recreation framework outlined in Chapter 1, WMAs do not fit perfectly into any single category. While they are certainly organized around the preservation of fish and wildlife habitat and populations, this is most often in service of sport hunting and fishing, which are recreational pursuits. Nonconsumptive uses of wildlife (such as bird or wildlife watching or photography) can also be considered recreational in nature. However, the extent to which agencies should and actually do stress nonconsumptive uses or the preservation of nongame species of wildlife in general is a hotly debated topic explored later in this chapter. Other than hunting and fishing (and perhaps viewing), WMAs tend to offer very few if any other recreational amenities, usually lacking visitor centers, developed campgrounds, and sometimes even hiking trails and parking lots. They also largely prohibit motorized and other high-impact forms of recreation.

Finally, WMAs in many states are subject to resource extraction, producing timber, grazing, and sometimes energy. In fact, Missouri and Rhode Island have taken this multiple use orientation a step further by merging their state forest/multiple use lands and wildlife areas into a single category.

Most states, however, are not quite so explicit in considering their WMAs as fully multiple use. Instead, they seem to occupy this nether region, not strictly single use like a state natural area or wilderness preserve and not fully multiple use in that "land-of-many-uses" framework that state forests usually operate within. Instead, wildlife conservation is usually the dominant overriding purpose, but where and when managers authorize, various recreational or extractive activities are allowed or even encouraged, provided they do not interfere with the primary use—at least in theory. In the case of controversial logging or other extraction projects on WMAs, it is this question of impact that often serves as the main bone of contention.

Wildlife Agencies and Wildlife Values

Progressive Era wildlife conservation, just like forest conservation, emerged from a firmly utilitarian mindset—wildlife needed to be saved from wanton slaughter and extirpation not so much for its own sake but so that well-regulated hunting and fishing could thrive as a valuable collective resource in the long term. As such, hunters and anglers have been the main constituency of wildlife agencies from the very start and remain so today.[8] These origins and orientations are deeply embedded in the DNA of nearly every state wildlife agency and provide them their foundational task of managing specific game and fish species and regulating their use (seasons, quotas, size limits, etc.) on behalf of hunters and anglers. However, more recently grafted onto this utilitarian approach is a second mandate to protect and nurture wildlife biodiversity of all kinds, including the vastly more numerous species that no one hunts or fishes (nongame species).[9] The challenges and controversies that beset nearly all state wildlife areas largely stem from the mismatch of these mandates, agency priorities, resource allocations, and constituent demands.

From their founding through most of the 20th century, state wildlife agencies were nearly perfectly in synch with the needs and interests of hunters and anglers, mostly because the agencies' professional values aligned with the hunting public so closely. Not surprisingly, then, the entire infrastructure of what the Association of State Wildlife Agencies calls "the State Conservation Machine"[10] was built to provide services to people who hunt and fish and to pay for it with the taxes and fees collected from those same people. However, with time and demographic change and the rise of the modern environmental movement, new voices began to emerge after 1970 that articulated some very different attitudes toward wildlife and demanded input and representation from those very same agencies. Edward Langenau and Charles Ostrom argue that this development required state wildlife agencies to adopt a "multiple satisfactions" approach in dealing with their now-expanded clientele.[11] The extent to which these different demands are equally weighed and prioritized, however, is subject to tremendous debate.

Those who study wildlife values term these newer attitudes *mutualism*—the belief that wildlife has inherent value aside from what use it provides to humans and thus people must learn to accommodate wildlife and share resources.[12] *Traditionalism*, on the other hand, signifies a utilitarian approach to wildlife that emphasizes wildlife's use and benefit to humans and sees animals' needs as secondary to human ones. According to 2018 Colorado State University survey research on wildlife values, mutualism has become the dominant wildlife attitude in the U.S., with 35% of the general public identifying as such as compared to 28% considering themselves as traditionalists. Another 21% are what the study's authors call *pluralists*, meaning they believe in aspects of both ideas depending on the context. Finally, 15% of the public are considered *distanced*, which means they do not think much at all about wildlife and do not have any particular interest or concern.[13] Not surprisingly, the polarization around wildlife values mirrors, to some extent, the larger political, geographic, and demographic divisions in the nation, with traditionalists strongest in the Mountain West, South, Great Plains, and Alaska while mutualists are strongest in the West Coast, Southwest, New England, and Florida. Mutualists are less involved with hunting and fishing and more racially and ethnically diverse. They are also associated with higher levels of education and income.[14] Furthermore, a mutualist orientation strongly correlates to concern over climate change and a preference for environmental protection over economic growth (by a two-to-one ratio compared to traditionalists), while traditionalism is correlated to support for predator control.[15]

Wildlife managers find themselves, therefore, between a rock and a hard place—with a traditional clientele who have waning trust and resent any policy deviations on one side and a rapidly changing population who demand new directions and see wildlife agencies as far too deferential to and closely tied to hunting interests on the other. On top of this is a funding system that disproportionately draws revenue from hunting fees and licenses, creating its own microclimate of incentives and disincentives. In fact, it is estimated that 90% of state fish and wildlife spending goes to the most common game species, which account for a minuscule percentage of species present (about 2%).[16] Conversely, just 5% of the budget of the Washington

Department of Fish and Wildlife goes toward nongame and endangered species conservation.[17]

More Similarities than Variation between States

Since the 1970s, it is certainly true that the rise in mutualist values toward wildlife as well as the growing prominence of ecological science have forced wildlife managers to broaden the scope of their concerns and pay at least some heed to the notion of biodiversity. However, this "multiple satisfactions" approach notwithstanding, most wildlife agencies are still well rooted in the utilitarian framework. In fact, state wildlife managers are more than four times less likely than the general public to espouse mutualist attitudes, according to survey data, with only 8% identifying with that concept versus 64% deeming themselves traditionalist.[18] Along similar lines, survey research comparing the attitudes of the Michigan public to the Michigan DNR on the use of lethal control of wildlife as a management tool found the latter significantly more supportive of using such measures.[19] While the 50 states' fish and wildlife agencies certainly vary in terms of the extent to which they balance their game and nongame responsibilities, their attitudes toward predators, and how enthusiastically they adopt ecosystem management approaches (if at all), it is ultimately not a stretch to say that state wildlife agencies tend to be more alike than different.[20] And where variation occurs, it seems to be a good deal less than that of, say, state park systems or an individual state's approaches to natural areas and wilderness. This homogeneity might be due to the rather narrow time period when game and fish commissions were developed and the quite singular focus at the time on game management and the specific needs of hunters and anglers. At a time so bedeviled by market hunters and rampant, unregulated killing, regulated hunting became a near synonym to conservation. Where some variation has crept in, it has been in those states where the residents now have mutualist majorities and have begun to pressure their agencies (or legislatures) to get what they feel are more balanced wildlife policies.

Differences between State and Federal Wildlife Managers

Chapter 4 showed how state and federal forest managers have come to diverge in some significant ways because of differences in the political context they operate in, and the same can certainly be said of wildlife managers. In the broadest sense, U.S. Fish and Wildlife Service (USFWS) staff do much the same as their state counterparts—manage wildlife refuges for hunting, habitat, and biodiversity. Yet, what survey data exists for the USFWS show some significant attitudinal differences and evidence that the shift to a more heterodox set of wildlife values has more readily taken root at the federal level with far less of the long lag seen at the state level. While this survey of 480 USFWS staffers did not directly ask respondents to self-identify as mutualists or traditionalists, it did measure on a 5-point scale (5 being *strongly agree*) their views on the mutualist proposition that "plants and animals do not exist primarily for human use" and found a mean score of 4.13.[21] Meanwhile, when asked what their top priority was for managing their wildlife refuge, 72.3% chose "habitat protection" or "restoration" as opposed to only 0.6% who chose "game management."[22]

As with the USFS, this more rapid evolution in agency culture can be traced to staff demographics, legal mandates, and the political environment in the federal context. As compared to state wildlife agency staff, the USFWS is considerably more diverse, with 40% female staff versus 28% for state agencies and 17% non-white versus 9% for states.[23] The USFWS also must contend with mandates such as the Endangered Species Act, the Migratory Bird Act, and the Marine Mammal Protection Act that obligate it to take ecological concerns and biodiversity much more seriously. As with the USFS example in Chapter 4, these laws have teeth and provide numerous avenues for public input and judicial review that the agency must take into account and adapt to. The National Wildlife Refuge Improvement Act of 1997 is the main law guiding the agency's management of its vast 89-million-acre system of federal refuges and, according to Robert Fischman, a major factor in making this agency uniquely attuned to ecological considerations.[24] In the language of the act, the role of wildlife refuges is "to sustain and, where appropriate, restore and enhance, healthy populations of fish, wildlife, and plants utilizing . . . methods and procedures associated with modern scientific resource programs."[25] This, according to Fischman, makes the agency uniquely focused on principles of ecosystem management and the protection of biodiversity:

> The most important aspect of the new refuge management regime is that it has a clear statutory goal of conservation, defined in ecological terms. The refuge conservation mission is defined by statute as being for animals, plants, and their habitats. This is a very different conception of conservation from the progressive-era, multiple-use, sustained yield missions that sought to conserve a steady stream of commodities to be extracted from the public lands. It also

embraces a broader land (and water) ethic that extends to plants and habitat than the earlier refuge goals, which focused on animals ("wildlife") almost exclusively.[26]

State wildlife agencies, for the most part, lack these same subtle and not-so-subtle pressures that push federal managers toward ecosystem-oriented thinking.

The Influence of Agency Structure

Table 5.2 shows whether a state wildlife agency is a division of a larger, more centralized DNR-type cabinet department or whether it is a more independent stand-alone entity, most often in the form of a commission (a legacy of the earlier days of fish and game administration). As the table shows, the two variations are equally divided, with 23 states having stand-alone commissions or agencies and 23 states having wildlife agencies as part of a larger and comprehensive environmental department. Another 4 states, Mississippi, Montana, Kansas, and Nebraska, meanwhile, have single hybrid "wildlife and parks" agencies in which the park system is relatively tiny and the wildlife functions are clearly dominant.

In their study, Langenau and Ostrom examined whether the structural characteristics of state wildlife agencies had any effect on performance, and although they found that the role of the governor and the composition of commissions were important factors, they found no significant difference between commission and division structures.[27] On the other hand, some critics find the commission structure to encourage isolated policy fiefdoms insulated from public opinion. Political scientist Bruce Rocheleau notes that commissions in many states earmark seats (sometime the majority) to be held by hunters, trappers, outfitters, or farmers. In fact, North Dakota and Mississippi prohibit any nonconsumptive wildlife users from their boards.[28] In all, an estimated 75% of all commission seats in 2021 were held by consumptive users.[29] For these reasons, some wildlife advocacy groups call for commissions to be abolished altogether, and if not, at least restructured so their boards feature a representative balance of consumptive and nonconsumptive users.[30] Vermont legislators attempted just this in 2024 with a bill that would add 2 board seats for nonhunters to the currently 14-member board, but facing vehement opposition from hunters, it stalled out in the house.[31] This opposition notwithstanding, the relative autonomy of the commission structure can cut both ways—by allowing them to function as either an assured and focused entity relatively immune from political inter-

TABLE 5.2 WILDLIFE AGENCY STRUCTURE		
Wildlife agency as division of much-larger cabinet-level department	Wildlife agency as dominant member of wildlife and parks agency	Wildlife agency as stand-alone commission or department
Minnesota	Nebraska	Alaska
Wisconsin	Kansas	Florida
Georgia	Montana	Louisiana
Utah	Mississippi	Missouri
West Virginia		California
Colorado		Washington
Hawaii		North Carolina
Alabama		Tennessee
Texas		Pennsylvania
Michigan		Arkansas
New Jersey		Oklahoma
South Dakota		Idaho
South Carolina		Virginia
New York		New Mexico
Iowa		Wyoming
Indiana		Massachusetts
Ohio		Nevada
Vermont		Oregon
Maryland		Kentucky
Illinois		Maine
Delaware		North Dakota
Rhode Island		New Hampshire
Connecticut		Arizona

ference (recall their aggressive, under-the-radar WMA land acquisitions) or as a tradition-bound "old boy" network impervious to ecosystem science or public opinion.

Conversely, wildlife divisions are integrated into larger natural resource departments who must presumably answer to a broader swath of the public. Those who favor such an arrangement argue that it makes them more responsive to external input and open to coordination across the entire department on scientific and policy priorities like climate change, biodiversity, restoration, or ecosystem management (or, maybe less positively for the environment, greater timber or energy production). Although they do not weigh in on the preferability of commissions versus divisions per se, Cynthia

Jacobson and colleagues call for agency structures that are more integrative and able to break out of compartmentalized professional or cultural silos—a position that might seem like an endorsement of the division model.[32]

Constituencies, Public Opinion, and the Representation of Interests

Fewer Hunters, Stronger Influence

According to Michael Manfredo and his collaborators, we are presently in the midst of a profound transformation of sociocultural values regarding wildlife.[33] They find that where mutualism as a belief orientation has increased, the number of hunters has tended to decline commensurately.[34] Overall, according to a 2022 USFWS survey, only 5.4% of Americans aged 16 and over currently hunt, which is down from 10% in the 1970s.[35] Speculation over the reasons for this decline include smaller rural populations, greater expense, social media, increasingly hyperorganized youth sports, and a demographic cliff of over-65 hunters aging out of the sport.[36] By contrast, the USFWS estimates that 57% of people 16 and over are wildlife watchers (and 28.2% travel to watch wildlife).[37] This is way up from 30% of the population in 2011 and includes a much more diverse cross section of Americans.[38] The same study compares total 2022 expenditures by category of wildlife recreation and reports $45.2 billion for hunting, $99.4 billion for fishing, and $250.2 billion for wildlife watching.[39]

This evolution in public attitudes and behavior toward wildlife means that there are now clear majorities against predator control policies (beyond regulated hunting seasons), leghold traps, baiting, dog chasing, and aerial hunting and in favor of endangered species protection, nongame conservation, and wolf reintroduction.[40] However, what the public professes to want is not even close to what it gets from its wildlife agencies. "General public opinion," as Rocheleau sums it up, "has limited impact on state decisions made by their wildlife management agencies."[41] Given the inexorable advance of these clear demographic trends, one might think that mutualist wildlife policy priorities would eventually seep into even reluctant state agencies. But on the contrary, there has largely been only a deepening chasm, hastened along by the intensifying political polarization that has begun to engulf this issue.

Because of this disconnect, wildlife advocates have at times tried to do end runs around agencies by using citizen-led ballot initiatives (in the states where this is feasible), as was successfully done in California with its mountain lion hunting ban and Colorado with wolf reintroduction. In fact, between 1990 and 2008, 10 of 13 citizen-led ballot initiatives regulating hunting practices were successful.[42] Although wildlife managers disparage this so-called "ballot-box biology"[43] as an uninformed affront to their supposed scientific expertise, it is also a measure of just how thoroughly they have frustrated the policy preferences of all but a select group of favored constituents.

As discussed in Chapter 2, scholars have long pointed out that narrowly focused interests seeking exclusive benefits will usually have a much easier time mobilizing resources and political will to influence policy than broad, diffuse groups that seek collective, nonexclusive benefits. To Rocheleau, this phenomenon translates into a "disproportionate impact of hunter interests on wildlife management."[44] Furthermore, in Jeanne Clarke and Daniel McCool's agency resource model, it is the ability to shape and manipulate the external political environment and mobilize supporters that most strongly influences agency power. It follows, then, that the politically stronger the constituent group it serves, the more powerful the agency is. Indeed, in Clarke and McCool's research, the USFS, an agency with some substantial and narrowly focused clients, was identified as a particularly powerful natural resource agency, while the National Park Service and the USFWS, representing only broad, diffuse, and politically weaker interests within the general public, are described as just "muddling through."[45]

By this same measure, we might better understand why state wildlife agencies, despite a decline in their hunting and angling constituency and a broad move toward nonconsumptive uses of wildlife, would be resistant to change. As a recreational activity, hunting might be on the decline, but as an organized interest, it has never been as strong or more intensely mobilized. And when joined by ranching and agricultural interests, especially in western states, this becomes an exceedingly powerful alliance. As of late, this movement has become even more powerful by its growing boldness and emulation of other groups on the populist right. In the last few decades, venerable old nonpartisan sportsmen's organizations like the National Wildlife Federation, Ducks Unlimited, Boone and Crockett Club, and the Isaak Walton League have been overshadowed by a much more polarizing and strident set of groups, such as Hunter Nation, the Safari Club, the National Rifle Association (NRA), and hundreds of subnational groups who are eager to dive into culture war politics and use tactics of extreme rhetoric and intimidation.[46] Manfredo and colleagues, in fact, explicitly draw a connection between wildlife traditionalists and the cultural angst of our current moment:

Those with traditionalist wildlife values feel left behind by change and as a result, have become increasingly vocal, discontent, and active in their defense of traditional values and lifestyles. . . . This phenomenon, described as "cultural backlash," was examined in the context of fish and wildlife management. . . . Findings suggest that those with traditional wildlife values have been "fighting back" against the rise of mutualist wildlife values and the institutions they viewed as supporting such a transition. . . . These results illustrate the challenge that managers will face amid a shift in values.[47]

State Wolf Policy as Culture War Proxy

Perhaps no area of wildlife policy is as contentious or revealing as wolf management. Wolves were largely extirpated in the 19th and early 20th centuries in the lower 48 states, save for a small population remaining in Minnesota. From the passage of the Endangered Species Act in 1973 until they were delisted many decades later,[48] wolves were a federally protected species under the strict oversight of the USFWS. Through a number of controversial wolf reintroductions as well as natural recolonization of their former range, the wolf population in the contiguous states is now approximately 7,500, with significant populations in the upper Great Lakes (Minnesota, Michigan, and Wisconsin) and the Northern Rockies (Montana, Wyoming, and Idaho) and slow migration into Oregon, Washington, California, and possibly Utah and South Dakota—a tremendous conservation success story.[49] Wherever the wolf has reestablished itself, ecological benefits have abundantly flowed, as described by one observer:

> Scientific findings emerged from Yellowstone on the impact of wolves' return to the landscape. In their long absence, coyotes had run rampant and the elk population exploded, overgrazing the willow and aspen. Without those trees, songbirds declined, beavers no longer built dams, and streams began to erode. In turn, water temperatures were too high for cold-water fish. Upon wolves' reintroduction, in what's called a trophic cascade, the elk populations began falling immediately. Within about 10 years, willows rebounded. In 20, aspen began flourishing. Riverbanks stabilized. Songbirds returned, as did beavers, eagles, foxes, and badgers. Wolf populations in Montana and Idaho began to grow and slowly disperse to other parts of the Rockies and beyond. Media and conservationists heralded it as the greatest rewilding event in history.[50]

In Wisconsin, meanwhile, a fatal prion disease, CWD, ravages the deer herd in the wolf-less southern part of the state but hardly exists in the northern herd, where wolves abound and keep largely keep deer free from such disease.[51]

Economic benefits also flow freely from wolf reintroduction, including wildlife watching and related tourism, reduced car-deer collisions, habitat improvements, and damage mitigation, not to mention the existence value to those who favor wolves on the landscape. In fact, researchers at Colorado State University estimated that $115 million in benefits would flow to Coloradans with wolf reintroduction in their state (in 2020 a referendum to that effect was narrowly approved)[52] and that this was approximately 50 times greater than the estimated losses that would need compensation.[53] In Yellowstone National Park, NPS biologists estimate that each of the park's resident wolves, given their value to the region's ecotourism and the ecological services they render to the park, is worth $1 million alive but only $200 dead.[54]

Given the clear abundance of the ecological and economic benefits that accompany healthy wolf populations, backed up by indisputable scientific consensus as well as strong public support, one might think that the careful, balanced, and supportive management of the wolf would be a no-brainer for wildlife agencies and their professionally trained staff. And yet, in many states with wolves, that would be a mistaken assumption. Wherever and whenever wolves have been delisted and removed from federal protection,[55] they have returned immediately to state management, and the record of that management in the last decade ranges from wary, begrudging acceptance to bristling and politically charged hostility. In fact, famed hunter and outdoors writer Ted Williams suggests that state agencies have opposed federal reintroduction efforts and the prospect of having wolves in their states "from the get-go."[56]

As far as most state wildlife agencies are concerned, the unforgivable crime that wolves commit is to prey on deer and elk, which makes them hated competitors of the main constituency of those same agencies. Consequently, in Wyoming, wolves are legally classified as *vermin* across 85% of the state and can be hunted without a license, without limits, and by any means, including bludgeoning, snares, poison, and explosives in their dens.[57] Only in the 15% of the state around Yellowstone are wolves treated as game animals with quotas.

Similarly, the neighboring states of Montana and Idaho have set long-term wolf population management goals for 80% and 90% reductions respectively and permitted motorized and aerial hunting. Idaho, meanwhile, makes payments to successful hunters that resemble bounties.[58] Alaska has also managed its wolves with a very heavy hand; it has long conducted extensive aerial hunts at the behest of the big game trophy-hunting lobby. Incidentally, the Alaska Board of Game, even more controversially, employs aerial hunting to kill brown bears in order to boost survival rates during caribou calving season (something biological research has shown as ineffective).[59] In spring 2023, nearly 100 of these giant bears (essentially coastal grizzly) were killed by state game personnel to supposedly bolster caribou hunting.[60]

Until wolves outside the Northern Rockies were put back on the endangered species list in 2022, South Dakota and Utah were so determined to keep wolves from establishing themselves that they were classified as nonresident varmints and shot on sight (if they had established themselves into a resident breeding population, the state would be legally obliged to not extirpate them).[61] With abundant suitable habitat, a similarly determined Colorado Parks and Wildlife agency fiercely resisted reintroduction of both timber and Mexican wolves until a successful referendum forced their hand.[62]

In the Great Lakes states, however, wildlife agencies have generally been much more balanced and careful regarding wolf management. Although the region's wolves are back under ESA protection as of 2022, for the period they were actively managed, Michigan, Wisconsin, and Minnesota oversaw more regulated hunts with relatively restrained quotas. However, in Wisconsin, that all changed in February 2021 after the wolf had recently been delisted by the Trump administration. While the DNR was cautiously planning for a hunt the following fall, impatient hunting groups sued on the basis of a standing state law to immediately trigger a hunt as soon as the species was delisted. A state judge agreed, and the DNR was ordered to immediately hold a hunt in February when females are pregnant and easy to track in the snow. The ensuing hunt resulted in sheer carnage as hunters killed so many wolves so fast that they blew way past the DNR's original harvest quota. As a result, 218 wolves (which translates to between 21% and 33% of the state's entire population) were killed in less than 72 hours.[63] The DNR was then further ordered by an external policy board to offer up an additional quota of 300 wolves for the coming fall season, making for two substantial hunts within eight months and a full halving of the state wolf population.[64] The public, and more quietly DNR biologists, angrily decried this unrestrained slaughter, and in an unprecedented move, the agency rejected the board's new quota and set a much lower one of 130 (56 of which are reserved by treaty rights to the Ojibwe people, who always allow their quota to go unhunted).[65] That hunt never happened, though, as pending lawsuits from tribes and environmentalists led to injunctions and eventually the reinstatement of the wolves in the Great Lakes on the endangered species list in early 2022.[66]

The story of state wolf management is one of uninhibited cultural grievance masquerading as wildlife policy. The newer brand of politically emboldened hunting enthusiast, according to Dan Ashe, the USFWS director in the Obama administration, "has become radicalized and imbedded with the gun culture and wolf persecution. . . . This isn't about elk, deer, livestock, or science. It's just old-fashioned persecution, hatred, and cruelty."[67] Battle lines on this issue are drawn along familiar demographic and political divides, which then allows the wolf (supported by largely urban mutualists) to serve as a villainous stand-in for everything the traditionalist disdains about liberals or city dwellers or . . . fill in the blank. The story stops being about predator-prey biology or carrying capacity or biodiversity but instead becomes about the wolf as an avatar for a deluge of marginally related resentments. To be clear, the greatest responsibility for these type of culture war flareups in wildlife policy lies with legislatures, governors, and the interest groups that incite them much more so than agency staff. The politicians and activists are the ones recklessly pouring fuel on the fire and always on the lookout for symbolic point-scoring opportunities. However, the differences in agency responses in the Great Lakes versus the Northern Rockies points to a certain acquiescence and culpability on the part of the latter that belies the mission they claim to uphold.

WILDLIFE MANAGEMENT AREAS: *Spotlight on Florida*

Florida has a massive 6.1-million-acre system of wildlife management areas in 184 separate units. In terms of total acres (owned, leased, or cooperatively managed), it is the largest in the nation by a wide margin—in fact, more than one in seven WMA acres across the entire country are in Florida. In terms of only those WMAs owned and directly controlled by a lead wildlife agency, Florida's 1.55 million acres is the nation's second largest, only behind Alaska.[1] The other 4.6 million acres in Florida's WMA system are comanaged by the Florida Fish and Wildlife Conservation Commission (FWC) in conjunction with other agencies and partners. About 2.46 million acres of these comanaged WMAs are on federal land, while another 2.06 million acres are on other types of state land, mostly state forests and water management district lands, which exist to provide water retention and flood control.[2] In fact, an estimated 60% of all Florida WMAs consist of wetland habitats, which acre for acre provide more intense ecosystem service provision than perhaps any other landscape. Indeed, with its extensive wetlands and freshwater habitats, long coast, and subtropical zones, Florida is one of the most important biodiversity hotspots in the U.S.[3] Despite its huge size, Florida's WMA system is, compared to many states, relatively new, with most of the units purchased or negotiated since about 1960.[4]

The FWC was created in 1999 through the consolidation of the Florida Game and Freshwater Fish Commission and several other marine and law enforcement agencies. What is quite unique about Florida is that this reorganization came about through constitutional amendment rather than the legislative authorization common to most states; thus, the FWC can be seen to have a constitutionally derived mandate. Its self-described mission is to manage "wildlife for their long-term well-being and the benefit of the people," which they work toward with 3,000 employees, including 848 law enforcement officers.[5] In FY 2022–23, the FWC had an operating budget of $115.3 million, with 39.2% of that figure provided by general funds, which is nearly five times the national average for wildlife agency funding sources,[6] a statistic that might indicate unusually high levels of political support for wildlife conservation in Florida.

As an independent commission in a state with very decentralized land management responsibilities (see Table 1.2), one might expect the FWC to maintain more autonomy and political insulation than wildlife agencies that exist as divisions in centralized departments of natural resources. In the context of wildlife management, this insulation has also, in most states, generally meant greater deference to traditional hunting constituencies and the needs of game species to the detriment of nongame species and ecosystem management as well as more resistance to broader public sentiments about wildlife. In Florida, however, this setup seems to have had the opposite effect—while game management is certainly a major priority, nongame and endangered species conservation, public recreational access, ecosystem-based management, and open and transparent decision-making processes are all vigorously emphasized as well.

In fact, according to the agency's 2020 strategic plan, its main initiatives are to build and maintain organizational capacity, incorporate techniques of landscape conservation, and work to create public engagement and the support of *broad* constituencies.[7] The plan further goes on to identify the characteristics of its "wildlife governance" as being adaptable and responsive to citizens' needs and interests, incorporating multiple and diverse perspectives, applying social and ecological science, and being accessible and transparent.[8] Needless to say, these are hardly statements of principles one would expect a typical politically insulated wildlife commission to espouse.

The FWC's more open and balanced approach can be seen in its internal organizational structure. The commission is subdivided into six separate units:

the Division of Law Enforcement, the Division of Freshwater Fisheries Management, the Division of Marine Fisheries Management (oceans), the Division of Hunting and Game Management, the Division of Habitat and Species Conservation (DHSC), and the Fish and Wildlife Research Institute. Most tellingly, responsibility for managing the huge WMA system is left in the hands of the DHSC and not the hunting and game division.[9] The DHSC also oversees the conservation and recovery of Florida's many threatened and endangered species, such as the manatee, the Florida panther, sea turtles, key deer, and alligators, drawing money from a number of species-specific (manatees, panthers) and general nongame trust funds the likes of which few other states can boast.[10]

Furthermore, the DHSC has a subunit, the Public Access Services Office, that is quite unique in the realm of wildlife management. The office exists to facilitate public enjoyment and use of the WMA system by managing trails, paddling routes, fishing docks, and viewing blinds. They also manage volunteer steward networks and citizen-science initiatives and assist rural communities in building ecotourism opportunities around wildlife access.[11] Thus, the FWC seems to have gone all in on the concept of wildlife broadly conceived (not just hunting and fishing) as an important social and economic asset. Nelson, in fact, argues that this notion of access to wildlife as an economic growth-enhancing amenity is the underlying reason for Florida's extremely aggressive land acquisition program since 1960.[12] A good portion of the resources for this have come from real estate transfer taxes; so ironically, the sprawl that comes from economic growth pays for the conservation thought to create yet more economic growth.[13]

This focus on public access and endangered and nongame conservation may also have roots in Florida's decidedly nontraditional wildlife values profile as a state with enormous ethnic diversity, urbanization, and a massive tourism and sport fishing industry. Using the values framework of Manfredo and colleagues, one can see that Florida has the nation's tenth-lowest ranking for people who identify as having *traditionalist* values concerning wildlife (24.8%) while conversely having the sixth-highest percentage of *mutualists* at 41.2%.[14] Among the quarter of the population in Florida that hold traditionalist values, trust in their state's wildlife agency is the third lowest in the country, suggesting that the FWC is seen by that sector as too aligned with progressive policy goals.[15] Ultimately, through some combination of the state's wildlife values and unusual biodiversity, and the FWC's constitutional mandate, internal structure, and the generous funding it receives from the state, there seems to have emerged a fairly strong and ideology-resistant consensus regarding the broad conservation of Florida's wildlife and the right of all Floridians to access and enjoy that wildlife.

NOTES

1. See Table 5.1.
2. For data sources, see appendix, under Florida.
3. Zenaida Kotala, "Florida Declared a Global Biodiversity Hotspot" in *UCF Today* (February 26, 2016), available at: https://www.ucf.edu/news/florida-declared-a-global-biodiversity-hotspot/.
4. Robert Nelson, *State-Owned Lands in the Eastern United States: Lessons from State Land Management in Practice* (PERC Public Lands Report, March 2018), p. 37.
5. Florida Fish and Wildlife Conservation Commission (FWC), *Strategic Plan 2020–2024* (Report, May 6, 2020), p. 13.
6. FWC, *Budget* (Webpage, 2024), available at: https://myfwc.com/research/about/budget/; for national average, see Figure 5.3.
7. FWC, *Strategic Plan*, p. 26
8. *Ibid.*, p. 5.
9. *Ibid.*, pp. 15–19.
10. FWC, *Budget.*
11. Florida Department of Environmental Protection, *Outdoor Recreation in Florida 2019* (Report, 2019), p. 58, available at: https://floridadep.gov/sites/default/files/1SCORP%20Chapters.pdf.
12. Nelson, pp. 40–41.
13. *Ibid.*, p. 41.
14. Michael Manfredo et al., *America's Wildlife Values: The Social Context of Wildlife Management in the U.S.* (Colorado State University Department of Human Dimensions of Natural Resources, 2018), p. 15.
15. *Ibid.*, p. 61.

Financing Wildlife Conservation

At the very heart of the close connections between hunting and conservation in the so–called North American model is the way state wildlife agencies and the WMAs they manage are financed. From the start, hunters have largely carried the financial weight of conservation, and their outsized influence within state agencies reflects that fact. "Historically funded by license sales and equipment taxes," report Manfredo and colleagues, "state wildlife agencies have developed client-based models of governance that attended primarily to hunters and anglers."[68] Now, with hunting in decline, the whole model is in danger of being upended.

Wildlife Conservation Budgets

In 2017, the collective budget of the 50 state wildlife agencies was $5.63 billion, which, in most states, comes in the form of a complex patchwork, as can be seen in Figures 5.2 and 5.3. Of that total, which includes both state and federal money, 58.8% was from fees or taxes related to hunting or

Figure 5.2 Portion of state wildlife funding provided by hunting and fishing (Data source: Association of Fish and Wildlife Agencies, *The State Conservation Machine* [Report, 2017], p. 9.)

Figure 5.3
Composition of state wildlife budgets
Note: Categories do not add up to 100% due to rounding.
(Data source: Association of Fish and Wildlife Agencies, *The State Conservation Machine* [Report, 2017], p. 9.)

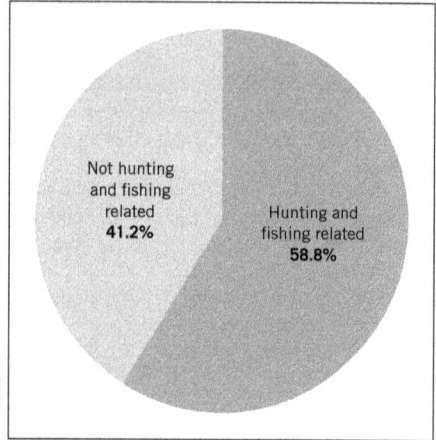

Not hunting and fishing related **41.2%**

Hunting and fishing related **58.8%**

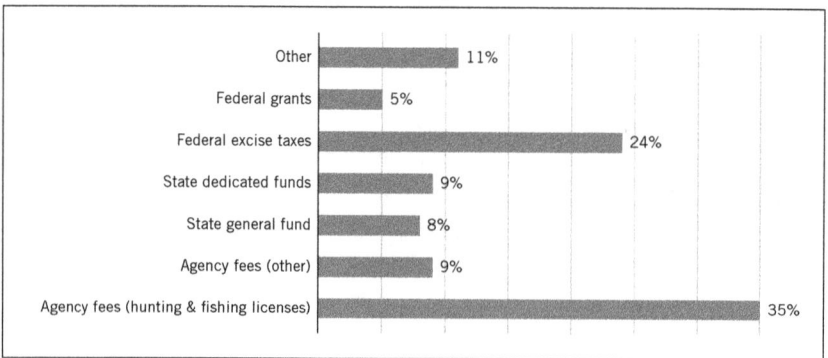

Other	11%
Federal grants	5%
Federal excise taxes	24%
State dedicated funds	9%
State general fund	8%
Agency fees (other)	9%
Agency fees (hunting & fishing licenses)	35%

fishing and 41.2% came from nonhunting-related sources. Specifically, 44% of total budgets were from fees and licenses collected by the state wildlife agency, four-fifths of that from hunting and fishing licenses and the rest from fees on ATVs, watercraft, and park entrance.[69] Another 28% of wildlife agencies' budgets was from federal funding, with most of that in the form of revenue from two federal excise taxes, one on firearms, ammunition, and archery equipment (Pittman-Robertson Act) and the other on fishing equipment (Dingell-Johnson Act). These two acts, passed in 1937 and 1950 respectively, have mostly been a stable pillar in the financing of wildlife conservation in the North American model.[70] The remaining portion of federal money (about one-sixth) comes from USFWS grants and a smaller amount from the Coast Guard. State governments pitch in about 16% of state wildlife budgets, with the money coming from general funds, dedicated funds, or targeted sales taxes depending on the state.[71] The remaining 11% is classified as "other" and includes revenues earned from commodity production like timber sales or gas leasing.

Because of the outsized role of hunting- and fishing-related fees and taxes, wildlife policy and WMA management have long been tilted toward game production. As mentioned before, less than 10% of all funding goes to the nongame species that account for 98% of species in the U.S. "Game species may be doing OK," says the director of the Missouri Department of Conservation, "but we are losing the battle on this non-game side, and losing the battle on habitat."[72] In fact, nongame species are precisely where the biodiversity crisis is most grave, with one-third of all species in the U.S. in some level of imperilment, with especially steep declines in bats, amphibians, butterflies, mussels, and freshwater fish.[73] Bird species have been hard hit as well, with an estimated 2.9 billion fewer birds in North America or a one-third total decline since 1970 and a 50% decline in grassland birds, according to scientists.[74] To attempt to address this disparity, in 2002, Congress began to provide states with federal grants for nongame species if they completed State Wildlife Action Plans to inventory and address the management needs of nongame species. While all 50 states have completed such plans, the grants are relatively small and have certainly not moved the needle on nongame conservation. Currently, Congress appropriates about $70 million annually, which accounts for a bit over 1% of all state wildlife funding. It is estimated that over $1.3 billion annually would be necessary to properly implement state action plans.[75] With this level of funding, State Wildlife Action Plans remain mostly aspirational.

Hunting Revenues in Decline and the Search for Alternatives

Like most other elements of state land management (i.e., parks or state forests), wildlife conservation is currently facing a funding crisis in which, according to one observer, "agencies barely have enough money to oversee hunting and fishing programs, let alone protect non-game species."[76] As the share of the population that hunts continues to decline, revenues from licenses and federal excise taxes have declined with it. For example, the share of the Vermont Fish and Wildlife Department's budget that came from hunting and fishing revenues declined from 64% in 1990 to 31% in 2019.[77] As funding gaps have opened up, states have had to either earmark more general funds (which most are loath to do), shrink budgets, or search for alternative sources of funding. In keeping with their hunting and angling heritage, though, many state wildlife agencies have put even greater effort into recruiting new hunters and trying to reach populations that do not hunt in any significant numbers, including children, women, and non-white people, through various promotions and educational and marketing campaigns.[78]

While recruiting more hunters and thus restoring hunting revenues might be their preferred solution, many state agencies and legislatures are beginning to see the demographic writing on the wall and have begun to propose and in some cases have already adopted alternative funding mechanisms. To nongame wildlife activists, this potential funding shift presents an important opportunity to achieve an accompanying shift in priorities toward general biodiversity and away from strict game management. These alternatives include the following:

- Outdoor gear tax—Of the $75.9 billion per year directly spent by wildlife watchers, virtually none of this is captured as revenue for wildlife conservation, unlike fees and taxes on hunting and fishing. Texas, Virginia, and Georgia have all recently passed legislation (constitutional amendment in Texas's case) that earmarks a portion of state sales tax on outdoor gear to create a dedicated funding line for wildlife conservation.
- General sales tax—As discussed in Chapter 2 regarding state park funding, Missouri, Arkansas, and Minnesota have all dedicated a portion of general sales tax on all goods specifically for conservation purposes, including state parks, WMAs, and wildlife conservation.
- Increasing general fund allocation—General funds make up an average of 8% of total wildlife funding.[79] As hunting-related revenue has declined, some states, like Oregon and Michigan, have bolstered wildlife budgets with one-time infusions of general funds. South Carolina, however, is one of the few states whose WMA and wildlife budgets get consistent and significant annual general fund allocations (25% in this case).
- Real estate transfer tax—Florida and South Carolina earmark revenue from their real estate transfer tax to fund wildlife conservation.
- Lottery revenue—As with state parks, some states, including Arizona, Colorado, Maine, and Oregon, dedicate a portion of lottery revenues to support wildlife conservation.
- Severance taxes on resource extraction—Most states collect severance taxes for fossil fuels and minerals extraction, but a few channel a portion of revenue to fund wildlife conservation.

- Voluntary programs—A number of states provide their residents with voluntary options for making donations to wildlife conservation, including special license plates (Texas and Wisconsin) or income tax refund check-offs (Connecticut, Alabama, North Carolina, and New Jersey, to name a few).[80]

Colorado has taken an unusual and somewhat controversial approach to bolster funding for WMAs and wildlife. Due to rapid population growth and the intense demand for outdoor recreation in Colorado, visitation to WMAs has skyrocketed in recent decades, and this has been driven mostly by nonhunters using the preserves for various sorts of recreation. As a result, the Colorado Parks and Wildlife department claims that numerous WMA units have been seriously degraded by the crush of new visitors and the resulting off-road vehicle use, vandalism, trash, and noise, all of which stress out and drive away wildlife.[81] As a result, the agency decided in 2020 to require all visitors to WMAs over 18 years of age to have a valid hunting or fishing license, even if they had no intent to hunt or fish. As it turned out, this was a very unpopular decision among the nonhunting public, some of whom were quite resistant to buying hunting tags. Rather than antagonize such a significant segment of users, the agency ended up creating a state wildlife area pass in 2021 that is priced roughly the same as a hunting license (hunters and anglers do not need a pass). Previously, the agency had been dissuaded by USFWS rules for federal matching funds that preclude other entrance fees, but that rule was changed in 2021.[82] In several ways, this new policy represents a tightrope balancing of uses and user groups—the agency is at once using the rationing of access to limit overuse of facilities intended for wildlife (prioritized over recreation) but also beginning to collect revenue from all users and not just hunters and anglers. Although no one likes user fees very much, the nonhunting public should welcome this indirect recognition of the validity of their nonconsumptive uses—their purchase of wildlife area passes now makes them a more visible constituency with skin in the game.

Colorado's approach, while bold, is trickier to pull off than it seems, as user-fee-generated revenue is not as obvious a solution as it is in the state parks. This is mainly because recreation (beyond hunting and fishing) is an afterthought in most WMAs. There are limits to what can be charged to access tracts with few or no trails, visitor centers, campgrounds, or facilities of any kind and numerous use restrictions around things like breeding seasons or nesting areas. In Colorado, charging access fees actually seems to be part of a strategy to *cool down* visitation levels rather than juice them up for additional revenue. WMAs, therefore, pose a funding paradox in that, for their intended conservation purposes, the best level of visitation might be *zero*—a fact that makes them quite hard to pay for strictly through on-site revenue generation. Ideally, rather than, or at least in addition to, on-site revenue generation, there needs to be a larger societal buy-in for funding wildlife, and polling strongly suggests there is.[83]

Generating Revenue through Resource Extraction

An even more politically fraught source of on-site revenue generation for WMAs comes in the form of resource extraction of timber, forage for grazing, or energy. As hunting and general revenues have declined, resource managers have faced increased pressure to approve such activities on their WMA units. This is potentially quite problematic as WMAs are not typically considered as true multiple use lands in the way that state forests are.[84] They might be more accurately thought of as a hybrid of primary use (wildlife habitat) and secondary use (any resource extraction that does not at all degrade the primary use). The National Wildlife Refuge Improvement Act, which governs federal wildlife refuges, is quite explicit about this distinction, and as a result, while resource extraction does occasionally occur on federal wildlife land, it is not very common and usually is not only compatible with wildlife management but improves it (for example, logging a closed woodland in the Upper Midwest to restore a more biodiverse open oak savanna).[85] State guidelines for WMAs are rarely so clear but do suggest, nonetheless, a hierarchy of uses that starts with wildlife.

This ambiguity, however, has allowed for all kinds of overtly resource-oriented management decisions as the scramble for revenue intensifies. For example, Florida generates 50% of the on-site revenue it collects from WMAs from timber harvests.[86] In Pennsylvania, logging on WMAs accounts for 20% of all Pennsylvania Game Commission revenue. According to Nelson, the WMA system there produces 40% of the timber that the four-times-larger state forest system produces.[87] While he applauds this high level of productivity, one might wonder how compatible it is with quality wildlife habitat for woodland species.

The Pennsylvania Game Commission has also been quite aggressive in selling natural gas leases on WMAs, which in 2014 accounted for another 20% of commission revenues.[88] While the governor at the time, Tom Wolf reinstated a ban on all new fracking leases on state forests and parks, he could not extend this to WMAs because he did not have authority over an independent commission as he could if the agency were a wildlife division in his own cabinet.[89] Given that mining and energy production have very high impacts on the water resources that are at the heart of most wildlife lands, such activities would seem to never be able to meet the "do no harm to the habitat" criteria that supposedly governs state WMA management, but in this case, the lure of revenue seems to have won out.

Such was the case as well in Tennessee's Bridgestone-Firestone Centennial Wilderness WMA, a celebrated and much-beloved tract of land, called by some "the Grand Canyon of the Cumberlands" and chock full of waterfalls, native pictographs, steep bluffs, and abundant old growth.[90] The land was gifted to the state by the tire company with all manner of restrictive covenants to keep it, in the words of the agreement, "pristine." However, third party monitoring responsibilities to enforce the covenants were placed with the Tennessee Wildlife Federation, a close, hunting-oriented client of the Tennessee Wildlife Resources Agency (TWRA).[91] In 2021, the TWRA announced plans to clear-cut 2,000 acres of mature and old-growth forest along a ridge in the heart of the preserve and adjacent to a state natural area in order to create habitat for quail, a species that prefers open grasslands and savannas. The TWRA cloaked this decision in strictly biological terms; it was merely meeting the needs of wildlife and following the science. The Tennessee Wildlife Federation, meanwhile, found these clear-cuts to be compatible with the deed's protective covenants.[92] What the TWRA did not mention was that unlike some wildlife agencies (especially those with a division structure), they would keep all the revenues from the very lucrative logging of old-growth timber within the agency. Especially galling to opponents was the fact that the WMA also included many nearby acres of regenerating farmlands and old pine plantations that would be perfectly suitable for restoring to grasslands for the quail.[93] But the TWRA insisted that only the exact location they chose in the heart of the mature forest would do.

What the TWRA did not count on, however, was the ferocious and broadscale backlash that this plan engendered. While many WMAs are quite obscure and inconspicuous, this one was well known and loved, heavily used, and the linchpin of the immediate area's economy. A local group, Save the Hardwoods, was soon formed as a coalition of hikers, hunters, environmentalists, and civic leaders. The nearest town council announced their opposition, as did the local chamber of commerce.[94] Threatened with a lawsuit and confronted by a bipartisan bloc of 34 state lawmakers, the agency reluctantly scaled back the plans in February of 2022, with the agency director defiantly proclaiming that "the decision is one that is being made in response to the community's opposition only and is not based on the best science or what's best for wildlife."[95] But the legislature did not turn away its spotlight on the agency, and by May 2022, its key leadership, including the director, deputy, and several counsels, were all terminated. Additionally, a law was passed bringing the procedure for planning and signing timber contracts in line with the more transparent process of the state forest division.[96]

While WMAs are not supposed to be explicitly considered as multiple use wherein all potential uses are weighed equally, the case of WMA logging in Tennessee brings to light a loophole often used to justify all manner of logging in WMAs—*we must do it for the good of the wildlife*. But this begs the question of which wildlife and why. For example, in 2023, the New Jersey Fish and Wildlife division authorized the logging of an old-growth swamp in the Glassboro WMA in order to provide additional open habitat for the American woodcock, a bird favored by hunters. However, the bulldozers that did the clearing destroyed fragile vernal pools that provided refuge for rare salamanders and took down nesting and roosting trees for imperiled barred owls and red-shouldered hawks. In fact, the destruction and damage to rare species was so egregious that the New Jersey Department of Environmental Protection, the wildlife division's parent agency, found them in violation of state environmental law and issued them a citation.[97]

There is no doubt that some species prefer clearings, grasslands, and young forests. Such areas offer abundant browse and other food sources. Many (but not all) of these species also happen to be game species, including deer, grouse, woodcock, pheasant, and rabbit. Other species, however, like pine martens, fishers, owls, woodpeckers, amphibians, and many neotropical migrants like warblers and vireos, require large patches of mature forests, and these are largely nongame species. A well-managed WMA would, of course, try to optimize habitats and offer a diverse and balanced array of appropriate ecotypes. However, mature and old-growth forests are not exactly abundant on most state WMAs, so any plans that sacrifice the latter and its species for former and its species might have a cynic wondering what the role of hunting tags and timber revenue has come to play in these supposedly "scientific" decisions.

Sometimes the pressure for revenue comes from outside the wildlife agency. Minnesota and Wisconsin, for example, have both faced external mandates to increase timber output from all forested lands (including those within WMAs), even over the objections of local wildlife managers. For example, when Minnesota increased its overall public timber harvest in

2017 (see Chapter 4), WMAs were expected to increase their contribution to the quota, which stands at about 12%. Because of a history of heavy logging on state forests, WMAs in Minnesota hold some of the last significant stands of old growth left on state lands, but the increase has forced some logging onto these forests, including a stand in a WMA near Bemidji of 80-to-120-year-old oaks with massive acorn production. Dismayed wildlife managers wrote in protest, "We see absolutely no wildlife management purpose, and instead a wildlife management detriment."[98] At the Polk WMA near Crookston, the raised quota led to plans to log unique tamarack wetlands. This case, in many ways, is the exact opposite of the Bridgestone-Firestone logging proposal in Tennessee. In Minnesota, the revenues go to the state, not the wildlife agency or individual WMAs, who are only left with the damage. Whereas the TWRA was adamant that good, scientific management required clear-cutting, the Minnesota wildlife managers see it as an unwelcome intrusion, forcing their hand and working against their mission, which they would also insist is scientifically derived. According to a letter to Minnesota DNR upper-level administration signed by 28 field managers,

> Harvesting at this level of intensity jeopardizes long-term conservation of many wildlife species, dependent on older forest for all or part of their life. . . . We do not believe it is scientifically honest or transparent to say that the 10 year plan is beneficial to wildlife.[99]

In response, a somewhat defensive DNR insisted that its overall management direction is to manage for biodiversity and a range of habitats, but it also conceded that WMA managers can be overruled on decisions about where and how much to cut.[100] This is a change noted by a retired Minnesota WMA manager who argues that only the on-site manager should have the final say:

> For all of my time in DNR, we were only allowed to do timber sales in wildlife management areas if there was a wildlife management purpose. . . . Now they're going to do timber sales even if the wildlife manager says it will harm wildlife. This is a pretty blatant example of how we have a public resource being managed for a single special interest industry. As a hunter, $4 of my small-game license goes to wildlife management areas, and I want them managed for wildlife, not for the timber industry.[101]

Recovering America's Wildlife Act—the Holy Grail of Wildlife Funding

Perhaps the biggest advance in state wildlife conservation funding would come about if the proposed federal Recovering America's Wildlife Act were ever to be enacted. The bill came tantalizingly close to passage in 2022; it passed the House 231–190, as well as the Senate Environment and Public Works Committee, but could not make it across the finish line in the Senate's huge end-of-the-year funding bill to which it was attached. Disagreements over funding mechanisms had not yet been settled as time ran out. The bill, overwhelmingly backed by state wildlife agencies, as well as hunting and conservation groups, would distribute $1.3 billion in annual funding to states and tribes for nongame species (with 25% in state matching funds).[102] This stable and significant new founding source would revolutionize states' capacity to conserve nongame species and their habitats. In essence, it would finally allow for states to act on their State Wildlife Action Plans, which had mostly been gathering dust for the last two decades. Despite the bill's focus on nongame species, mainstream hunting groups tended to support it because habitat improvements and land acquisition would benefit game species as well. Also, the flood of new money would take the pressure off of game management budgets by altering the current zero-sum competition within agencies over conservation funding priorities.[103] While the bill has enough state and bipartisan support to yet be passed, it is probably not a high priority for the GOP majority that took control of the House in 2023. If it were to pass, however, it would profoundly improve the financial picture for wildlife and WMA management.

Despite fast-approaching changes in demographics, attitudes about wildlife, and funding mechanisms, the bureaucratic infrastructure of state wildlife conservation can still be considered one overwhelmingly built for hunters and a narrow array of game species. The example of the USFWS, though, shows us that wildlife agencies can be balanced and attend to the needs of hunters and nonhunters, traditionalists and mutualists, and game and nongame species alike—and do so with ecological integrity. Jacobson and colleagues identify what they see as the "leverage points" for achieving such transformation and balance within state wildlife agencies as leadership, hiring and retention, agency structure, expertise and capacity, and diversity of thought.[104] By exploiting these points of leverage, the authors believe that state wildlife agencies can much better serve the fullest cross section of society:

The state wildlife conservation institution has begun to acknowledge its exclusivity and need to broaden its boundaries to maintain public support and ultimately ensure the success of its conservation and management efforts into the future. In broadening its boundaries, the state wildlife conservation institution and individual [state fish and wildlife agencies] will benefit from proactively engaging its traditional constituencies and promoting a shared understanding of the need for connecting with and serving the interests of a broader segment of society.[105]

Mill Bluff State Park, Wisconsin (Photo by author)

6

State Trust Lands

The Sort of *Public Lands*

> These are not now, nor were they ever, established as publicly accessible
> lands. . . . They were intended as a savings account for the states to fund
> schools and public education. The main purpose of the state trust lands
> is to generate revenue for the state, not to give hunters additional places
> to hunt.
>
> —Dan Harrison, quoted in Andrew McKean,
>   "Are State Lands Really Public?"

> You'll hear that states established these trust lands in order to generate
> revenue for a specific purpose, whether public schools or land-grant
> institutions. That is their common history. But over time, states have come
> to recognize that the public purpose of state lands transcends just
> maximizing annual receipts from grazing or mining or timber harvest.
> They've defined the longer-term benefits as more sustainable,
> contributing to improved water quality, wildlife habitat, viewscapes, and
> public recreation.
>
> —Joel Webster, quoted in Andrew McKean,
>   "Are State Lands Really Public?"

Trust lands of one kind or another make up nearly 70% of all state land, with 139 million acres, as Table 6.1 shows. Despite this massive size, Souder and Fairfax contend that trust lands "exist in a quiet corner of public resource management, only occasionally coming into view."[1] This might have something to do with their unique history, relative isolation, and lack of public awareness. Nevertheless, they are some of the oldest public lands of any kind in the United States—their origins can be traced to the land grants made by the federal government to each new state starting in 1803. With the exception of Alaska and Hawaii, the main purpose of these grants at the time they were made was to provide states with the basis for funding schools and other public institutions. Fairfax, for one, is quite enamored with the trust land approach and what she sees as its transparency and flexibility and reliance on leasing, finding that it has "a great deal to teach us about management institutions and tools."[2] Others, like Melinda Bruce and Teresa Rice, come to the

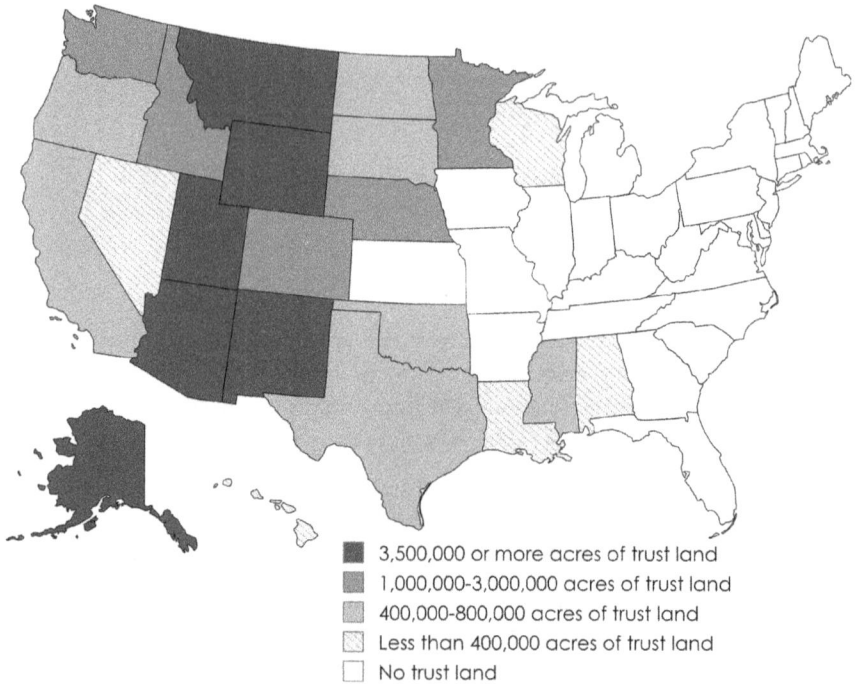

Figure 6.1 State trust land systems by acreage (Data sources: See Table 6.1 and appendix.)

opposite conclusion, criticizing trust lands as an archaic throwback that has not adapted to changing scientific understandings or public expectations:

> In contrast to the federal government's relative responsiveness to the rhythm of change, a numbing sameness pervades state governments' approach to managing the bulk of state lands. [Trust lands] are managed for the same purpose and in the same manner as they were when the states were first admitted to the Union. . . . Once the idea of economic exploitation of state land grants was imbedded in state statutes and particularly state constitutions, the concept became difficult to change.[3]

Figure 6.1 shows that 23 states possess trust lands, though the clear majority of large holdings are in the West. This is because eastern states either did not receive grants (pre-1803 states) or sold them off before Congress made this harder to do in subsequent grants. In the eastern half of the U.S., only Louisiana, Wisconsin, Minnesota, Mississippi, and Alabama retain any school trust lands. For more than half of the states with trust land (13 of 23), these lands make up two-thirds or more of their state-owned lands, and for 6 of them (Alaska, Arizona, New Mexico, Montana, Wyoming, and Nebraska) over 90%.

Alaska and Hawaii as Outliers

Interestingly, as Table 6.1 shows, the largest chunk of state trust lands (89.7 million acres, or nearly 45% of all state-owned land in the U.S.) exists in a class all by itself and does not exactly fit in with all the other trust lands discussed in this chapter. That is because by the time our newest states, Alaska and Hawaii, were admitted to the Union in 1959, almost all restrictions on federally granted land were dropped from their statehood acts. Hawaii was actually granted back all their former royal lands from before annexation (including about 200,000 acres put into trust), and Alaska, partly as a function of its enormous size and near-total federal ownership, was given a massive and unrestricted 105-million-acre land grant.[4] After carving out state park, state forest, and WMA systems and a 1.25-million-acre institutional trust, Alaska was left with approximately 89.7 million acres of uncategorized state land held in trust, some of which may eventually be sold or transferred to tribes or local governments.[5] This mind-boggling figure needs to be kept in mind because it is so large as to distort all other facts and figures about state land ownership in the U.S. if not kept front of mind. It also needs to be differentiated from the other 49 million acres of school and other institutional trust lands that are the focus of this chapter.

A Brief History of State Trust Lands

According to Fairfax, state trust lands are "our oldest and most durable land management regime."[6] Their roots go back to the General Land Ordinance of 1785 and the Northwest Ordinance of 1787, which outlined the process by which the frontier was to be delineated, settled, and transitioned to statehood. Without providing any detailed guidelines, the former law specified that a one-square-mile section of each township be reserved to support public schools. At the time, Jeffersonian notions of agrarian democracy largely held sway, and for this vision to function, it absolutely required an educated citizenry and ongoing social improvement. In the words of the Northwest Ordinance, "Religion, morality, and knowledge, being necessary to good government and the happiness of mankind, Schools and the means of education shall forever be encouraged."[7] This was no easy task, though, on the raw frontier with little to no established property tax base and a federal government with a minuscule budgetary capacity. This was also seen as a matter of equity between the newest states with little to no infrastructure and the established states on the Eastern Seaboard that had been building educational institutions for more than a century.[8] Thus, this

TABLE 6.1 STATE TRUST LANDS

State	State trust land acres (in thousands)	Trust land as percentage of all state-owned natural resource land	Public access allowed?
Alaska	90,931.0[1]	90.4%	Yes
Arizona	9,200.0	98.5%	Yes (w/ fee)
New Mexico	8,373.9	90.1%	Yes (w/ fee)
Montana	5,213.5	92.3%	Yes (w/ fee)
Utah	4,861.9[2]	89.4%	Yes
Wyoming	3,500.0	90.8%	Yes
Washington	2,800.0	72.6%	Yes (w/ fee)
Colorado	2,800.0	85.8%	No (unless specified)
Minnesota	2,500.0[3]	29.8%	Yes
Idaho	2,400.0	89.3%	Yes
Nebraska	1,254.0	92.2%	NA
Oregon	774.1	44.9%	Yes
South Dakota	750.0	65.8%	Yes
Oklahoma	726.0	65.7%	No
Texas	719.0	41.8%	No
North Dakota	706.0	85.6%	Yes
Mississippi	640.0	59.2%	No
California	458.8	15.6%	NA
Hawaii	200.0[4]	13.1%	NA
Louisiana	157.7[5]	11.0%	NA
Wisconsin	77.0	4.9%	Yes
Alabama	45.0	8.5%	Yes
Nevada	2.9	0.9%	NA
Total U.S.; institutional trust land only	139,077.9 49,196.9	69.7% 24.6%	

Data sources: See appendix and Philip Cook, Michelle Benedum, and Dennis Becker, "Recreation Access and Leasing of State Endowment Lands" in *University of Idaho College of Natural Resources Issue Brief* (No. 19, September 2016).
Note: NA = information not available.

[1] Alaska's land trust stems from the 105.5 million unrestricted acres it was granted at statehood. Of this, 100.6 acres have been actually transferred to date. Approximately 1.25 million acres are in trusts specifically focused on mental health, universities, and schools. The rest is general purpose—in fact, Alaska's state park, state forest, and wildlife refuge systems have largely been carved out of this huge grant of land. The remaining 89.7 million acres are used for economic development, resource extraction, and revenue generation, including sale.

[2] Utah trust lands consist of 3.4 million acres of school trust and the 1.45-million-acre state sovereign trust, which largely lies under the bodies of water in the state and is managed to benefit the state generally.

[3] This figure does not include the so-called tax-forfeited lands, which is a 2.8-million-acre trust of forest lands held for and managed by counties.

[4] These are leftover lands from the original statehood grant and are earmarked for homesteading. These are not school trust lands.

[5] Louisiana's school trust lands are not actually managed by the state but rather by individual school districts.

land-based strategy for providing support for education and leveling the states was conceived by a federal government that was, as Sean O'Day puts it, "land rich and cash poor."[9]

Starting with Ohio's statehood in 1803, states began to receive the 16th section per township for school trust lands.[10] But the experience of the earliest states that received trust land grants was not promising. Their granted sections tended to be rich and well-watered land with high agricultural potential, which was something in great demand. Consequently, the land was quickly sold to immediately benefit schools, and in some places, portions of the proceeds were also put into educational trust funds, but without the influx of any additional revenue, these funds were quickly depleted.[11] Some scholars, like George Coggins, even suggest that these early eastern trust lands were sold at below market prices simply to encourage settlement. Whatever the reason, eastern states, with a few scattered exceptions, had entirely squandered their land grants in fairly short order.[12]

In response to this experience, Congress, by the middle of the 19th century, began to place more restrictions on the use and disposal of granted trust lands in subsequent statehood acts (mostly west of the 100th meridian).[13] Additionally, Colorado's enabling act in 1875 also required the creation of a permanent fund to place undistributed revenues.[14] Fairfax argues that the impetus toward retention over disposal of trust lands came from the states themselves as they came under pressure from educational interests in their states and also realized that liquidating their trust lands would make the goal of sustaining ongoing funding impossible.[15] Therefore, state constitutions also began to stipulate stricter obligations regarding how trust lands were to be handled.[16] As a result, western states, with a few exceptions, held onto a far larger percentage of their granted trust land. Arizona, New Mexico, Idaho, Washington, and Wyoming have all maintained at least 70% of their original grants, while Utah and Colorado held onto about half. California, Oregon, and Nevada are the outliers, having lost the vast majority of their trust lands.[17]

By 1859, with Oregon's statehood act, Congress also raised the school trust grant to two sections of land (the 16th and 36th) per township. This was at least partly because of the West's greater aridity, which Congress felt necessitated more land to produce adequate revenue. In 1910, this was raised again to four sections per township for the even more arid new states in the desert Southwest (see Figure 6.2).[18] The statehood acts of Arizona and New Mexico also featured the most fully realized version of the modern trust doctrine and all its requirements.[19]

Figure 6.2 Allotment of school trust sections within a township

Note: Until 1859, states received only Section 16; for the rest of the 19th century, they received Sections 16 and 36. The last states, around the turn of the century, received Sections 3, 16, 32, and 36. Each section is 640 acres. A township is 36 square miles, or 23,040 acres. (Data source: Peter Culp et al., *State Trust Lands in the West: Fiduciary Duty in a Changing Landscape* [Lincoln Institute of Land Policy Report, 2015], p. 9.)

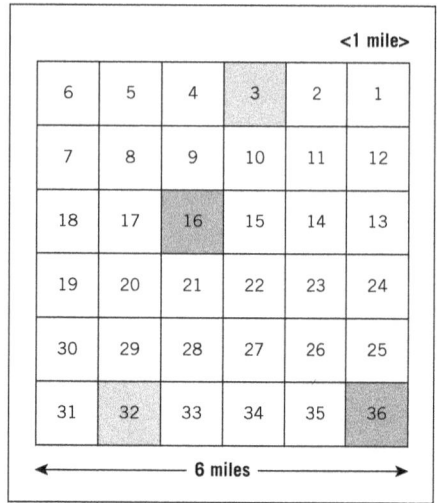

State Trust Lands in the Modern Context

Among state-owned lands, trust lands are quite distinct in how they are used, what they are for, and how the public relates to them. Because they are strictly intended to raise revenue for trust beneficiaries, trust lands cannot in any way be considered as multiple use land.[20] Their use is determined by what land managers consider to be the most lucrative revenue-generating activity for that particular unit of land. This generally makes them what should be considered dominant-use resource-extraction lands. For the most part, conservation explicitly occurs only when it is the use that can generate the most revenue (a lease for hunting land, for example). The fact that the ecological health and productivity of land are explicitly tied to its long-term economic value has been an idea quite slow to catch on in this management realm, as more fully explored later in this chapter.

Confronting the "Blue Rash"

The unique, and perhaps somewhat archaic, mechanisms for bestowing state land grants—that is, allocating the 16th and 36th sections of each township—have had some profound effects on the modern-day management of state trust lands. As a result of this process, large portions of the states' trust land holdings have been left as evenly scattered square-mile parcels arrayed in checkerboard fashion across the landscape. Because of the way these dispersed lands traditionally showed up on color-coded western land use maps, they are sometimes referred to as the "blue rash."[21] Perhaps

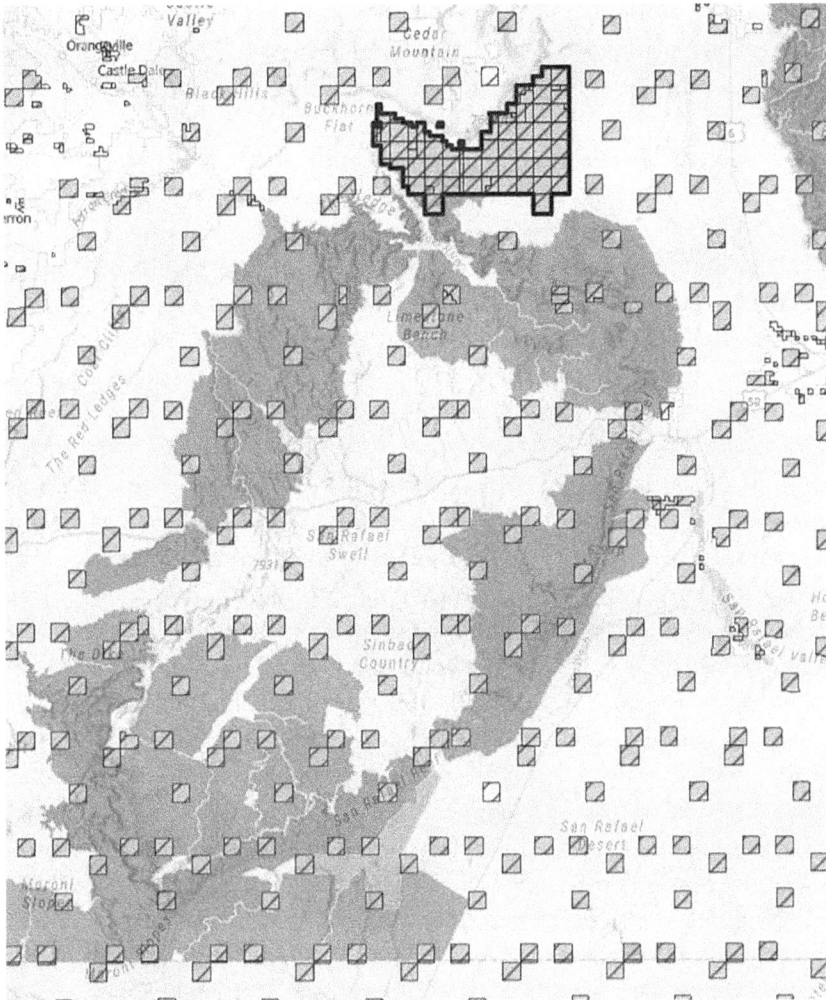

Figure 6.3 Map of state trust lands in portion of Emery County, Utah

Note: The small scattered squares are trusts lands as originally granted in Sections 3, 16, 32, and 36 of each township. Notice that some of these are trapped within the darker shaded national forest lands. The cluster of squares at the top left has been consolidated through exchanges since statehood into a bigger unit. (Source: Utah Trust Lands Administration.)

no state has a more splintered inventory of trust lands than Montana, which has its 5.2 million acres scattered across 16,000 isolated parcels.[22] One can see this very same fragmentation of parcels clearly in the map of the trust lands of Emery County, Utah, in Figure 6.3. One of the more dramatic consequences of this fragmentation is that about 6 million acres of trust land (or about one in eight) is unreachable by roads and surrounded by federal or private land, rendering it inaccessible to the public and often even land managers.[23] In Minnesota, nearly a quarter-million acres are landlocked and inaccessible, surrounded as they are by private land.[24] This obviously makes management quite challenging and inefficient, as Bruce and Rice point out:

> These grants impose a management burden that was doomed to failure almost from the start. . . . The unvarying grant of particular sections within each township also creates unmanageable tracts, isolated and intermixed with federal and private lands across the face of each state. This pattern of distribution . . . causes hardship for those who must manage the lands to produce income. Isolated one square mile tracts of land, often lacking legal access, are not, for the most part, successful income-producing properties.[25]

Not all states suffer as extensively from the blue rash. Oregon and Washington, for example, embarked long ago on an aggressive program of consolidation of their fragmented holdings, swapping, selling, and buying lands to create more contiguous units on roughly the same total acreage.[26] The federal government has mostly been a sympathetic partner in this endeavor as the significant state trust land inholdings in so many large federal tracts are a headache for them as well. Usually, these state inholdings found themselves embedded within national parks or forests created after statehood grants were made. Western states and the federal government have long traded parcels, with the latter transferring more contiguous chunks of federal land in exchange for numerous small park inholdings. Another source of consolidation, especially for states that joined the Union relatively late, have been the so-called in lieu lands, which gave states the ability to select tracts of land of equivalent acreage from the federal inventory when the legally allotted numbered sections were already spoken for as protected federal land or private land homesteaded before the statehood grants were made. Naturally, when choosing in lieu lands, states selected larger contiguous blocks, as Arizona very presciently did around the future sprawl of Phoenix.[27]

Trust Land Uses and Revenue

Generally, trust land managers are understood to be obligated to identify the use of a particular unit of land that will return the greatest revenue.[28] Geography, geology, and the random distribution of land grants all conspire to make the usage of trust land wildly variable between and within states. For example, Nebraska's and Oklahoma's trust lands are almost entirely leased for agricultural production,[29] and the Washington DNR is the larg-

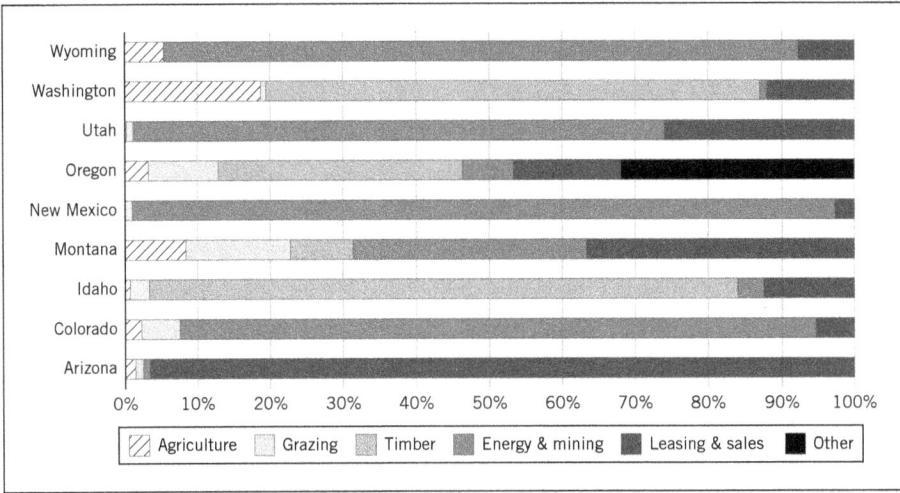

Figure 6.4 Portion of revenue by source for selected state trust land systems
(Data sources: Peter Culp, et al., *State Trust Lands in the West Fiduciary Duty in a Changing Landscape* [Lincoln Institute of Land Policy, Policy Focus Report, 2015], pp. 54–62; Wyoming Office of State Lands and Investments, *Business Plan and Annual Report* [2021], p. 26.)

est wheat producer in the entire state.[30] Figure 6.4 shows the proportion of revenue generated by various trust land activities across selected states. Interestingly, there is not necessarily a close relationship to how much land is allocated to a given use and how revenue is generated. For example, grazing is by far the single biggest use of trust land overall in terms of acres devoted (at around 77%),[31] and yet it is a negligible source of revenue, with only Montana (14%) and Oregon (10%) posting percentages of total revenue in the double digits. Timber production is the dominant revenue producer in Washington, Oregon, Idaho, Wisconsin, and Minnesota. By far the most lucrative activities on trust land are energy production/mining and commercial leasing and land sales, with the former being especially dominant in New Mexico, Texas, Colorado, Montana, Wyoming, and Utah. In fact, New Mexico and Texas, on the basis of their aggressive oil and gas production on state trust land, lead the nation in revenue, permanent funds, and distributions to schools, as can be seen in Table 6.2. In Montana, it is hardrock mining and coal production that dominate, while Utah produces oil from tar sands on over 32,000 acres of trust land.[32]

Sales and commercial leasing, meanwhile, are major revenue producers in Arizona (93%), Montana (37%), and Utah (26%). Land sales tend to generate the most revenue when they are adjacent to fast-growing urban areas where demand and land values are high. The reason that Arizona's trust

TABLE 6.2 FY 2021 STATE TRUST LANDS DISTRIBUTIONS, REVENUES, AND PERMANENT FUNDS FOR SELECTED STATES

State	Total trust distributions (in millions of $)	Total trust revenues (in millions of $)	Permanent fund value (in millions of $)
Alaska	31.2	44.0	844.7
Arizona	384.8	409.2	7,620.0
New Mexico	1,234.7	1,251.9	23,960.4
Montana	55.5	107.3	760.7
Utah	97.4	202.6	3,193.1
Wyoming	253.0	100.6	4,078.5[1]
Washington	167.4	239.8	1,305.8
Colorado	138.7	148.6	1,334.9
Minnesota	36.0	54.6	1,940.0
Idaho	84.5	74.9	3,107.8
Oregon	60.1	34.0[2]	2,249.1
South Dakota	16.0	16.0	375.0
Oklahoma	116.1	572.7	2,874.9
Texas	345.0	1,842.8	46,600.0
North Dakota	194.3	179.5	6,057.6
Wisconsin	82.5	NA	NA
Nevada	74.5	5.1	396.8

Data sources: National Association of State Trust Lands, *FY21 Member State Data* (Report, 2022), available at: https://www.statetrustland.org/uploads/1/2/0/9/120909261/report_-_topic_compilations.pdf. Wyoming Office of State Lands and Investments, *Business Plan & Annual Report* (Report, September 1, 2021), available at: https://drive.google.com/file/d/1b5Xufa5RZgyTNTE5Gsw476GZKiru2z9d/view; National Association of State Trust Lands, *FY20 Member State Data* (Report, February 28, 2021), available at: https://www.statetrustland.org/uploads/1/2/0/9/120909261/report_-_topic_compilations_02-28-21.pdf; National Association of State Trust Lands, *FY19 Member State Data* (Report, April 29, 2020), available at: https://www.statetrustland.org/uploads/1/2/0/9/120909261/report_-_topic_compilations_04-29-20.pdf; Wyoming Legislative Service Office, *Wyoming School Land Revenues* (Presentation, May 24, 2022), available at: https://wyoleg.gov/Interim Committee/2022/05-202206062-01WyomingStateSchoolLandsRevenues_AgStatePublicLandsWater ResCommittee_FINAL.pdf; Wisconsin Board of Commissioners of Public Land, *2019-2021 Biennial Report* (Report, 2021), p. 3, available at: https://bcpl.wisconsin.gov/bcpl.wisconsin.gov%20 Shared%20Documents/Agency%20Info/2020-2021%20Biennial%20Report.pdf.

[1] Wyoming permanent fund data is from 2019.
[2] Oregon's trust revenue figure is from 2020 rather than 2021.

revenues are almost entirely from land sales is because the state has a lot of trust land surrounding the Phoenix and Tucson metro areas. Unlike grazing or logging, it does not actually take the sale or commercial leasing of many acres to generate a lot of revenue. Bruce and Rice calculated the ratio of revenue per acre produced by grazing versus commercial sales/leasing and found results ranging from 1:10 all the way to 1:5,000.[33] Because of this bonanza, Arizona has managed to sell off more than 10% of its trust holdings over the years.[34]

What is important to remember about sales or leases of any kind (except recreational) is that they allow lessees to exclude the public, as these are most definitely not multiple use lands and do not necessarily bear the obligations of all other public land to ensure public access. According to the Colorado State Land Board, if an individual is not the lessee of a particular piece of trust land, "the land is just as off limits to the public as a piece of private land."[35] This is not the case in every state, however; the third column in Table 6.1 shows which states allow public access to trust lands, require a fee, or prohibit it altogether. An alternative revenue-generating use on some state trust lands is leasing land for recreation or conservation (whereby the lessee is usually a state wildlife agency or perhaps an environmental organization or organized group of hunters). Because such leases could theoretically outbid certain other resource-extraction uses (especially grazing), a few states try to head off this scenario and actually prohibit leases that are exclusively for recreation.[36]

Table 6.2 shows a fiscal year (FY) 2021 snapshot of state trust revenues, disbursements to beneficiaries, and the size of the permanent fund that each system is required to have. While figures can significantly vary from year to year, what these data show is that depending on the extent of trust land holdings, their dominant uses, and perhaps local decisions regarding the land or the permanent fund, there is wide divergence between the states in the terms of the funds they can bestow upon their beneficiaries in a given year. While public K–12 schools are the main beneficiary in most states, other endowed public institutions include universities, prisons, state hospitals, state libraries, state buildings, veterans' homes, and mental health institutions.[37] Annual distributions to beneficiaries (Table 6.2, column 1), it should be noted, come from two sources: revenue from renewable resources (grazing, timber, agriculture) plus some portion of interest from the permanent fund investments. Revenue from nonrenewable sources (energy production, mining, or the sale of land), meanwhile, goes straight into the permanent fund. Conversely, if a state land board was to purchase land for its trust portfolio, it would be paid for out of the permanent fund.[38] There are, it should be noted, two exceptions to this rule: (1) Utah, which invests revenue from both renewable and nonrenewable resources in its fund and only pays distributions through the fund, and (2) Colorado, which splits all revenue regardless of type evenly between beneficiaries and the permanent fund.[39]

While initial land grants were conceived of in 1785 as *the* way to fund public schools on the frontier, centuries of development and modernization have rendered this system very much obsolete as the financial needs of modern public schools have wildly outgrown this system's capacity. Most states' trusts provide only low-end single-digit percentages of support for their school systems.[40] In fact, the only outliers in this regard are New Mexico, with its energy production juggernaut and massive permanent fund, which provide about a quarter of the public school budget, and lightly populated Wyoming, which hits 15.3%.[41] So, for the most part, this enormous, complex, and elaborate system of land management and resource production has evolved to serve a distinctly subordinate and supplemental role in modern public school financing. Bruce and Rice are far less charitable with their characterization of the whole trust land system as "a largely failed notion," while another observer in Washington State derides funding essential services with timber as a "19th century mentality."[42] For western state budget writers, on the other hand, any extra funding is doubtlessly welcomed.

A Closer Look at the Trust Doctrine

The modern trust doctrine that largely guides today's trust land managers holds that they have a strict fiduciary duty to the trust beneficiaries and no one else. It also requires the creation of permanent funds to maintain the trust endowment (though not necessarily the actual trust acreage) in perpetuity. The modern version of this doctrine has its roots in the last two state enabling acts that distributed school lands—New Mexico and Arizona.[43] These two acts articulated a much more precise version of the trust doctrine than the vague and underdeveloped notions found in earlier statehood acts. Further clarification and solidification of these ideas were subsequently achieved through state constitutional provision and even more so through a number of significant state and federal judicial rulings.[44] Perhaps the most impactful case, *Lassen v. Arizona Highway Department* in 1967, revolved around whether the state highway department could gain rights-of-way for roads across trust land without compensating the trust.[45] The U.S. Supreme Court ruled that the trust authority did indeed have to be compensated, and in doing so, it laid out the basic framework for the modern trust doctrine: (1) sales and leases on trust land must be at full market value, and (2) trust lands had to be managed for maximum economic productivity.[46]

Besides articulating such a strict trust doctrine, *Lassen* is also important in that, soon afterward, many state courts began to explicitly apply this standard. For example, in *Oklahoma Education Association v. Nigh* in 1982, the Oklahoma Supreme Court struck down legislatively imposed limitations on the terms for leases and sales of agricultural trust land, ruling that "a State may not use school land trust assets to subsidize farming and ranching."[47] There have, however, been some notable exceptions, too. California state courts have long interpreted state authority over their trust lands as unconditional, thus giving the legislature broad discretion, and indeed, 1980 legislation requires land use planning, recreational access, and multiple use principles to be applied to all parcels of trust land, almost as if *Lassen* did not exist. Thus far, this interpretation has gone unchallenged in federal court.[48]

Another exception to the strict application of the modern trust doctrine has been in Colorado, where, in 1996, the public approved a constitutional amendment to carve a 300,000-acre stewardship trust out of the larger 2.8-million-acre system to focus on wildlife habitat, open space, and scenic beauty.[49] Several school districts sued, but in *Branson School District v. Romer*, the federal district court ruled that although Colorado did have to abide by federal requirements on trusts, good stewardship can actually enhance the value of the land and thus it does not necessarily violate the trust doctrine.[50] This ruling has potentially cracked the door open somewhat to initiatives to make trust management more environmentally sensitive, as explored in more depth further on in this chapter.

Politics and the Trust Doctrine

The trust doctrine demands that trust lands be managed for the good of beneficiaries, not leaseholders, but when those lessees are politically powerful and well connected, the latter scenario is indeed what sometimes happens. Headwaters, an economic think tank, points to an array of performance audits that have shown that in many western states, economic returns are not being maximized. They cite cases with no competitive bidding or poor or sometimes no appraisals to determine the value of leased properties.[51] In Arizona, for example, grazing fees for state trust lands are set by an external board appointed by the governor and subject to all sorts of typical interest group lobbying and pressure. Furthermore, these grazing fees are rarely adjusted to keep up with inflation, and so, consequently, rates have fallen in 2018 dollars to $2.76 AUM (animal unit/month) as compared to $15 in Nevada and $14.51 in Colorado, which have set prices closer to market value.[52]

This becomes less surprising when one considers the revolving doors in some states, like Wyoming, between trust managers and members of local stock growers associations.[53] This can be seen as creating some serious conflicts of interest, considering that those interests often view subsidized leases as a birthright of sorts. In fact, according to Erin Pounds, below-market grazing leases are so ubiquitous on western public lands that it may never even dawn on trust managers that it could be a problem:

> Land managers may be unwilling to impose fair market value on grazing leases of their own volition because the practice of issuing grazing leases below market price is so engrained that land managers may not view it as a violation of the trust.[54]

More evidence of this bias toward grazing can be seen in Idaho and Arizona, where environmental groups set upon a strategy to outbid ranchers for certain grazing leases in a quest to give overgrazed land a chance to recover. However, in both states, trust land agencies tried to reject these high bids, which led to legal action. Eventually, these cases made it to each state's supreme court (in 1996 and 2001 respectively) and were resolved in favor of the plaintiffs in rulings that found that the trust doctrine requires that the high bid be accepted even if it comes from a politically disfavored bidder.[55]

Another good example of the entrenched power of politically connected lessees can be seen in the political conflict over the slow shift of leases away from grazing. Wind and solar projects are rapidly becoming a widely exploited new use for state trust lands given their very high demand and the sunny, windswept acreage that makes up so many trust parcels. In Montana, it has been reported that a roughly 1,300-acre tract that earned $2,430 in revenue from a grazing lease now earns $480,000 from leasing for renewable energy.[56] While displaced ranching leaseholders loudly protested, the trust doctrine absolutely demanded this shift. Unlike federal lands or state multiple use lands, there is no obligation to serve any clientele besides the trust beneficiary. However politically, socially, or economically important ranching is perceived to be in any given state and regardless of the clout that ranching interests may wield, below-market grazing (which Pounds claims is a very common occurrence)[57] can never be considered anything but an unquestionable violation of the trust doctrine that comes directly at the expense of trust beneficiaries. For the trust doctrine to work, Headwaters argues, there must always be competitive bidding, sufficient monitoring, and aggressive negotiation.[58] According to trust doctrine purists, there should be no place in the administration of trust lands for the types of interest group advocacy that animate most all other realms of public lands politics.

Permanent funds and how they are managed are another way that political considerations sometimes intrude on the trust doctrine, and the result is often that current beneficiaries become favored over future ones. For the trust funds to sustain themselves into perpetuity, there is an optimal distribution that should not be exceeded, but the huge coffers brimming with billions of trust fund dollars often prove too tempting for politicians of all stripes under pressure to increase school supports (Democrats) or avoid tax increases (Republicans). Utah, Colorado, and Arizona, in particular, have been accused of letting political expediency and short-term thinking harm the long-term viability of their permanent funds.[59] In fact, Utah spent down its permanent fund so aggressively in the 1980s that it has subsequently had to sharply cut back on distributions and divert incoming revenue back to rebuilding the fund, thus denying current beneficiaries their due in favor of the ones who preceded them.[60] Washington, on the other hand, has a reputation of managing their trust fund by the book in terms of optimal distributions.[61] Another controversy over permanent funds involves who should rightly be considered a beneficiary, with some pushing for a much broader interpretation. For example, Oregon rerouted distributions in 2018 to shore up its teachers' pensions, which critics said was not directly for schools and their students.[62]

The Trust Doctrine and Conservation: Is It Even Possible?

The revenue maximization imperative of the trust doctrine has generally been interpreted by land managers in ways that guarantee the brutalization of the land's ecological systems. Conservation, for the most part, has not been seen as any kind of obligation for trust management; rather, it is viewed as an impediment standing in the way of good returns on revenue. This notion is so strong that some states even prohibit conservation *leases*, which actually earn revenue (often more than grazing), let alone voluntary conservation measures. To be clear, there is a certain baseline for environmental protection on trust land that may be imposed by external forces such as state regulations to protect drinking water supplies, federal endangered species act protections, state environmental review where it exists (like Montana), or even local counties' land use plans, as was determined in a 1990 Colorado court case.[63] That said, the mandate for aggressive revenue maximization has taken a heavy toll, with damage from overgrazing, mining, and energy production the most notable.

Michael Loring and John Workman, for example, compared the ecological condition of grassland habitat on adjacent tracts of rangeland owned by the USFS, the Bureau of Land Management (BLM), the Utah Trust Lands Administration, and private ranchers. What they found was that USFS rangeland was in the best shape ecologically and benefited from the most investment, while BLM and private lands had substantially less investment and were in equally poor shape. They found state trust lands, however, to be in the very worst shape of all and with the least investment.[64] In another federal-state trust land comparison, Cally Carswell reports on a population of endangered gypsum wild buckwheat found in a remote area of the Chihuahuan desert on land divided between the BLM and New Mexico trust land. On the BLM side, with its existing federal protocols for flagging rare species, following Endangered Species Act requirements, and doing environmental impact statements, the plant is fully protected, with no roads, drill pads, or pipelines. On the state side, though, it is business as usual, with an active fracking site and its abundant infrastructure blasted right through the buckwheat colony, despite the fact that biologists had previously brought the plant to the state's attention.[65] "There's no infrastructure for protecting plants," says a biologist from the NM State Land Office. "The state statute is pretty ambiguous, and it doesn't give anyone any particular authority to stop anything from happening."[66] Similarly, a dense colony of endangered Tharp's bluestar was also discovered in the same area and reported to trust land authorities by state biologists, and soon after, a drill pad was built right on top of the site.[67]

Energy production is certainly a lucrative use for trust lands, and indeed, New Mexico's massive permanent fund and generous annual distributions are almost entirely a function of its energy wealth. There are two problems with this bounty, however. First, the resource production in this case is nonrenewable—when it's gone, it's gone—and second, when it's gone, all that is left is damaged land desperately in need of remediation. It is estimated that New Mexico maintains assurance bonds for energy production damage and clean-up on trust lands that cover only 2.4% of the actual $8.3 billion that is projected to be needed—a staggering $8.1 billion shortfall.[68] Are these costs to be compensated by the permanent fund? By the general taxpaying public? Or will the land, after its one-time bounty of gas is drained, be left to trust beneficiaries as a poisoned and devalued wasteland?

The Land That Time Forgot

With one-square-mile land grants dating back to the Northwest Ordinance and trust doctrines articulated around the turn of the last century, land trust management can seem a bit frozen in time. Indeed, what Pounds calls "static management" has, in most states, utterly failed to keep up with growing social movements, evolving public values, and advances in ecological science that have all pushed toward conservation, biodiversity, and greater recreational access.[69] These discrepancies that have developed have become increasingly problematic and have put additional pressure on trust land managers. The general public, especially in rapidly growing urban areas like Denver, Phoenix, or Boise, cannot always discern between types of public land or appreciate the nuances of trust doctrine mandates, especially when they want a popular mountain bike trail extended further onto public (trust) land or when Arizona proposes sales or commercial leasing on scenic tracts of wildland right outside crowded cities yearning for more public space. The challenge for trust land managers is how to accommodate at least some of these growing demands while staying true, legally and otherwise, to the obligations imposed by their unique fiduciary mandate. To trust doctrine purists, though, such calls for enhanced conservation are just another form of external political pressure, no different than the ranchers seeking below-cost grazing. Those with more expansive conceptions, however, would argue that especially if one applies more appropriate time frames, the ecological health of land is inextricably tied to its value and the ultimate return on that value.

Unlike state parks acquired for their spectacular landscapes or wildlife management areas set aside for their wetlands or rich habitat, statehood acts distributed trust lands in a completely random and haphazard manner with absolutely no attention paid to the land's characteristics, assets, or economic potential. This means that trust lands, especially the large portion that remain unconsolidated, run the gamut—some teeming with biodiversity and others largely barren, some blessed with heart-stopping natural beauty and others monotonous and mundane. Unfortunately, the trust doctrine framework is not at all equipped to evaluate and discern what might make a particular parcel precious in ways that transcend the traditional and exceedingly narrow framework for revenue generation through commodity production. "The focus on particular section numbers, with little or no attention paid to the land's character," claim Bruce and Rice, "ensure that land granted for the support of schools will include some tracts with significant value other than the ability to produce income."[70]

Making matters worse, many states have astonishing poor inventories of the natural and scenic assets on their trust lands such as rare plant or animal populations or biodiversity generally.[71] Instead of making well-informed decisions in a holistic way, each square mile is considered in isolation, with managers seeking out revenues by choosing from the usual very limited buffet of choices—grazing, logging, energy production, or commercial development. This is why three-quarters of trust lands are used for grazing even though grazing revenues are but a minuscule portion of overall revenues. In the big picture, it might be a highly destructive action not worth the pittance it earns, but for that one square mile in the desert without minerals, oil reserves, or commercial prospects, it is perceived as the only way to maximize revenue as the trust doctrine seems to demand.

A perfect example of this "penny-wise and pound-foolish" approach to revenue maximization can be seen in the agricultural leases that trust land administrators have sold to Fondomonte, a Saudi company, in the scorching, drought-plagued desert of west-central Arizona's Butler Valley and that earn the trust about $50,000 annually. Because of Arizona's libertarian water policy, which leaves rural water unregulated and considered a fundamental property right, Fondomonte, since the lease began in 2015, has pumped 16,415 acre-feet of water (or 5.35 billion gallons) annually from the valley's limited aquifer to grow water-intensive forage crops to export back to Saudi Arabia for dairy production (as pumping water to grow forage crops is not legal in equally dry Saudi Arabia).[72] Not only is Arizona's trust land being permanently damaged and devalued, but many billions of gallons of scarce water are being denied to the neighboring residents of a parched state and many millions of dollars of untapped wealth are not flowing to beneficiaries. On paper, though, assuming the state did indeed earn somewhere close to market rates for an agricultural lease on a patch of desert with no oil, gas, or minerals and with unpriceable water, then this arrangement is perfectly aboveboard and technically compatible with the trust doctrine.[73]

Stewardship Reconceived as Long-Term Value Enhancement

When the Colorado public voted in 1996 to amend the state constitution to put about a tenth of the state's trust lands into a stewardship trust, it also changed the language of the fiduciary obligation for all trust holdings from generating the "maximum possible amount" of revenue to "providing for prudent management."[74] The amendment language further stated,

> Economic productivity of all lands held in public trust is dependent on sound stewardship, including protecting and enhancing the beauty, natural values, open space, and wildlife habitat thereof for this and future generations.[75]

In the inevitable legal challenge to this significant policy alteration, the Colorado Supreme Court ruled that while the fiduciary obligations of the trust lands are real, there is flexibility in how to achieve and sustain those returns for the long haul.[76] The importance of this ruling is that it opened the door within the trust doctrine to incorporate alternative forms of valuation and time horizons. Most importantly, however, was that it implicitly acknowledged that revenue maximization in the short term can sometimes irreparably damage that tract of land's ability to generate revenue in the future. Could the exhaustion of a parcel in order to wring out every last dollar as quickly as possible really be the intent of a trust doctrine conceived to be perpetual? Or might a more modest revenue flow that can be sustained indefinitely be more in line with trust principles? Such an idea recognizes the natural capital on trust land as not just the commodities that roll off the assembly line but the machinery that produces it all. Therefore, to take care of this natural infrastructure is to provide long-term value to the trust and its ability to generate wealth long into the future. Thus, according to Pounds, the *maximum* economic production of the trust doctrine does not necessarily have to mean *immediate* economic production.[77]

This was exactly the thinking behind the Washington legislature's reforms of trust land management in the 1990s, which explicitly added the protection of wildlife habitat to the list of obligations. These laws were particularly focused on the 1.1 million acres of dry grassland and shrub/steppe ecosystems on trust land in eastern Washington that were severely degraded after many years of grazing and agricultural leasing that left the sage grouse and pygmy rabbit in great jeopardy.[78] Armed with the new laws, the Washington DNR set out not to overturn existing land uses as much as to introduce better practices and greater restrictions (something generally unheard of on trust lands) for erosion control, soil fertility, and the preservation of biodiversity. These practices included temporarily withdrawing some land from production to let it rest and heal, something the DNR argued was fully consistent with their trust obligations as it restored the productivity of severely damaged land.[79] The fact that leases in eastern Washington earned so little revenue to begin with and yet caused so much degradation not only made the DNR's reforms easier to sell but in a larger sense called some aspects of the whole trust model (at least for the dry steppes of Washington) into question. Thus Washington, California, Oregon, and Colorado have all taken steps legislatively or constitutionally to redefine trust obligations in ways that leave room for basic conservation practices.

Interestingly, Washington is one of only four trust land states (along with Colorado, Montana, and Minnesota)[80] that has an integrated cabinet-level DNR-type department rather than an independent agency or board administering trust lands. Not surprisingly, at least three of these states take a much broader view of trust obligations and seem much more sensitive to public opinion. For example, Minnesota maintains 51,000 acres of highly protected state natural areas within its trust land system[81]—something that would be nearly inconceivable within most state trust land systems. This inevitably raises the question of whether these larger integrated agencies with other environmental responsibilities besides trust land management (like wildlife biology, state park management, etc.) are more knowledgeable, more sympathetic, and more aware of ecological concerns, not to mention more subject to public opinion, than the rather specialized and politically isolated state land offices that typically manage trust lands. In Washington's case, this phenomenon might be even more pronounced due to the fact that their DNR is not led by a gubernatorial appointee but rather the elected commissioner of public lands.

Strategies for Conservation

Beyond this kind of powerful reimagining of the trust doctrine, which seems to be very slowly but steadily gaining traction, there are other more immediate strategies that reformers have advocated for to achieve better conservation outcomes on trust land.

Land Exchanges and Buyouts

Perhaps the most direct thing that a trust land agency can do to conserve a particularly scenic or biodiverse tract of land is swap with (or sell to) another agency or non-profit who can conserve it without having to wrestle with the complications of the trust mandate. For example, the Wisconsin Bureau of the Commissioner of Public Lands (BCPL) has scoured its modest 77,000-acre timber holdings for old-growth stands and then trades them with the DNR for state-owned forests more suitable for timber production, preferably adjacent to other blocks of BCPL trust land. They have also sold

old-growth tracts to nonprofit organizations and used the proceeds to buy commercial timberlands to replace their inventory.[82] Although a one-time liquidation of old growth would certainly provide a jolt to revenues, the BCPL, which is governed by a small board of elected officeholders, has instead shown admirable restraint and engendered goodwill in sparing this precious biodiversity without losing access to productive timberland.

Similarly, environmental groups in Washington in the 1990s raised $20 million to buy 30,000 acres of old-growth lynx habitat in the trust lands that comprise Loomis State Forest.[83] What this purchase achieved was to remove the land's trust status so it could be conserved without running afoul of trust requirements; the trust fund, meanwhile, received full market value to either purchase new land or invest in the permanent fund. This scenario also played out in 2006 when a timber sale was planned for trust land near a popular trail in Washington's Blanchard Mountain and citizen opposition led to a buyout, which allowed the trust to buy other less controversial private timberlands to replace that acreage.[84] This strategy offers a conflict-tempering safety valve of sorts when citizens speak out and mobilize against a particular proposal for resource extraction on especially popular and valued parcels. As Fairfax says, "If you have the money, you can buy your way out of many environmental conflicts."[85]

An even bigger (and more expensive) version of this maxim at work might be the recent case of the Elliott State Forest in Oregon, also trust land.[86] Despite having a lot of mature forest, this unit's timber program was losing money, so, in keeping with its fiduciary duties, the trust managers decided to sell the land to a consortium of private timber companies. However, the idea of privatizing such a well-known and heavily visited forest did not sit well with a mobilized public.[87] To quell the outcry, the state felt it had no choice but to figure out a way to finance a $100 million payout to the permanent trust. After several years of painstaking negotiation, the state created a unique status for Elliott as a nontrust public research forest governed by a diverse board of stakeholders.[88]

Forest activist Andy Kerr thinks what happened with the Elliott State Forest should be a model for all trust lands with high-quality conservation assets, which he claims have much more value to the public than their financial returns to beneficiaries. At least in his state of Oregon, he argues that trust lands are relatively poor financial performers with return of asset values in FY 2018 of 1.05% for agriculture leases, 0.48% for timber, 0.49% for rangelands, and 0.70% for industrial/commercial leasing. "A rational financial manager," he argues, "would sell them, take the cash, and put it in better investments."[89] He would prefer the federal government to be the buyer of most of this land, using now-enhanced funding from the newly reauthorized LWCF.[90]

As previously mentioned, state trust agencies and the federal government have long exchanged land, and, in fact, the Federal Land Policy and Management Act of 1976 explicitly encourages and authorizes the BLM and USFS to make such exchanges where applicable.[91] States, however, routinely complain that federal bureaucratic rigidity and budgetary complications have made the process far longer and more tedious than it needs to be.[92] The most common scenario with state-federal exchanges involves state trust land inholdings within units of federal land. This is actually quite common, with hundreds of thousands of stranded acres each in Wyoming, Utah, and Arizona alone.[93] When land grants were made at statehood, much of the federal domain that surrounded these trust lands was intended to be eventually homesteaded as private land, but then the conservation movement blossomed and succeeded in retaining much western land as national forests and parks, thereby stranding the granted sections within high-value protected areas. For example, the 1.9-million-acre Grand Staircase-Escalante National Monument in Utah contained nearly 377,000 acres of stranded trust land when the monument was dedicated in 1996. Utah was bitterly against the creation of the monument for many reasons, but partly because it made the prospect of being able to develop its trust land within the protected monument pretty much out of the question. Consequently, the Clinton administration gave Utah 139,000 acres of federal land elsewhere in the state and $50 million for the permanent fund.[94]

Similarly, Minnesota and the federal government are in negotiations to compensate Minnesota for the 83,000 acres of trust land trapped within the federal Boundary Waters Canoe Area Wilderness through exchange and monetary compensation.[95] Incidentally, exchanges need not be acre for acre, as could be seen in the trade the BLM made with Utah for 950 acres of trust land within a larger federal recreational area for only 330 acres of BLM land near Cedar City but that had very lucrative potential for commercial leasing.[96] If they can be pulled off, exchanges tend to be win–win situations as states get to consolidate trust lands into bigger, more efficiently managed chunks and the federal government removes scattered inholdings from their more protected parks and wilderness areas for which there is always the ongoing threat of legal or environmental hijinks.[97]

Unfortunately, as political polarization intensifies, the purposeful creation of such mischief seems to have become more important in some western states than the very real benefits of consolidating trust lands. For example, in early 2024, Utah abruptly derailed a long and painstakingly negotiated swap of

130,000 acres of trust land within the Bears Ears National Monument to protest the federal government's newly released management plans for the monument, and then approved a 460-foot telecom tower for a state trust parcel embedded within the monument. In this case, Utah seems to be wagering that keeping its parcels within Bears Ears allows it continued leverage and the chance to undermine the monument they so adamantly oppose.[98]

Conservation Leases

Another strategy for introducing conservation into trust land settings where it normally does not appear is for government agencies or private nonprofits to directly lease tracts of trust land for an explicitly conservation-related purpose, such as wildlife habitat, scenic open space and recreation, or hunting. While trust managers have historically shown great resistance to conservation leases,[99] and a few states, such as Montana, explicitly disallow them,[100] they have nevertheless become more commonplace due to favorable court rulings (requiring highest bid) and public pressure. For example, Colorado has seen a 93% increase in conservation/recreation lease revenue in just the four-year period between FY 2013 and FY 2017.[101] Idaho is another state in which the fish and game agency commonly leases state trust tracts for wildlife habitat (and sometimes even WMAs). However, conservation leasing will only work in situations where it competes against other fairly low-revenue activities like grazing, agriculture, or some marginal-value timber harvesting, leading to a better chance of what O'Day refers to as "beating revenue maximization at its own game."[102] Obviously, conservation leases will rarely, if ever, be the high bid against energy, mining, or commercial leasing proposals. Critics, however, dislike this idea of one element of state government paying another for leases that used to be paid by private lessees and liken it to "robbing Peter to pay Paul."[103]

Of course, one of the bigger obstacles to conservation leasing is how to finance it. This is especially true considering that generally cash-strapped state wildlife agencies would most often be the public sector lessee (though passage of the Recovering America's Wildlife Act—see Chapter 5—and the unlocking of its huge pot of funding might ease this problem). In some cases, more nimble nonprofits have taken the lead in bidding for leases using a combination of their own funds, LWCF grants, and state matching grants. Arizona, in fact, created the Arizona Preserve Initiative (API) in 1996 for just this reason—to allow groups to match funds for leasing or buying out previously identified priority conservation areas on trust land. For a time, Arizona was in a league by itself in inventorying conservation assets on trust land and then offering up that land for sale or lease, mostly to conservation groups and county and municipal governments in fast-growing urban areas. By 2012, 46,511 acres had been reclassified as eligible for conservation, another 36,000 were awaiting consideration, 16,343 acres had been formally protected, and another 10,000 acres were awaiting final approval and financing.[104] In 1998, Arizona voters also passed Proposition 303 to dedicate more funding to cities to lease or buy trust land (through the API process) to meet their local open space and recreation needs.[105] All told, this program of conservation sales and leasing earned the Arizona permanent fund nearly $389 million just between 2008 and 2013.[106] Unfortunately, lawsuits and changing political winds in Arizona state politics tremendously slowed the program in subsequent years as critics began to frame these conservation leases arrangements as "cactus vs kids."[107]

STATE TRUST LANDS: *Spotlight on Wyoming*

After the Arapaho, Arikara, Blackfeet, Cheyenne, Crow, Kiowa, Nez Perce, Sioux, Shoshone, and Ute tribes were displaced from their lands, the federal government moved to bestow statehood on portions of the former Wyoming Territory.[1] The enabling act that authorized this in 1890 also granted the new state the 16th and 36th sections of every six-square-mile township across the state to support its schools and other public institutions. This statehood grant amounted to 4.2 million acres, and Wyoming is one of a small cluster of states that have held onto most of their trust lands—specifically, 83% (3.5 million acres). While Wyoming ranks fourth in the nation in terms of institutional trust land acreage,[2] it has amassed the third-largest permanent trust fund, which provides the second-highest percentage of school budget support (at 15.3%) of all the trust land states.[3] Over a five-year period (2017–2021), these distributions totaled more than $810.4 million.[4] This trust mostly supports K–12 schools, but other beneficiaries include the University of Wyoming, the State Hospital, and the State Veteran's Home, as well as state fish hatcheries, prisons, and buildings and grounds.[5]

The permanent fund is fed by revenues from leases and royalties of $100.6 million in 2021, though this figure can be quite variable year to year—the 2017–2021 average was $182.1 million annually.[6] Of the 2021 revenues, a full two-thirds (65.7%) were from oil and gas production, 14.4% from coal, and 4.6% from other mining activities. While only negligible amounts of revenue came from commercial sales/leasing in 2021, in other years, this was a more important source of revenue, especially for lands in the Jackson Hole and Grand Teton National Park areas.[7] Another 5.2% of revenue in 2021 came from grazing, which may seem substantial until you consider the fact that grazing leases covered 98% of all trust land surface acres as Wyoming often "stacks" leases with grazing leases overlaid upon energy- or mineral-leased lands.[8] The fact that nearly 3.5 million acres of grazing earned only $5.2 million is testament to how unproductive this ecologically impactful activity is. Wyoming's trust lands tend to have been subject to less consolidation and fewer land exchanges than in some other Western states. Therefore, like its neighbor Montana, much of its trust land acreage remains as it was when granted in 1890—as a highly dispersed scattering of individual 640-acre parcels. In fact, a fair number of these parcels are landlocked and not readily accessible. One study estimates 1.1 million such acres in Wyoming (not all these acres, though, are necessarily state trust land).[9]

Wyoming trust lands are administered by an independent agency, the Office of State Lands and Investments (OSLI), overseen by the Board of Land Commissioners. The OSLI had 103 employees in FY 2021–2022 and a net operating budget of $22.1 million.[10] As in many states with trust lands, the extent to which conservation can be incorporated or even considered is a perpetual issue regarding their management. For example, there has been great controversy recently over the possibility that OSLI would sell the 640-acre Kelly parcel inside Grand Teton National Park. There were several such state tracts trapped within the Tetons that the National Park Service slowly moved to buy out, but they ran out of funds before they could purchase the Kelly parcel. The land currently has a grazing lease earning $2,845 a year, but if the land were developed for low-density housing, its appraisal in 2022 was set at $62.4 million.[11] Given the preponderance of billionaires who live in the surrounding Jackson Hole region, some argue it is worth even more.[12] So, on one hand, trust doctrine would seem to require this drastic but very lucrative land use decision, and yet bringing a housing development for the ultrarich with all its attendant traffic, noise, and habitat fragmentation to the middle of a most beloved and economically important national park is quite unpopular and seen by many as nothing less than obscene. Due to widespread opposition, officials backed away from an open auction of the parcel and after initially asking the federal government for $750 million for the square-mile tract, in early 2024 the legislature authorized the sale to the NPS for $100 million. The not-yet-finalized arrangement contains several potentially deal-killing stipulations imposed by Wyoming upon federal land use in the broader area outside the park managed by the Bureau of Land Management.[13]

Another example of the difficulty that conservation faces, at least under Wyoming's interpretation of the trust doctrine, is with conservation leases. Unlike some neighboring states, Wyoming does not explicitly lease trust land for conservation purposes such as hunting or wildlife habitat, even though most land is leased only for low-revenue grazing. In November 2020, an advocacy group, the

Wyoming Outdoor Council (WOC), won (as the only bidder) a bid on an oil and gas lease in the Honeycomb Buttes area of the Northern Red Desert, which is a rugged and very wild area with some of the state's best habitat for sage grouse, an imperiled species. The WOC did its homework and purposefully chose to bid on an area with very high conservation values and low probability of striking oil or gas (exactly why it had no other bidders).[14] Despite this, the WOC found that its lease was soon canceled by the state as it was found impermissible. Apparently, an active conservation lease is less desirable than a speculative mineral lease very unlikely to ever produce oil and gas royalties. The WOC admits that the reason they made this irregular bid was due to their desire to draw attention to the fact that conservationists have no real tools at their disposal (besides protest) when it comes to protecting high conservation value areas within Wyoming trust lands.[15]

More than anything, this seems to be the result of the fairly one-dimensional and unchanging way that many trust administrators have long approached their obligations; what some go as far as to call "an institutional bias."[16] According to one observer, speaking of Wyoming,

> Conservation is a very new fish in this pond, up against 130 years of historical practice . . . the state is extremely accustomed to its revenue streams from traditional uses, so trying to develop a revenue stream that might supplant those existing uses is a very hard conversation and a very slow starter.[17]

Bruce and Rice report much tension between Wyoming park and game land managers from other agencies and trust managers, with the former sharing in the conservationists' frustration at the lack of coordination and the overall disinterest in conservation priorities.[18] Without adequate funding to buy high-value parcels outright, there is little the park or game managers can do. Very slowly, however, this resistance may be starting to break down as the OSLI has begun recently to take very modest and incremental steps toward the consideration of conservation leasing in the future as many neighboring states have incorporated.[19]

Legally, what it would take for Wyoming to change how it interprets its trust doctrine may not be as onerous as it seems. While the later enabling acts for Arizona and New Mexico laid out strict requirements close to our present understanding of the trust doctrine, Wyoming's enabling act was far vaguer about the state's exact obligations in managing trust lands and how much leeway it had in regulating such land. In fact, a 2003 case, *Riedel v. Anderson*, tested this very issue. The case evolved around whether preferential rights to renew leases violated the trust requirements in the 1890 enabling act and the state constitution. The Wyoming Supreme Court found that both the enabling act and the state constitution leave the legislature with broad discretion to regulate leases and it is only the subsequent passage of ordinary statutes that codified the modern understanding of trust obligations.[20] As such, Pounds argues,

> In light of these recent decisions in . . . Wyoming, it appears that other western states may revisit their adoption of the trust doctrine with regard to the management and disposition of their state lands and potentially discover that their management restrictions under the trust doctrine are not as limiting as previously thought.[21]

According to Pounds, all it would take to change the nature of trust land regulation in Wyoming would be a willing legislature.

While Wyoming has heretofore been reluctant to incorporate conservation goals or initiatives, it has been far more open about recreational access. Unlike some of its neighbors, Wyoming allows public access on its trust lands by default unless otherwise noted. Most trust lands are open to hunting, fishing, hiking, and horseback riding (but not camping) and without fees.[22] While some might see this as "leaving money on the table" for trust beneficiaries, it actually shows that Wyoming already takes into account subsidiary concerns related to the public's interests. Surely it can do the same thing with conservation priorities in a way that still allows it to honor its trust obligations.

NOTES

1. For a brief overview, see, Gregory Nickerson, "Before Wyoming: American Indian Geography and Trails" in *Wyoming History Encyclopedia* (Wyoming Historical Society, July 30, 2019), available at: https://www.wyohistory.org/encyclopedia/wyoming-american-indian-geography-and-trails.

2. See Table 6.1. Technically, Utah has more trust acres at 4.86 million acres, but only 3.4 million is school trust acreage. The rest underlies bodies of water and does not benefit specific institutions.

3. Wyoming Legislative Service Office, *Wyoming School Land Revenues* (Presentation, May 24, 2022), p. 6, available at: https://wyoleg.gov/InterimCommittee/2022/05-202206062-01WyomingStateSchoolLandsRevenues_AgStatePublicLandsWaterResCommittee_FINAL.pdf.

4. Jenifer Scoggin, *Wyoming State Trust Lands* (Presentation, April 21, 2021), p. 2, available at: https://wyoleg.gov/InterimCommittee/2022/03-2022042703-01WyomingStateTrustLands.pdf.

5. *Ibid.*, p. 16.

6. *Ibid.*, pp. 29–32.

7. Wyoming Office of State Lands and Investments, *Business Plan and Annual Report* (Report, 2021), p. 26; Peter Culp et al., *State Trust Lands in the West: Fiduciary Duty in a Changing Landscape* (Lincoln Institute of Land Policy, Policy Focus Report, 2015), p. 20.

8. Wyoming Office of State Lands and Investments, p. 26; Culp et al., p. 45.

9. Theodore Roosevelt Conservation Partnership, *Inaccessible State Lands in the West* (Report, August 15, 2019), p. 6.

10. Wyoming Office of State Lands and Investments, pp. 4, 22. This budget figure does not include grants disbursed to local communities.

11. Jason Blevins, "A Proposed Auction of State Trust Land Sale in Wyoming Could Start a National Trend" in *Colorado Sun* (November 21, 2023).

12. *Ibid.*

13. Another obstacle is the significant fundraising required of the NPS's nonprofit conservation partners. Chris Clements, "Obstacles Remain to Complete the Sale of the Kelly Parcel to Grand Teton National Park" in *Wyoming Public Radio* (July 12, 2024).

14. Birch Malotky, "A New Lease on State Land: How Conservation Is Hoping to Buy a Seat at the Land Management Table" in *Western Confluence* (March 24, 2022), available at: https://westernconfluence.org/a-new-lease-on-state-land/.

15. *Ibid.*

16. *Ibid.*

17. Jason Crowder quoted in, *Ibid.*

18. Melinda Bruce and Teresa Rice, "Controlling the Blue Rash: Issues and Trends in State Land Management" in *Land and Water Law Review* (Vol. 29, No. 1, 1994), p. 39.

19. Malotky.

20. Erin Pounds, "State Trust Lands: Static Management and Shifting Value Perspectives" in *Environmental Law* (Vol. 41, 2011), pp. 1347–1348.

21. *Ibid.*, p. 1348.

22. Scoggin, p. 26.

Contributory Value

If the problem with conservation on trust lands is that decisions are made parcel by parcel in an isolated, piecemeal way, then one solution that is very slowly taking root is the principle of *contributory value*—that is, the idea that the value of one piece of land is all bound up with and contingent upon the value of the adjacent (in this case, wild) land. The principle is most relevant when trust land is sold for residential development, as is quite common in Arizona, Utah, and Montana. Whereas the trust managers can sell any particular tract of land on the outskirts of a metropolitan area for a given price, that price might be substantially enhanced if the preservation of a large adjoining tract of open space (also trust land) was included in the deal. Typically, the developer buys all the land and then transfers development rights through a conservation easement on the open space portion of the project. As long as the residential development with its adjacent preserve is sold at a premium, then the trust doctrine is being honored despite the fact that some of the land is being preserved.[108] Successful examples of this sort of master planning that features large-scale conservation have occurred on state trust lands throughout the urban West, including Phoenix, Albuquerque and St. George, Utah.[109]

Calculating Ecosystem Services

For those who believe that public lands contain and actively spin off many billions of dollars of unpriced *ecosystem services* (see Chapter 2), such as water filtration and retention, erosion control, biodiversity, and carbon sequestration, it is infinitely frustrating to consider the trust doctrine's very narrowly conceived revenue-maximization obligations. Not only do they omit from consideration these massive stores of nontraditional, noncommodity-based value, but trust managers' supposedly "legitimate" revenue sources (grazing, mining, fracking, logging) actively degrade and devalue those very same ecosystem services. The reason that this framework has so far gained so little traction in trust land management is simply because actual markets for these services are so underdeveloped or even nonexistent. State or national park administrators can and do use the ecosystem services framework in a more theoretical way to calculate and illustrate the actual value of their parks in the fullest measure, which often include things like economic spin-off activities, enhanced growth, existence value, costs *not* incurred, or disasters, like floods, that were avoided. This is an especially useful analytical tool when used to justify an agency's work and public land's worth when funded with tax dollars. The trust doctrine, on the other hand, demands actual fungible revenue to be both distributed and invested on behalf of beneficiaries. And for this to happen, there must be readily accessible and functioning markets.

No matter how vital and spectacularly valuable, *in real terms*, a functioning wetland on state trust land may be, there is usually no way to monetize it for the beneficiaries except to drain it to lease to a farmer to grow soybeans or divert and pollute it in service of a nearby mine or fracking site. That is, there are presently (with a few exceptions) not really any markets that can translate their nearly priceless value in terms of water purification, retention, absorption, habitat, and climate regulation into actual money. This would take a wholesale restructuring and rethinking of markets for environmental goods and services as well as policies that forcefully prevent negative environmental externalities to be foisted onto bystanders and force their costs back onto market participants. This is a transformation far beyond the scope and responsibility of most trust managers' jobs as they would see them. And even if markets began to more rapidly evolve in this direction, it would still take state trust managers fluent in the ecosystem services concept and armed with the ability to understand and inventory ecological assets and alert to new possibilities and partners. In fact, nearly all of the Sonoran Institute's recommendations for moving forward with ecosystem service projects on trust land involve internal capacity building within state trust agencies.[110]

That is not to say that ecosystem service projects do not exist at all on trust land but rather they tend to be quite small scale and tentative at this point. One often-cited example would be prairie dog habitat banks established on trust lands in Utah where the Division of Wildlife Resources paid

$1,636 per credit for 154 credits (based on the estimated prairie dog population in the area) for easements to protect habitat.[111] Another example would be wetland mitigation banks for when developers destroy wetlands and must, according to federal and some state regulations, protect or restore additional replacement wetlands.[112] This would allow trust lands to monetize their wetlands by offering developers an actual place to "spend" the mitigation credits they were forced to buy in the first place. However, with the U.S. Supreme Court's recent decision severely limiting the extent to which wetlands fall under the Clean Water Act's protection, the need for these mitigation banks will undoubtedly decline.

As the climate crisis deepens and accelerates, carbon credit markets are beginning to take center stage among various nascent ecosystem service markets. They are, in fact, likely to become mature and more fully developed faster than any other such markets. What is noteworthy about carbon sequestration markets is that they have the potential to allow trust lands to take advantage of significant financial opportunities that require conservation rather than commodity production. The most obvious application for generating revenue for carbon credits would be for forests on trust lands. However, if this is done much like it currently is on state forests (see Chapter 4)—that is, to sell credits for existing forests without changing anything regarding how they are managed—then it may earn revenue for a while but will ultimately not amount to any actual reduction in carbon emissions and thus may eventually be unmasked as wasteful or even fraudulent. If, on the other hand, credits are sold that require trust managers to lengthen the time between logging rotations or even forgo logging of mature and old-growth forests on trust lands in the service of greater carbon sequestration, then this would become a use of trust land that both enhances conservation goals and makes a handsome profit for trust beneficiaries.

This very point is made at a larger scale by Adam Davis, who argues that of all types of public land, trust land is perhaps the best suited to employ an ecosystem services framework. He suggests that this is because it aligns "financial incentive with measurable environmental performance," the latter of which ecosystem service markets demand.[113] Trust lands, according to Davis, "alleviate the common conflict between 'doing the right thing' from a fiduciary perspective vs. 'doing the right thing' for the environment."[114]

Alternative Energy

In many ways, alternative energy projects are the perfect use for trust land with their abundant wind and sunshine and revenue-generation mandate.

Unlike ecosystem services, alternative energy already has fully developed markets and is thus quite lucrative and fully compatible with even the most restrictive interpretation of the trust doctrine. And yet, when thought of in the context of our dramatically worsening climate crisis, it can also be considered a use that strongly advances conservation goals. As of 2022, 4.2 gigawatts of power have been generated by 116 wind and 73 solar projects on state trust land, earning $16.8 million in revenue.[115] While this is an impressive start, it pales in comparison to fossil fuel production on state trust land, and advocates argue that it has barely begun to scratch the surface of both what is needed and what trust lands are capable of. The problem, according to Ada Montague, Samuel Panarella, and Peter Yould, is much the same as with ecosystem services—trust managers' knowledge, inclination, and capacity.[116] The technical challenges inherent in such complex and intensive (and, to trust managers, novel) land use are greater than agencies are able to handle (at least as they are currently set up). The authors stress that agencies will need to adapt and gear up to this new, more complicated type of leasing.[117]

Montague, Panarella, and Yould also identify a few other impediments standing in the way of alternative energy projects. The first thing that is largely missing is a rigorous inventory of trust lands for their solar, wind, and geothermal potential. Also, the isolated (and sometimes inaccessible) one-square-mile parcels that make up the "blue rash" are not always conducive to large-scale, land-intensive projects, especially involving large solar arrays. Setting up and servicing the infrastructure is also hard if the land is hard to access by road, and this remoteness from the grid poses challenges as well. Finally, prior uses can complicate the picture when a project is proposed for a particular suitable spot but the land has long been used for other activities.[118] Whether through inertia, a lessee's misguided notion of squatter's rights, or downright political favoritism, trust managers may be reluctant to abruptly change course. In fact, some states specifically prohibit surface uses on trust land that competes with mining or energy production.[119] Given that alternative energy leases are good revenue generators in their own right and are infinitely renewable and do not create pollution, trust managers might do well to reconsider some traditional uses, especially in light of the damage and reduced future productivity that mining and fossil fuel production bring upon trust land in the long term.

Washington Oaks State Park, Florida (Photo by author)

7

Appraising State Management of Public Land

The Good, the Bad, and the Ugly

> State lands are dispersed, resource rich, ecologically important, and underappreciated for their unique environmental, economic, and recreational significance.
>
> —Uma Outka, "State Lands in Modern Public Land Law"

State Public Lands: Patterns of Similarity and Difference

As has been suggested throughout this volume, the 50 states and how they organize and manage their public lands are simultaneously quite similar and almost infinitely variable. Some areas of convergence where strong, across-the-board patterns emerge include a wildlife management and financing regime that strongly privileges game species over general biodiversity, a state park budget process that labors under severe and near-universal constraints, fairly aggressive practices in forest and other resource management to maximize production, and, of course, trust land requirements and practices uniformly imposed (with a few exceptions) by modern legal understandings of the trust doctrine. These common patterns also help differentiate state management practices from that of the federal government, as shown in previous chapters.

Despite these common patterns, though, *homogeneity* would certainly be the wrong word to describe how the various states handle their public lands. Besides the vast differences in landscapes, biodiversity, political culture, demographics, and the twists and turns of each state's unique history, there are some areas of state land management that stand out as particularly divergent. First, states wildly differ on the characteristics of their state land portfolios and which types of land jurisdictions (forests, parks, WMAs, trust lands) tend to dominate their holdings. Another area of great divergence is the question of how much priority states give to programs of land acquisition—some, like

Florida and New Jersey, have been enthusiastic assemblers of vast and diverse systems while others in the South, Great Plains and Mountain West seem to barely give it a thought. Another important area of policy divergence would include the extent to which states have embraced preservation as an explicit management goal. Has a given state established binding natural areas programs and/or wilderness systems? Some have done so (often with great vigor) and many others not at all. Also, how do states reconcile the conflicting demands of recreation versus preservation on their state parks? Do they develop complex revenue-generating tourist infrastructure, or do they stay true to the original *state park idea* of quiet and pristine wildlands offering the harried citizen refuge close to home? And if revenue generation is indeed the holy grail, how open are states to schemes of privatization and outsourcing? Again, some states are very inclined to experiment with this, while others are far more cautious and even resistant.

What Explains the Variation between States?

The common patterns across the states are fairly easy to explain. Big historical events (like the Northwest Ordinance, progressive reform, or the passage of major relevant legislation like the Pittman-Robertson Act or the LWCF), broad-scale cultural and demographic change, the effect of national economic conditions on state budgeting trends, and the natural policy diffusion that accompanies federalism have all pushed state land management policies and practices in certain common directions.[1] Much less settled, however, is the question of what best explains policy *variation*. A simple answer would harken back to Justice Brandeis's "laboratories of democracy" framework; different states with different natural resources, populations, and policy demands toil away to solve problems in innovative ways unique to their situation.[2] However, an alternative explanation might focus on the fact that American politics since at least 2010 has been beset by intense polarization and increasing political radicalism. This, in turn, has had profound effects on the very make-up of state legislatures as aggressively partisan redistricting and polarized and nationalized state elections create massive, often veto-proof majorities. In this scenario, one would expect, rather than a true "laboratory of democracy" type of policy variation, a sort of dual-track, red state/blue state sorting of land management policies as state public lands, despite strong and relatively broad-based public support, get swept into this ideological maelstrom.

A case in point might be Wisconsin, perhaps the nation's swingiest, razor's-edge state with a long and proud tradition of public lands and environmental protection. Since achieving one of the nation's most aggressive and efficient gerrymanders in 2011, Republicans held as of 2024 a remarkably stable majority of more than 63 of 99 seats in the assembly and a veto-proof 22–11 majority in the Senate, despite earning only between 46% and 54.6% of all votes cast for legislature in recent election years.[3] Not surprisingly, this period has coincided with drastic changes in state environmental and land management policies, including an unprecedented zeroing out of general funds for the state parks, public land privatization, heavily increased logging on state forests, and dramatic reductions in land acquisition and conservation budgets. None of these measures enjoys much public support, but the stranglehold on policymaking and budgets that gerrymandering affords largely renders public opinion moot. Conversely, one could argue that this great ideological sorting has also led West Coast and northeastern states to increasingly move toward greater adherence to principles of ecosystem management and concern over biodiversity. And as discussed in Chapter 5, perhaps nowhere are the effects of ideological frenzy more evident than in the extreme and divisive rhetoric and attitudes that swirl around state wolf management policy. Not surprisingly, Colorado's successful reintroduction referendum and Wyoming's policy of near-total liquidation neatly adhere to the blue-red sociopolitical divide.

And yet, despite how persuasive this argument seems at times, upon closer scrutiny, reality reveals itself to be far more complex and nuanced. One thing that muddies the waters a bit is the evolution of the Republican Party's ideological leanings. It is important here to distinguish between the small-government, free market emphases of the earlier and more traditional manifestations of GOP ideology and today's more anti-corporate and culture war–oriented populism. The older free market ideologies are not necessarily synonymous with the more recent polarization that has marked our politics from the 2010 Tea Party movement to the Trump era, and these current lines of division no longer track cleanly along the traditional lines of debate about the role of markets. While both wings can often espouse explicitly antienvironmental views, there are subtle and not-so-subtle differences between them when it comes to public lands. While the populists lash out at any issue that they identify with "elite" culture (such as wolf protection, climate change, or limits on land use), they are a good measure less antagonistic to the very *idea* of public land than their more libertarian counterparts in the party. It is the free market, libertarian wing of the party that is most interested in slowing down or stopping land acquisition, pushing aggressive revenue-generating activities on parks and forests, and implementing various privatization schemes, and this cohort has been at it since the 1980s, well before the current era of polarization. For this reason, a simple Trump-era, red state/blue state framework for understanding policy variation does not always quite fit.

In fact, some of the more populist-conservative states offer some surprising policies that one would not expect in a simple ideological polarization model of state land management. For example, state parks in Tennessee, Missouri, Oklahoma, Arkansas, and Kentucky all have no entrance fees. Kentucky, meanwhile, is the only state with a cabinet-level nature preserves agency overseeing its substantial natural areas program, and 6 of the top 15 states in Table 3.3's ranking of the preservation orientation of state land inventories are deep red in their politics. Oklahoma and South Carolina, meanwhile, have wilderness areas, and Florida (which ranks fifth nationwide in percentage of public land) has assembled a massive inventory of public land practically from scratch in the last 50 years. Tellingly, Governor Ron DeSantis, a populist conservative, has worked to dismantle or otherwise shake up voting rights, LGBTQ civil rights, higher education, K–12 education, and public health, he has largely not lifted a finger against Florida's massive inventory of state land or its funding or its rather biocentric wildlife agency. Conversely, some progressive states have fairly lackluster records on public lands whether one considers inventory and acquisition (Illinois and Virginia), the vigor of their energy development (New Mexico and Pennsylvania), or their commitment to heavy logging (Washington and Minnesota). Deep-blue California, meanwhile, has gone further with park privatization than many other more conservative states.

Policy variation, therefore, is perhaps best characterized as being influenced by a host of factors including, but not limited to, ideology and polarization. Aspects of the "state laboratory" model seem to be equally relevant, at least in terms of understanding policy variations as the result of idiosyncratic local histories and geographies, previous policy, and unique political dynamics around particular public land assets. These randomly dispersed "facts on the ground" that develop over the years in particular states go a long way in scrambling ideological patterns. For example, while the Oklahoma of today might never have legislatively established the McCurtain Wilderness, it did do so in 1953, and now it is quite doubtful that anyone would threaten the status of so storied a landscape with such firmly established protection.[4]

Further confounding the role of polarization is the fact that the free market ideas that have gained currency since the Reagan era have, over the last four decades, actually seeped into nearly all states' policymaking, as witnessed by the widespread acceptance of the principle of park revenue generation and self-sufficiency. Another complicating factor that must be considered has been the role of state referenda and other ballot measures to force wildlife protection policies, land acquisition programs, and tax and bond authorizations onto often reluctant and resistant policymakers. Interestingly, these ballot measures tend to be as successful in red states as in blue. This, for example, is how Missouri and Arkansas achieved their very steady dedicated lines of park funding, and it serves as a reminder that despite all the culture war polarization out there, conservation still has a large and broad base of support among ordinary citizens. As a result, the 50 states' policy environments regarding public lands are actually a complex and somewhat heterodox mélange of ideological and economic trends alongside unique local political, geographic, and sociocultural circumstances.

The Transfer of Federal Lands to the States

Almost as soon as the federal government began to retain some of its holdings for conservation purposes around the 1870s, fierce opposition to that prospect sprang up, as did voices calling for the "return" of land to the states that was never legally theirs to begin with. And the lands demanded were, of course, in addition to the tens of millions of acres that actually were granted by the federal government as institutional trust lands (see Chapter 6). Organized movements to formally transfer federal land to the states have periodically risen and have at times come tantalizingly close to realizing their goals, with significant pushes in the late 1920s, the late 1940s, the so-called Sagebrush Rebellion of the 1980s, and, most recently, a spurt of activity between 2015 and 2018.[5] This most recent period saw transfer advocates employing a two-pronged approach of pushing for federal legislation authorizing transfer as well as state legislation demanding it by set dates and relying on dubious legal theories regarding the constitutionality of federal land ownership.[6] While the former efforts were ultimately unsuccessful, Utah and Idaho—in 2012 and 2013 respectively—passed laws demanding the transfer of the federal lands within their borders to the state. Utah also passed legislation outlining how it would manage its new lands and set aside tens of millions of dollars for the legal battle they expected.[7] Arizona also passed similar legislation only to be vetoed by the governor. Montana, Nevada, and Wyoming, meanwhile, all passed laws authorizing further study of transfer options. In all, 10 of the 11 contiguous western states took up transfer legislation. Furthermore, 2 eastern states, Georgia and South Carolina, also passed their own resolutions calling for the transfer of western lands (interestingly, though, not for the transfer of the federal lands in their own states).[8] At perhaps the peak moment, the 2016 Republican National Committee platform statement clearly reflected this concerted push for transfer:

> Congress shall immediately pass universal legislation providing for a timely and orderly mechanism requiring the federal government to convey certain federally controlled public lands to states. We call upon all national and state leaders and representatives to exert their utmost power and influence to urge the transfer of those lands, identified in the review process, to all willing states for the benefit of the states and the nation as a whole. The residents of state and local communities know best how to protect the land where they work and live.[9]

By the next year, however, faced with a powerful and well-orchestrated countermobilization of environmental groups, hunters and anglers, Native American tribes, and the tourist and outdoor industries, this latest transfer movement lost steam legislatively, though it might just have gained new life in the courts. In August 2024, the state of Utah appealed directly to the U.S. Supreme Court to rule on whether the federal government had the authority to hold the 18.5 million acres of federal lands in the state not formally protected as parks or wilderness areas.[10] According to Martin Nie and Patrick Kelly, the transfer movement is morphing into something more stealthy and politically palatable—a movement for direct state management of federal lands rather than actual ownership title. Indeed, Nie and Kelly point to at least six bills introduced in the 115th Congress that would transfer important aspects of federal management to direct state control, including energy leasing, endangered wildlife management, and national monument creation and management.[11] While understanding state land management is important for its own sake, this task becomes even more vital when considering the potential consequences of land transfer were it to occur, especially given how durable the movement has been for over a century. Some scholars are quite bullish on the prospect of states gaining control of the federal estate. Nelson, for example, finds state management more efficient, accountable, and innovative while federal management is bogged down in "acrimony and endless litigation."[12] He concludes,

> As instruments of state governments, state-owned lands have better-defined constituencies and clearer purposes that promote a stronger sense of land management accountability in response to citizens' needs and preferences at the state and local level.[13]

Although she never explicitly calls for transfer of federal lands, Sally Fairfax similarly admires the way state land management, specifically the trust model, operates, and she believes that states "have a great deal to teach us."[14] What she specifically admires about the trust model and believes all public lands management would do well to emulate are its four main principles of 1) clarity, 2) accountability, 3) enforceability, and 4) perpetuity.[15] She finds this model transparent and self-directing without all the conflict, opaqueness, and subjectivity that she and others (like Nelson) find so objectionable with federal management.

Holly Fretwell and Shawn Regan, meanwhile, argue that state land managers are far more efficient than their federal counterparts. They point to data from 2009 to 2013 that compares revenue per dollar spent on operations and find an average on state trust lands of $14.51 versus $0.73 on federal land.[16] Revenues per acre, meanwhile, were $37.16 on state trust land versus $11.79 on federal land. Specifically, for grazing, the gap for revenue per dollar spent was $0.10 for the USFS, $0.14 for the BLM, and $4.84 for the states, while for timber, it was $0.32 for the USFS, $0.38 for the BLM, and $2.51 for the states. Even with recreation, they find states vastly outearning the federal government, with revenue per dollar spent at $0.28 for the USFS and $0.20 for the BLM as compared to $6.31 for Montana and $9.51 for Idaho.[17] It should be noted, however, that in this analysis, Fretwell and Regan are comparing all federal lands, which are managed for a multitude of purposes for the public, against state trust lands, which have a fiduciary duty to raise maximum revenue for beneficiaries at the exclusion (as shown in the last chapter) of all other goals and purposes. It is perhaps for this reason that libertarian analyst Randall O'Toole calls for federal lands to be similarly managed as a fiduciary trust, though with the American people rather than schools or other institutions as the stated beneficiary, an idea broached by Fairfax as well.[18]

The prospect of the transfer of federal land raises questions of *which*, *where*, and *how*. If one looks to the most advanced proposal—Utah's 2012 transfer legislation—it calls for the transfer of all federal land except for national park units,[19] congressionally designated wilderness areas, Defense Department lands, and tribal lands (together, less than 6.2% of Utah's federal land).[20] Less settled is the question of whether congressional transfer legislation would be offered to all relevant states or just the western ones who have agitated for it. Would more politically liberal states like California, Oregon, Washington, and Colorado, for example, have the right to roundly reject the invitation to acquire their abundant federal lands? And what about a particularly eager eastern state—could West Virginia, for example, simply gain title free and clear to the Monongahela National Forest, which was not simply retained like western federal lands but rather painstakingly pieced together from 1915 to 1920 through purchase with money from taxpayers coast to coast? The legal questions this raises are profound and unsettled. The Utah legislation also stipulates that the transferred land could be either retained or sold. It is this latter scenario that has many critics accusing Utah's transfer proposal of being, in reality, nothing more than a stalking horse for the eventual privatization of federal land as the costs of managing 31.2 million acres of arid land become untenable. Without privatization, Robert Keiter and John Ruple find, in their analysis of Utah's proposal, that the state would need to replace $432 million in operational costs, federal payments in lieu of taxes (PILT), and lost federal revenue sharing.[21] They argue that only the most aggressive scenarios of energy production (including full-on mining of coal seams and uranium at Grand Staircase-Escalante) at the highest possible market prices (over which Utah has no control) would allow the state to come close to covering this gap.[22] "Economic imperatives," they claim, "make anything other than a massive increase in development unrealistic."[23] Furthermore, such an approach would fully preclude all other management goals, such as those related to recreation, water quality, wildlife habitat, and biodiversity. "The economic shortfall that would occur under all but the most optimistic of scenarios and its associated imperative to develop public land," they conclude, "should concern everyone who values state fiscal responsibility or our public lands."[24]

In states like Idaho, without the same degree of potential energy resources, the numbers are even harder to square. According to one 2014 analysis, federal transfer might cost Idaho between $60 and $111 million annually; only the highest-end scenario—logging a billion board feet (bbf) of timber annually at consistently high market prices—would realize a $24 million dollar surplus.[25] For context, the total USFS volume of national forest timber sold system-wide from coast to coast in 2021 was 2.8 bbf,[26] so Idaho alone would need to log within its own borders more than a third of the entire national forest harvest to essentially break even. In their analysis of the costs of transfer, Headwaters Economics noted the often-overlooked expense of fire prevention, control, and suppression in increasingly tinder-dry, drought-stressed forests for which the federal government now allots nearly $3 billion a year.[27] Federal PILT expenditures come to another $500 million annually, which states would either need to replace or forego.[28] If it is the latter, small towns with a limited tax base and their economies would disproportionately suffer. With all these subsidized costs (resource management, fire suppression, USFS road maintenance) and revenue-sharing (PILT, shared extraction revenues), the reality is that federal ownership of land offers a pretty fantastic deal for states. When the burden for federal lands is shared nationwide, it comes out to about $4 a year per taxpayer, but if these costs were foisted onto just the taxpayers in a handful of relatively lightly populated states where the vast majority of federal land is, the burden becomes highly concentrated—for example, a Utah taxpayer's share would rise to $54.[29]

Faced with these limitations, then, states would need to earn levels of revenue that are nearly impossible to raise without completely trashing the underlying resource base and forgoing pretty much every other goal of land management besides resource extraction, including recreation, biodiversity, aesthetics, public access, tourism, and, perhaps most importantly, ecosystem service provision. For example, dirtier water from increased logging, mining, fracking, or other short-term revenue-generating activities would lead to either substantial future outlays for water treatment plants or else the incurring of equally substantial health or productivity costs imposed by untreated water pollution. Reflecting on such subtler, long-term factors, Headwaters Economics argues that the multifaceted and substantial economic benefits that issue forth from public lands would both shrink and narrow in a state land transfer scenario.[30]

If this development-oriented style of land management seems reminiscent of how state trust lands are handled, it is because a number of states have explicitly claimed the trust doctrine as their model for the management of the new lands should transfer ever be authorized.[31] If states were instead to manage their newly acquired lands as they do state parks or wildlife management areas or even state forests, they would quickly be crushed under an avalanche of management costs in a budgeting context that does not permit deficit spending, unlike the federal government. In the very likely event that states found themselves unable to fully cover the costs of properly managing their lands, there is no reason to believe that they would not proceed to sell them (at least those with less extractive potential). Even if they fully employed the trust model and aggressively maximized revenue, it is important to remember that land sales are an important and commonly used tool in the trust manager's toolbox, especially when it is determined that if a certain tract was sold and its proceeds reinvested in the trust, it would earn more than resource extraction on that land.

In sum, if large-scale public land transfer were ever to transpire, we could reasonably expect from states the following:

- Much more aggressive resource extraction and revenue generation necessary to cover the substantial costs of inheriting so much additional public land.
- Reduced emphasis on, investment in, and capacity for the work of enhancing biological diversity and resource conservation. Ironically, it is those states like New York, Maryland, Washington, California, Minnesota, and Hawaii with the most interest, expertise, and capacity in conservation and preservation for whom transfer would be either a moot point (New York and Maryland with almost no federal lands) or something they are resolutely against (California and Washington). Instead, states like Wyoming, Arizona, and Idaho, with relatively low institutional conservation capacity (but millions of trust acres), would stand to inherit the federal bounty.
- Reduced public access due to sharply increased fees and/or resource-extraction activities that preclude such access. The trust model relies on leasing arrangements that grant quasi-private property rights with exclusive use and restrictive access.[32]
- Much less environmental impact assessment and procedural safeguards to protect environmental quality, ecosystem services, or biodiversity. Only a handful of states have any kind of equivalent to NEPA that requires careful consideration of environmental impacts. This is the basis of the "efficiency" of the states that transfer advocates like to brag about while, carefully weighing impacts is, in their language, what constitutes an interminable and sclerotic federal bureaucracy.
- Far less public input in decision-making processes and grounds for administrative or legal appeal. Very few state laws require the sort of guaranteed public input and participation that federal environmental laws do. Consequently, there are very few grounds for legal challenge. Ironically, it is the federal process that offers the most decentralized and granular-level input often at the most local level.
- Incredibly constrained budgets. Federal land management budgets, while themselves quite constrained, bring a much greater economy of scale, which can better absorb the costs of environmental protection, allow for investments in the resource base (like stream rehabilitation, forest restoration, and controlled burns), and achieve a more varied and ambitious set of goals, from fire-

fighting to public education to cultural/historical preservation to low-cost recreational access of every kind. Federal budget writers, furthermore, are not constrained by balanced budget requirements, which, at the state level, seem to come at the expense of public lands before practically any other line item.

This comparison is not at all intended to besmirch state land management as a whole. However, when one considers the federal land transfer debate, it quickly becomes apparent that rather than a high-minded discussion of the virtues of federalism or local control, it rather tends to be driven by an ideologically focused and pointedly political movement to dismantle the federal estate. Again, it is important to remember that most transfer proposals involve only a handful of relatively low-population states from among the 50. For most states, this issue does not apply except insofar as their citizens would lose the precious federal public lands that are currently held on their behalf and which they currently have some potential input.

Considering State Lands in Their Own Right

While it is certainly a vital task to adequately analyze the prospect of federal land transfer to the states, this issue is also, in many ways, a huge distraction from fully appreciating the state lands for the important system that they currently are, distinct from and parallel to the federal lands. First of all, land transfer is largely a moot point for most states; in fact, half of all states have 5% or less of their land owned by the federal government.[33] For many eastern states with strong public lands systems, like New York, New Jersey, Maine, Pennsylvania, or Minnesota, public land largely *is* state land. And analyses of how well Utah or Idaho would do in taking control of tens of millions of acres of federal lands within their borders is not particularly relevant in helping us understand these nonwestern states. Transfer politics aside, then, it is perhaps more useful to perceive of state lands on their own terms—as reflections of each states' history, geography, and political culture, which have, in turn, shaped values and priorities regarding conservation, recreation, and economic development. Nevertheless, federal lands will always loom as state lands' big sibling, with roughly parallel structures (i.e., parks, forests, wildlife refuges) managed for some combination of roughly the same goals (preservation, recreation, resource development). So, for these reasons, it might be profitable to compare what each system does particularly well.

What the States Can Learn from the Federal Government

The period from 1960 to 1980 was a transformative era in American environmental law, especially regarding federal land management. The laws passed during this time include the Multiple-Use Sustained-Yield Act, the National Environmental Policy Act, the Endangered Species Act, the National Forest Management Act, the Federal Land Policy and Management Act, and then, several decades later, the National Wildlife Refuge Improvement Act of 1997. They were hardly perfect, but they all in their own way helped steer federal land management toward a much more authentic and nuanced balance regarding the handling of resource conflicts. Some of this was through direct guidance and mandate, but much was indirect through avenues of widened participation and legal access that enabled citizens and interest groups to hold managers to account. To free market ideologues and extraction industries used to unfettered access, this has been nothing less than an unmitigated disaster of legal acrimony, bureaucratic red tape, and paralysis. To supporters of these laws, however, they are more like speed bumps or railroad crossing gates, forcing policymakers to fully consider environmental consequences and all aspects of diverse management directives. To that end, some specific areas in which state land managers might do well to emulate their federal counterparts include the following:

- Integrated ecosystem-based management. When making complex decisions, federal managers are encouraged and, in many cases, directed to embed consideration of things like water quality, soil health, climate change, and biodiversity more holistically into their calculations. This tends to increase the chances that environmental concerns get serious consideration when planning timber sales or energy leases or selling grazing allotments or settling conflicts over recreational usage. Outka further argues that federal land management statutes give policymakers far more discretion in responding to previously unforeseen needs like climate adaptation.[34] State legal frameworks, on the other hand, are often far too underdeveloped to be useful—or, if related to trust lands, far too rigid and static. Regarding the transition to a low-carbon future, she claims that "changing course on dated approaches to land management may be easier for federal lands than for state trust land."[35]

- Openness to the ecosystem services framework. Federal land managers have made great strides in the last few decades in using the ecosystem services framework as both a specific micro-level tool for the sorts of valuations necessary for decision-making and also as a broader paradigm-shifting macro-level tool for reshaping how to talk about their parks and justify budgets and programs to legislators and the public. It is important to note, however, that the federal government's widespread adoption of this valuation tool has not, for the most part, led to a subsequent development of actual ecosystem services markets for the many valuable services that federal lands supply.

- Greater openness to all stakeholders. Because of its underlying mandates, federal land management tends to offer a much broader, more varied, and more significant opportunity for various stakeholders (recreationists, resource users, preservationists) to have input. While this certainly can be seen to introduce a certain amount of inefficiency to the decision-making process, federal land management decisions are almost always much more thoroughly vetted by a broader range of the public than state decisions and this, in turn, makes such a process more authentically democratic.

- Greater commitment to the notion of parks as public goods requiring investment. Federal managers seem to have a greater comfort level with the notion of parks not having to "pay for themselves" except by serving the public and providing ecosystem services. As shown earlier in this chapter, the federal government earns less in revenue on most of its acreage than what is spent on operations, and this is always framed by critics as "losing" money. But this can also be seen as simply an investment in much in-demand public goods and environmental services. Does the Pentagon "lose" money when it buys an F-35? Do local governments "lose" money when they repair the roof of the fire station, pay teachers, or buy library books? State land managers, under the intense pressures and constraints that their austere budgeting environments impose, have perhaps more readily internalized this notion of state lands as some sort of extraneous luxury needing to pay for themselves as much possible, a notion that denies their public goods functions. And for state trust lands, of course, this notion of paying for yourself (and then some) is legally mandated. It should be remembered that from the earliest days of the state parks movement, the notion of parks as collectively provisioned public goods was the norm and the default. It was not until the

1980s that libertarian notions of "self-sufficiency" led to the widespread advent of user fees and other revenue-generation schemes.

What the Federal Government Can Learn from the States

- Accessibility matters. Perhaps the very best thing about state lands is their greater physical accessibility to those who live and work nearby. Indeed, a "state park every 100 miles" was one of the foundational notions of the state parks movement. Mather knew that the national parks could never be all things to all people. By virtue of this dispersal across all states, and generally all parts of those states, this country has been bestowed with a public land system that is widely accessible (at least geographically) to a much broader spectrum of Americans than the federal lands. Especially because federal lands are so densely concentrated in one region and often in more remote and inaccessible areas, this poses a greater barrier to the three-quarters of the population that does not live in the West. Simply put, state public lands are much more within reach of ordinary people in their everyday lives, and the proof of this is the vastly higher visitation per acre on state parks versus federal ones.

- State natural areas programs. Although identifying, inventorying, and preserving biodiversity tends not to be the top priority for many states, where this task does get done at the state level is though SNA programs. Despite their chronic underfunding, understaffing, and low visibility, these programs have doggedly carried the flag for fragile places with outstanding biological, geological, and botanical qualities with great care and knowledge and affection. Despite all the ways that SNAs are hamstrung by resource constraints and/or hostility from external policymakers, these programs bring tremendous focus and expertise onto relatively small areas, which makes transformative ecological restoration a rather viable goal. Surprisingly, this framework is truly unique to state lands. While federal managers certainly act to preserve and restore rare ecological assets (maybe even to a greater extent), this particular type of designation and the attention, care, and restoration that often accompany it do not have a direct federal analog.[36] In fact, in states with highly developed SNA programs, like Illinois, Wisconsin, and Minnesota, the ecologically special places within the national forests in those states are generally protected by overlapping state natural area status rather than any sort of internal USFS status (though this is certainly done with the USFS's cooperation).

- Innovation and partnership. Perhaps because of the pressures of chronic deprivation, state managers have had to become quite adept at seeking innovative solutions to keep their parks running and their biodiversity protected. Nowhere has this been more apparent than in the ways that complex, flexible, and mutually beneficial partnerships have often been forged with nonprofit conservation organizations. While this is often a sign of advanced neglect in a park system, it is also a last-ditch defense mechanism that has served to protect the most important aspects of wild and fragile places. The mutual trust and coordination present in these relationships extend to everything from parks operation to science and restoration to land acquisition. There is not an aspect of managing state land that has not been helped along by legions of volunteers, citizen-scientists, and experts from nonprofits. In an era of budget austerity and even defunding, this is often the only alternative to that very different other sort of "partnership"—with for-profit recreation corporations, concessionaires, resort developers, and other sorts of financially motivated "service providers." State managers, at least in places with strong volunteer and private conservation networks, can teach all managers quite a bit about extending one's terribly circumscribed reach by partnering with true friends.

- The transparency and clarity of the trust model. Although this volume argues that the trust model falls quite short when it comes to incorporating important ecological considerations into land management, there is no denying the appeal, as Fairfax describes it, of the trust model's transparency and clarity. At its best, it is a seemingly incorruptible framework for allocation decisions without subterfuge or drama or conflict. The problem, of course, is that its revenue maximization logic contains the seeds of its own destruction—that is, the short-term industrialized development it pushes toward hastens the future collapse of the land's long-term productivity and ecological service provision. Because of the anachronisms and narrowness found in its framework, it is blind to all sorts of real value. While California, Colorado, and Washington have made some great strides in opening up the trust concept enough to incorporate broader notions of value on longer time horizons, they are the exception and not the rule. Nevertheless, it might help to ask if land managers and policymakers have the necessary imagination, as Fairfax hopes, to redeploy and repurpose this idea to new applications. Can we reconceive who a beneficiary is and the trust manager's obligation to them? Can we redefine how we measure the direct, tangible values that come from proper-functioning ecological systems and how these accrue to the identified beneficiaries?

Conclusion: Realizing the Potential of State Lands

State public lands account for hundreds of millions of acres of natural resource lands spanning practically every geographic corner and ecological niche on this vast continent. There is hardly a soul living in the U.S. who is not within an easy drive of at least some unit of state public land. For this reason alone, they provide the bulk of basic access in this country to wildland and natural landscapes. A glimpse of the potential of state public lands can be provided, ironically, by looking *backward*—more than a century back to the time when Progressive Era reformers and conservationists came together to articulate a *state park idea* that rooted itself in notions of access, democracy, natural integrity, and an intergenerational public interest. While it originally concerned state parks, this stance is actually applicable to all state public lands—specifically, how to find a balance between responsiveness and accessibility on one hand and the wise stewardship and restraint necessary to protect a natural system's integrity on the other. If there is a single theme running through the history of state public lands since that first state parks conference in 1921, it is how far state public land systems have strayed from those founding principles.

Parks historian Ney Landrum, bemoaning all the present-day touristic development and financial challenges besetting state parks, argued, in the concluding chapter of his great history of the state parks movement, for "getting back to basics," by which he meant ready and affordable access to beautiful, inspiring, and minimally altered wild landscapes close to home:

> State parks . . . were never intended to be adaptable to the whims of ephemeral or constantly changing recreational interests. They have their own special legacy and their own distinct purpose. They are founded on the essential principle of resource preservation and management to support certain forms of compatible outdoor recreation.

As priceless specimens of an ever-diminishing resource base, they must not be appropriated and manipulated for the exclusive use of the people of today or of any particular time; they must instead be kept aesthetically and functionally intact for equivalent use and enjoyment by all generations yet to come. It is in this context that the state parks of every state should be expected to acknowledge and adhere to certain absolute and inviolable principles common to them all.[37]

Because of their geographic dispersal and their relative proximity to large urban centers, state public lands play an outsized role in providing recreational access to wild nature to a diverse array of ordinary people and especially those who lack the wherewithal to travel across the continent to distant national parks because of all kinds of financial, geographic, or cultural barriers. Furthermore, the experience of the COVID pandemic made abundantly clear how essential to basic physical and mental health that meaningful interaction with nature is. Access to state public lands (i.e., the closest wildlands to most people) is nothing less, therefore, than a basic issue of social justice. And yet, if one superimposes onto this fact the disinvestment, neglect, and steep user fees that increasingly mark the state public land experience, it becomes quite clear that access to these basic and essential public goods is now directly threatened by state governments that increasingly seem unmoved by the issue.

As discussed previously, the free market ideas of "self-sufficiency" and internal revenue generation have become so ingrained and widely accepted across the ideological spectrum that the previously common notion of paying for conservation land from general funds, as governments would pay for any other public good like bridges, fire protection, or education, is now seen as an outlandish prospect. This guarantees the physical deterioration of public land infrastructure, harms active conservation measures, and limits access, and changing it will require nothing less than a wholesale paradigm shift on the part of state policymakers. States currently spend 0.16% of their budgets on their state park systems, which is a ludicrously minimal outlay if one compares that to the outsized benefits that emanate from the parks (see Chapter 2).

Perhaps the best way to shine a spotlight on this value is to consistently adopt the ecosystem services framework in all places, at all times, as that might be the only thing that can even begin to speak to the enormity of value protected by and streaming from our public lands. State land advocates are slowly beginning to realize this. For example, in Michigan in May

2020, when two dams near Midland failed, the flooding along the Titta-bawassee River was not nearly as bad as feared, mostly because of the extensive state wetlands and forests along the river that soaked up and held tremendous amounts of water.[38] Normally, the counterfactual of avoided disaster and saved clean-up costs would simply go unnoticed and unremarked on—part of the "free goods" that free marketers love to assume that nature infinitely provides. This time, however, in the context of increased hostility toward public land in the then GOP-dominated state legislature, the Michigan League of Conservation Voters made sure that these services and measurable value would no longer go unaccounted for:

> We're going to pay particular attention to bringing the lens of natural capital on the state of Michigan and say what ecosystem services our public lands [are] delivering Michiganders right now that need to be recognized, monetized and elevated in the strategy.[39]

States sit on a treasure trove of value on their public land systems in terms of natural resources, recreation, physical and mental well-being, biodiversity, geology, history, scenic beauty, economic spin-off (from tourism and recreation), and every other aspect of ecosystem service. Some of these things have developed markets and some do not, but all are real and measurable. In an era when states give away tens or even hundreds of millions of dollars for luring corporate relocations, inking sports stadium deals, and lavishing tax incentives on key constituencies, the idea that taxpayer money might be invested in things that are claimed to "pay off" should not be a foreign concept to state legislatures or governor's offices. For example, in 2023, the Wisconsin legislature authorized spending $500 million in public money to renovate and upgrade the Milwaukee Brewers stadium.[40] The breathless press releases cited a 2005 study showing the team generated 4,683 jobs and $327.3 million in annual economic impact (or $526.5 million in 2024 dollars).[41] Meanwhile, in 2013, Prey, Marcouiller, and Kim released their study of the Wisconsin State Park System's economic value (see Table 2.3) and found total economic impact of $626.9 million ($845.5 million in 2024 dollars) and 8,251 jobs created.[42] That is nearly double the jobs and 160% more economic impact for something that the state has decided to spend zero dollars on, having stripped all operating funds for state parks out of the general budget in 2015.

Perhaps even more egregious was the fact that just two years later, in 2017, the same GOP-controlled legislature authorized $3 billion in tax incentives and infrastructure spending to entice the Taiwanese electronics giant Foxconn to build a plant near Racine.[43] Even if the promised jobs were to materialize (which they did not), this would have come to about $231,000 in subsidies per job created. By this job-investment ratio, the state park budget ought to be set at $1.9 billion! Instead, that same year, the state park's overall and entirely self-generated budget shrank to a paltry $19.6 million, proportionally the lowest in the country,[44] while overall conservation budgets in the state have declined 41% since 1995 (60% adjusted for inflation).[45] In 2021, the operating budget for the entire Wisconsin DNR overseeing 1.5 million acres with untold billions of dollars of ecological service value was $197.5 million, or 15 times less than the proposed Foxconn "investment."[46] Only the most perverse and blinding ideological hostility could explain the illogic that ignores such obvious economic, environmental, and social value.

As discouraging as that "tale of two budget lines" is, there is certainly hope that states are slowly beginning to realize how valuable and well loved their public land assets are. With dogged advocacy and a laser-beam focus on their measurable values, the state bias against sufficiently investing in public lands can perhaps slowly be turned around; indeed, the pandemic has started just such a reappraisal in some places. If fully and properly measured, the myriad benefits to the public interest all but guarantee a robust return on investment for each tax dollar spent on state public lands operations or acquisition. With that, the very idea of state public land can reach its fullest potential.

Appendix

Data Sources for State Lands Tables

Alabama: Alabama Department of Conservation and Natural Resources, *State Lands Division* (Webpage, 2022), available at: https://www.outdooralabama .com/about-us/state-lands-division; Alabama State Parks, *Fact Sheet* (Fact Sheet, 2022), available at: https://www.alapark.com/2021-fact-sheet; Alabama Department of Conservation and Natural Resources, *Wildlife Management Areas* (Webpage, 2022), available at: https://www.outdooralabama.com/hunting/wild life-management-areas; Jo Lewis, Natural Heritage Section Chief, State Lands Division, Alabama Department of Conservation and Natural Resources, email correspondence (April 20, 2022); Mary Yahn, "State Forests of Alabama" in *Encyclopedia of Alabama* (Auburn University, 2022), available at: http://encyclo pediaofalabama.org/article/h-4094.

Alaska: Alaska Department of Natural Resources, *Alaska's State Forests* (Webpage, undated), available at: http://forestry.alaska.gov/stateforests.htm; Alaska Department of Fish and Game, *Conservation Areas* (Webpage, undated), available at: http://www.adfg.alaska.gov/index.cfm?adfg=conservationareas.main; Alaska Department of Natural Resources, Division of Parks and Outdoor Recreation, *Ten-Year Strategic Plan 2007–2017* (Report, November 30, 2006), p. 2, available at: http://dnr.alaska.gov/parks/plans/strategicplan/compltplan.pdf; Alaska Mental Health Trust Authority (Homepage, 2022), available at: https://alaskamental healthtrust.org/; Alaska Department of Natural Resources, Division of Mining, Land, and Water, *Fact Sheet: Land Ownership in Alaska* (Fact Sheet, July 2021), available at: https://dnr.alaska.gov/mlw/cdn/pdf/factsheets/land-owner ship-in-alaska.pdf; Alaska Department of Natural Resources, Division of Forestry, *Who Owns/Manages Alaska* (Webpage Map, 2007), available at: http://for

estry.alaska.gov/Assets/pdfs/posters/07who_owns_alaska_poster.pdf; Lacy Hamner, Statehood Entitlement Manager, Alaska Department of Natural Resources, Division of Mining, Land, and Water, email correspondence (June 8, 2022).

Arizona: Arizona State Land Department, *Our Agency and Mission* (Webpage, undated), available at: https://land.az.gov/our-agency-mission; Jordan Smith, Anna Miller, and Yu-Fai Leung, *2019 Outlook and Analysis Letter* (National Association of State Park Directors Report, February 2020), p. 12; Jorge Canaca, Land Resources Program Manager, Arizona Game and Fish Department, email correspondence (April 17, 2007); Arizona State Parks, *Natural Areas Program Advisory Committee* (Webpage, 2022), available at: https://azstateparks.com/nat ural-areas-program-advisory-committee-napac; Headwaters Economics, *Public Land Ownership in the United States: Land Ownership by State* (Interactive Webpage Data for Arizona, June 2019), available at: https://headwaterseconomics.org /public-lands/protected-lands/public-land-ownership-in-the-us/.

Arkansas: Arkansas State Parks, *About Arkansas State Parks* (Webpage, 2022), available at: https://www.arkansasstateparks.com/about; Arkansas Department of Agriculture, Forestry Division, *Poison Springs State Forest* (Webpage, 2022), available at: https://www.agriculture.arkansas.gov/forestry/poison-springs-state-for est/; Randall Puckett, GIS Analyst, Arkansas Game and Fish Commission, email correspondence (April 12, 2022); Thomas Saccente, "Arkansas Natural Heritage Buys Nearly 1,200 Acres for River Valley Natural Area" in *Arkansas Democrat Gazette* (July 17, 2022), available at: https://www.arkansasonline.com/news/2022 /jul/17/arkansas-natural-heritage-buys-nearly-1200-acres/; Headwaters Economics, *Public Land Ownership in the United States: Land Ownership by State* (Interactive Webpage Data for Arkansas, June 2019), available at: https://headwaters economics.org/public-lands/protected-lands/public-land-ownership-in-the-us/.

California: California Department of Parks and Recreation, *Meeting the Park Needs of All Californians: 2015 Statewide Comprehensive Outdoor Recreation Plan* (Report, 2015), p. 6, available at: https://www.recpro.org/assets/Library/SCORPs /ca_scorp_2015.pdf; California Department of Fish and Wildlife, *Lands Inventory Fact Sheet* (Fact Sheet, May 2, 2023), available at: https://nrm.dfg.ca.gov/File Handler.ashx?DocumentID=160405&inline; California Department of Forestry and Fire Protection, *Demonstration State Forests* (Webpage, 2022), available at: https://www.fire.ca.gov/programs/resource-management/resource-protection -improvement/demonstration-state-forests/; Miranda Holeton and David Takacs, "U.S. State-Based Wilderness Law: An Evaluation" in *Hastings Environmental Law Journal* (Vol. 28, No. 1, Winter 2022), p. 34; California State Lands Commission, *Annual Staff Report on the Management of State School Lands* (Report, 2021), p. i, available at: https://slcprdwordpressstorage.blob.core.windows.net/wordpressdata /2021/12/SL_2020-2021.pdf; University of California, Natural Reserves System,

Growth (Webpage, 2022), available at: https://ucnrs.org/find-a-reserve/growth/; Headwaters Economics, *Public Land Ownership in the United States: Land Ownership by State* (Interactive Webpage Data for California, 2019), available at: https:// headwaterseconomics.org/public-lands/protected-lands/public-land-ownership -in-the-us/.

Colorado: Colorado State Land Board, *Stewarding Colorado's Trust Lands for Generations* (Report, Spring 2020), p.1, available at: https://slb.colorado.gov/steward ship-report; Colorado Parks and Wildlife, *State Trust Lands: About the State Trust Land Public Access Program* (Webpage, undated), available at: https://cpw.state.co .us/placestogo/Pages/StateTrustLands.aspx; Colorado Parks and Wildlife, *Natural Areas Information* (Webpage, undated), available at: https://cpw.state.co.us/about us/Pages/CNAP-Info.aspx; Colorado Parks and Wildlife, *Strategic Plan* (Report, November 2015), p. 5, available at: https://cpw.state.co.us/Documents/About /StrategicPlan/CPWStrategicPlan.pdf; Rebecca Ferrell, Branding and Communications Section Manager, Colorado Parks and Wildlife, email correspondence (July 5, 2022); Colorado State Forest Service, *Colorado State Forest* (Webpage, 2022), available at: https://csfs.colostate.edu/colorado-state-forest/.

Connecticut: Paul Aresta, Executive Director, Connecticut Council on Environmental Quality, email correspondence (May 10, 2022); Connecticut Department of Environmental Protection, *Statewide Comprehensive Outdoor Recreation Plan 2005–2010* (Report, September 2005), p. 16, available at: https://portal.ct.gov /-/media/DEEP/outdoor_recreation/scorp/SCORP2005WebVersionpdf.pdf; Dawn McKay, Environmental Analyst, Natural Diversity Data Base Program, Wildlife Division, Bureau of Natural Resources, Connecticut Department of Energy and Environmental Protection, email correspondence (May 9, 2022); Karen Zyko, Database Manager, Wildlife Division, Bureau of Natural Resources, Connecticut Department of Energy and Environmental Protection, email correspondence (May 18, 2022).

Delaware: Delaware Department of Natural Resources and Environmental Control, Division of Parks and Recreation, *Delaware State Parks 2019 Annual Report* (2020), p. 6, available at: https://destateparks.com/wwwroot/downloads /publications/2019AnnualReport-DEStateParks.pdf; Delaware Department of Agriculture, *Delaware State Forests* (Webpage, undated), available at: https://ag riculture.delaware.gov/forest-service/state-forests/; Delaware Department of Natural Resources and Environmental Control, Division of Fish and Wildlife, *Wildlife Area Maps and Regulations* (Webpage, undated), available at: https://dnrec .alpha.delaware.gov/fish-wildlife/wildlife-areas; Delaware Department of Natural Resources and Environmental Control, Division of Parks and Recreation, *Visiting Nature Preserves* (Webpage, undated), available at: https://dnrec.alpha .delaware.gov/parks/natural-areas/nature-preserves/; Delaware Department of Natural Resources and Environmental Control, Division of Parks and Recreation, *Building an Outdoor Legacy in Delaware* (Report, 2018), p. 37, available at: https://destateparks.com/wwwroot/downloads/SCORP/SCORP%202018.pdf.

Florida: Florida Department of Environmental Protection, *State of Florida Lands and Facilities Inventory Search* (Interactive Webpage, December 3, 2022), available at: https://prodenv.dep.state.fl.us/DslPi/stateLandDashboard.action; Florida Natural Areas Inventory, *Summary of Florida Conservation Lands* (Fact Sheet, January 2022), available at: https://www.fnai.org/PDFs/Maacres_202201_FCL_plus _LTF_final.pdf; email correspondence (June 22, 2022); Florida Department of Environmental Protection, *Outdoor Recreation in Florida 2019* (Report, 2019), p. 46, available at: https://floridadep.gov/sites/default/files/1SCORP%20Chapters.pdf.

Georgia: Elizabete Vasconcelos, "Georgia State Parks" in *New Georgia Encyclopedia* (Georgia Humanities, University of Georgia Press, April 9, 2021), available at: https://www.georgiaencyclopedia.org/articles/geography-environment/georgia -state-parks/; Georgia Forestry Commission, *Large Tracts of Land Are Maintained and Preserved by the State* (Webpage, undated), available at: https://gatrees.org /forest-management-conservation/state-managed-forests/; John W. Bowers, Special Projects Manager, Wildlife Resources Division, Georgia Department of Natural Resources, email correspondence (April 22, 2022); Savannah Archaeological Alliance, *Georgia Heritage Preserve-Designated Properties* (Document, March 31, 2020), available at: https://savarchaeoalliance.files.wordpress.com/2020/06/ga-heritage preserves-and-senate-districts.pdf.

Hawaii: Hawaii Department of Land and Natural Resources, Division of State Parks, *Welcome to Hawaii State Parks* (Webpage, 2022), available at: https://dlnr .hawaii.gov/dsp/; Hawaii Department of Land and Natural Resources, Division of Forestry and Wildlife, *Forest Reserves* (Webpage, 2022), available at: https:// dlnr.hawaii.gov/forestry/frs/reserves/; Hawaii Department of Land and Natural Resources, Division of Forestry and Wildlife, *Natural Areas Reserve System* (Webpage, 2022), available at: https://dlnr.hawaii.gov/ecosystems/nars/; Department of Hawaiian Home Lands, *About the Department of Hawaiian Home Lands* (Webpage, 2022), available at: https://dhhl.hawaii.gov/dhhl/; Blake Propst and Chad Dawson, "State-Designated Wilderness in the United States: A National Review" in *International Journal of Wilderness* (Vol. 14, No. 1, April 2008), p. 24; Hawaii Department of Business, Economic Development, and Tourism, *The State of Hawaii Data Book 2018* (Report, 2018), table 7.43, available at: https://files.ha waii.gov/dbedt/economic/databook/2018-individual/07/074318.pdf; Hawaii Department of Land and Natural Resources, *Hawaii Statewide Comprehensive Outdoor Recreation Plan 2015 Update* (Report, May 2015), p.15, available at: https:// www.recpro.org/assets/Library/SCORPs/hi_scorp_2015.pdf.

Idaho: Idaho Department of Parks and Recreation, *2018–2022 Idaho Statewide Comprehensive Outdoor Recreation Plan* (Report, 2018), pp. 10–11, available at:

https://parksandrecreation.idaho.gov/wp-content/uploads/scorp/Idaho-State wide-Comprehensive-Outdoor-Recreation-Plan-2018-1.pdf; Idaho Fish and Game Commission, *Director's Annual Report to the Commission FY2019* (Report, January 2020), p. 16, available at: https://idfg.idaho.gov/sites/default/files/direc tors-report-commission-2019.pdf; Idaho Fish and Game Commission, *Idaho's Wildlife Management Areas* (Webpage, undated), available at: https://idfg.idaho .gov/wma; Jordan Smith, Anna Miller, and Yu-Fai Leung, *2019 Outlook and Analysis Letter* (National Association of State Park Directors Report, February 2020), p. 21.

Illinois: Illinois Department of Natural Resources, *FY20 Land and Water Report* (Report, 2020), p. 1, available at: https://www2.illinois.gov/dnr/publications /documents/00000912.pdf; Friends of Illinois Nature Preserves, *Our History* (Webpage, 2022), available at: https://friendsofillinoisnaturepreserves.org/about -us/our-history/.

Indiana: Jill Flachskam, State Land Office Director and Division of Forestry GIS Coordinator, Indiana Department of Natural Resources, email correspon- dence (May 9, 2022); Natural Areas Association, *State Natural Areas Program Roundtable: State Reports* (Indiana State Natural Areas Video Report, November 17, 2021), available at: https://www.naturalareas.org/2021_state_natural_areas _progr.php.

Iowa: Iowa Department of Natural Resources, *Iowa Department of Natural Re- sources Land Inventory* (Interactive Webpage, January 28, 2022), available at: https://storymaps.arcgis.com/stories/d64a8c9f561f4a868407a59ae7eab553; Iowa Department of Natural Resources, *Iowa's State Forests* (Webpage, undated), avail- able at: https://www.iowadnr.gov/Places-to-Go/State-Forests; Iowa Depart- ment of Natural Resources, *Iowa State Preserves* (Webpage, undated), available at: https://www.iowadnr.gov/Places-to-Go/State-Preserves; Iowa Department of Natural Resources, *Wildlife Management Areas* (Webpage, undated), available at: https://www.iowadnr.gov/Hunting/Places-to-Hunt-Shoot/Wildlife-Manage ment-Areas; Michelle Wilson, REAP Coordinator, Conservation and Recre- ation Division, Iowa Department of Natural Resources, email correspondence (June 21, 2022).

Kansas: Stuart J. Schrag, Public Lands Division Director, Kansas Department of Wildlife and Parks, email correspondence (May 19, 2022); Kansas State Uni- versity, Horticulture and Natural Resources Department, *Enhancing Kansas' Out- door Parks Recreation Heritage 2021–2025* (Report, 2020), p. 7, available at: https:// ksoutdoors.com/State-Parks/S.C.O.R.P; Kansas Department of Agriculture, *Public Lands in Kansas* (PowerPoint Document, 2018), available at: https://agri culture.ks.gov/docs/default-source/pp-noxious-weed-control/schrag-nox ious-weeds-powerpoint.pdf?sfvrsn=4.

Kentucky: Debra Gibson Isaacs, "Modernizing Kentucky's State Parks" in *Lane Report* (October 12, 2017), available at: https://www.lanereport.com/82358 /2017/10/modernizing-kentuckys-state-parks/; Office of Kentucky Nature Preserves, *Kentucky Heritage Land Conservation Fund 2021 Annual Report* (Report, 2021), pp. 9–11, available at: https://eec.ky.gov/Nature-Preserves/About_Us /news/Reports/KHLCF%20OKNP%202021%20Annual%20Report.pdf; Kentucky Energy and Environment Cabinet, Forestry Division, *Kentucky's State Forests* (Webpage, 2022), available at: https://eec.ky.gov/Natural-Resources/Forest ry/ky-state-forests/Pages/default.aspx; Lee McLellan, "Kentucky Afield Outdoors: Explore Wildlife Management Areas over the Holidays" in *Northern Kentucky Tribune* (December 24, 2019), available at: https://www.nkytribune.com /2019/12/kentucky-afield-outdoors-explore-wildlife-management-areas-over -the-holidays/; Kentucky Department of Fish and Wildlife Resources, *Wildlife Action Plan* (Report, 2013), appendix 1.4, available at: https://fw.ky.gov/WAP /documents/1.4%20public%20land%20ownership.pdf.

Louisiana: Tripp Fairly, Historical Records Manager, Louisiana State Land Office, email correspondence (May 18, 2022); Louisiana Department of Wildlife and Fisheries, *Master Plan for Wildlife Management Areas and Refuges* (Report, 2014), p. 2, available at: https://www.wlf.louisiana.gov/assets/Resources/Pub lications/Wildlife_Management_Areas_and_Refuges/LDWF_Master_Plan _for_Wildlife_Areas_and_Refuges_2014.pdf; Louisiana Department of Wildlife and Fisheries, *Louisiana's Natural Areas Registry–2022* (Document, 2022), available at: https://www.wlf.louisiana.gov/assets/Conservation/Protecting_ Wildlife_Diversity/Files/natural_areas_registry_2022.pdf.

Maine: Maine Department of Agriculture, Conservation, and Forestry, Bureau of Parks and Lands, *2020–2024 Maine State Comprehensive Outdoor Recreation Plan* (Report, 2019), p. 36, available at: https://www.maine.gov/dacf/parks/publica tions_maps/docs/2020_ME_SCORP_final_1_2_2020.pdf; Natural Resources Council of Maine, *Maine's Public Lands and Ecological Reserves* (Webpage, 2022), available at: https://www.nrcm.org/programs/forests-wildlife/maines-pub lic-lands-ecological-reserves/; Maine Department of Agriculture, Conservation, and Forestry, Bureau of Parks and Lands, *Fiscal Year 2021 Annual Report* (Report, 2021), p. 4, available at: https://www.maine.gov/dacf/parks/publications_maps /docs/2021BPL-AnnualReport.pdf; Miranda Holeton and David Takacs, "U.S. State-Based Wilderness Law: An Evaluation" in *Hastings Environmental Law Journal* (Vol. 28, No. 1, Winter 2022), p. 42.

Maryland: Maryland Department of Natural Resources, *Fiscal Year 2021 DNR Lands Acreage Report* (Report, 2021), pp. 3, 7, 22–25, available at: https://dnr .maryland.gov/land/Documents/Stewardship/CurrentAcreageReport.pdf.

Massachusetts: Brian Hawthorne, Habitat Program Manager, Massachusetts Division of Fisheries and Wildlife, email correspondence (June 2, 2022); Massachusetts Department of Conservation and Recreation, Division of Water Supply Protection, *DCR Watershed Natural Resources Program* (Webpage, 2022), available at: https://www.mass.gov/orgs/dcr-watershed-natural-resources-program; Massachusetts Department of Conservation and Recreation, *A Summary: Landscape Designations for DCR State and Urban Properties* (Fact Sheet, undated), available at: https://www.mass.gov/doc/landscape-designations-fact-sheet/download.

Michigan: Michigan Department of Natural Resources, *Your Public Lands* (Webpage, 2022), available at: https://www.michigan.gov/dnr/managing-resources /public-land; Michigan Department of Natural Resources, *Natural Resources at a Glance* (Webpage, 2022), available at: https://www.michigan.gov/dnr/about /natural-resources-at-a-glance; Miranda Holeton and David Takacs, "U.S. State-Based Wilderness Law: An Evaluation" in *Hastings Environmental Law Journal* (Vol. 28, No. 1, Winter 2022), pp. 36–37; Amy Clark Eagle and Kim Herman, *Natural Areas Program Strategic Plan* (Michigan DNR Report, March 29, 2000), p. 3, available at: https://www.csu.edu/cerc/researchreports/documents/Michigan Natural AreasProgramStrategicPlan2000_000.pdf.

Minnesota: Minnesota Department of Natural Resources, *Public Lands In-Depth* (Report, version 1.4, June 27, 2019), available at: https://files.dnr.state .mn.us/aboutdnr/public_lands/public-lands-in-depth.pdf; Minnesota House of Representatives, House Research Department, *State-Owned Land in Minnesota* (Short Subjects Report, October 2002), available at: https://www.house.leg .state.mn.us/hrd/pubs/ss/sssoland.pdf; Blane Klemek, Northwest Region Wildlife Manager, Minnesota Department of Natural Resources, email correspondence (May 19, 2022); Rick Walsh, Land Acquisition Consultant, Minnesota Department of Natural Resources, Division of Fish and Wildlife, email correspondence (June 3, 2022); Miranda Holeton and David Takacs, "U.S. State-Based Wilderness Law: An Evaluation" in *Hastings Environmental Law Journal* (Vol. 28, No. 1, Winter 2022), p. 43.

Mississippi: Mississippi Secretary of State Office, *Public Lands by Agency* (Document, July 29, 2020), available at: https://www.sos.ms.gov/content/docu ments/lands/SummaryPublicLandsAgency.pdf; Jordan Smith, Anna Miller, and Yu-Fai Leung, *2019 Outlook and Analysis Letter* (National Association of State Park Directors Report, February 2020), p. 33; Russ Walsh, Wildlife Chief of Staff, Mississippi Department of Wildlife, Fisheries, and Parks, telephone interview (June 30, 2022); Mississippi Secretary of State Office, *16th Section Lands* (Webpage, 2022), available at: https://www.sos.ms.gov/public-lands/16th-sec tion-lands.

Missouri: Department of Natural Resources, Division of State Parks, *Parks, Historic Site Offices and Other Designations and Acreage Report* (Document, January 24, 2022), available at: https://mostateparks.com/sites/mostateparks/files/Mis souriStatePark_Designation_Acreages.pdf; Chris Scheppers, Equipment and

Purchasing Manager, Missouri Department of Conservation, email correspondence (June 3, 2022); Miranda Holeton and David Takacs, "U.S. State-Based Wilderness Law: An Evaluation" in *Hastings Environmental Law Journal* (Vol. 28, No. 1, Winter 2022), p. 37; Natural Areas Association, *State Natural Areas Program Roundtable: State Reports* (Missouri State Natural Areas Video Report, November 17, 2021), available at: https://www.naturalareas.org/2021_state_natural_areas_progr.php.

Montana: Lisa Bickell, *Interpretive Media and Exhibits at Montana State Parks Review and Priority Recommendations* (Montana State Parks Report, October 2020), p. 6, available at: https://fwp.mt.gov/binaries/content/assets/fwp/stateparks/documents/visitor-center-evaluation-report-2020.pdf; Montana Code Annotated, 77-5-102, *Designation of State Forests* (2021); Montana Department of Natural Resources and Conservation, Trust Lands Management Division, *Annual Report Fiscal Year 2021* (Report, 2021), p. 26, available at: http://dnrc.mt.gov/divisions/trust/docs/annual-report/fy-2021-trust-lands-annual-report.pdf; Yellowstone Public Radio, *Montana Land Board to Vote on Addition of Wildlife Management Area* (Transcript, July 17, 2020), available at: https://www.ypradio.org/environment-science/2020-07-17/montana-land-board-to-vote-on-addition-of-wildlife-management-area.

Nebraska: Board of Educational Lands and Funds, *72nd Biennial Report* (Report, 2020), p. 4, available at: https://belf.nebraska.gov/pdf/reports/belf2018-20.pdf, Charla Rasmussen, Realty Coordinator, Nebraska Game and Parks, email correspondence (January 6, 2023).

Nevada: Mike Zahradka, Wildlife Staff Specialist, Nevada Department of Wildlife, email correspondence (May 23, 2022); Department of Administration State Public Works Division, *Real Property Inventory List: State Lands Inventory* (Data Spreadsheets, 2021), available at: https://publicworks.nv.gov/Services/Leasing_Services/Real_Property_Inventory_List/; Amelia Pak-Harvey, "Opportunity Lost: Nevada Began with Millions of Acres of School Trust Land to Help Pay for Public Education. What Happened to Them?" in *Las Vegas Review-Journal* (December 21, 2019), available at: https://www.reviewjournal.com/local/education/opportunity-lost-nevadas-school-trust-lands-sold-off-over-150-years-1905104/.

New Hampshire: New Hampshire Department of Resources and Economic Development, Division of Forests and Lands, Forest Management Bureau, *Reservation Land Use* (Document, June 6, 2022), sent as file by Robert Spoerl, Land Agent, New Hampshire Forests and Lands, email correspondence (June 6, 2022); New Hampshire Fish and Game Department, *New Hampshire Wildlife Management Areas* (Webpage, undated), available at: https://www.wildlife.state.nh.us/maps/wma.html.

New Jersey: New Jersey Department of Environmental Protection, *2018–2022 New Jersey Statewide Comprehensive Outdoor Recreation Plan* (Report, September 2018), p. 12, available at: https://www.state.nj.us/dep/greenacres/pdf/scorp_2018 .pdf; New Jersey Department of Environmental Protection, New Jersey Fish and Wildlife, *Wildlife Management Areas* (Webpage, November 23, 2022), available at: https://www.nj.gov/dep/fgw/wmaland.htm; New Jersey Department of Environmental Protection, New Jersey State Park Service, *New Jersey's State Parks, Forests and Historic Sites* (Webpage, December 1, 2022), available at: https://nj.gov /dep/parksandforests/; New Jersey Department of Environmental Protection, Office of Natural Lands Management, *Natural Areas Program* (Webpage, April 15, 2022), available at: https://nj.gov/dep/parksandforests/natural/naturalareas/about .html.

New Mexico: New Mexico Energy, Minerals, and Natural Resources Department, *EMNRD 2021 Annual Report* (Report, 2022), p. 73, available at: https:// www.emnrd.nm.gov/officeofsecretary/wp-content/uploads/sites/2/EMNRD _AnnualReport_2021.pdf; New Mexico Energy, Minerals, and Natural Resources Department, State Parks Division, *Viva New Mexico: A Statewide Plan for Outdoor Adventure* (Report, December 2015), p. 3, available at: https://www .recpro.org/assets/Library/SCORPs/nm_scorp_2016.pdf.

New York: New York State Office of Parks, Recreation, and Historic Preservation, *New York Statewide Comprehensive Outdoor Recreation Plan 2020–2025* (Report, August 28, 2019), pp. 20, 25, available at: https://parks.ny.gov/documents /inside-our-agency/20202025StatewideComprehensiveOutdoorRecrea tionPlan.pdf; Robert Messenger, Chief, Bureau of Forest Resource Management, Division of Lands and Forests, New York State Department of Environmental Conservation, email correspondence (May 25, 2022); Katherine Barnes, Cartographic Technician, New York State Department of Environmental Conservation, email correspondence (June 27, 2022); Miranda Holeton and David Takacs, "U.S. State-Based Wilderness Law: An Evaluation" in *Hastings Environmental Law Journal* (Vol. 28, No. 1, Winter 2022), p. 39.

North Carolina: North Carolina Department of Natural and Cultural Resources, *N.C. State Park Lands and Waters Now Total 250,000 Acres* (Press Release, January 20, 2021), available at: https://www.ncdcr.gov/news/press-releases /2021/01/20/nc-state-park-lands-and-waters-now-total-250000-acres; North Carolina Department of Environmental Quality, *N.C. Coastal Reserve and National Estuarine Research Reserve* (Webpage, undated), available at: https://deq.nc.gov /about/divisions/coastal-management/nc-coastal-reserve-and-national-estua rine-research-reserve; North Carolina Forest Service, *State Forests* (Webpage, undated), available at: http://www.ncforestservice.gov/index.htm; North Carolina Wildlife Resources Commission Agency, *Organizational Overview 2021* (Report, December 6, 2021), p. 52, available at: https://www.ncwildlife.org/Portals/0

/About/documents/Commissioners/Agency-Organizational-Overview-FINAL -2021-REDUCE.pdf?ver=Y_Zr9yBV_xSTa7DQYZXblQ%3d%3d; Natural Areas Association, *State Natural Areas Program Roundtable: State Reports* (North Carolina State Natural Areas Video Report, November 17, 2021), available at: https://www.naturalareas.org/2021_state_natural_areas_progr.php.

North Dakota: North Dakota Parks and Recreation Department, *By the Numbers* (Webpage, undated), available at: https://www.parkrec.nd.gov/business /numbers; North Dakota Forest Service, *Explore Your State Forests* (Webpage, undated), available at: https://www.ag.ndsu.edu/ndfs/programs-and-services /explore-your-state-forests-2; Dale Repnow, Procurement Officer, North Dakota Game and Fish Department, telephone interview (May 27, 2022); North Dakota Parks and Recreation Department (Homepage, undated), available at: https://www.parkrec.nd.gov/; North Dakota Department of Trust Lands, *Mission, Vision, and History* (Webpage, 2019), available at: https://www.land.nd.gov /mission-vision-history; North Dakota Legislative Council, *State-Owned Real Estate—Background Memorandum* (Fact Sheet, August, 2005), available at: https:// ndlegis.gov/files/resource/committee-memorandum/79037.pdf.

Ohio: Ohio Department of Natural Resources, *Ohio 2018 Statewide Comprehensive Outdoor Recreation Plan* (Report, 2018), pp. 18–26, available at: https://ohiod nr.gov/static/documents/real-estate/2018_SCORP_Appendices.pdf; Ohio Department of Natural Resources, Division of Wildlife, *About the Division of Wildlife* ("Wildlife Management" Webpage Tab, undated), available at: https:// ohiodnr.gov/discover-and-learn/safety-conservation/about-ODNR/wildlife /about-the-division; Ohio Secretary of State, *State Agencies* (Webpage, undated), available at: https://www.ohiosos.gov/profile-ohio/government/state-agencies/.

Oklahoma: Oklahoma Office of Management and Enterprise Services, *2021 Oklahoma Real Asset Property Report* (Report, 2022), p. 4, available at: https:// oklahoma.gov/content/dam/ok/en/omes/documents/2021RealPropertyAsset Report.pdf; Oklahoma Department of Tourism and Recreation, *Oklahoma's State of Health: The People, the Economy, and the Environment 2018–2022* (Report, 2017), p. 55, available at: https://geog.okstate.edu/images/DOCS/RMP_GIS /SCORP/2017-12-15_SCORP.pdf; Kristen Gillman, Wildlife Lands and Minerals Coordinator/GIS Supervisor, Oklahoma Department of Wildlife Conservation, email correspondence (June 17, 2022); Commissioners of the Land Office, *2021 Annual Report* (Report, 2021), p. 5, available at: https://clo.ok.gov/wp -content/uploads/2021/12/2021-Annual-Report-1.pdf; Miranda Holeton and David Takacs, "U.S. State-Based Wilderness Law: An Evaluation" in *Hastings Environmental Law Journal* (Vol. 28, No. 1, Winter 2022), p. 42.

Oregon: Oregon State Parks and Recreation, *State Parks Guide* (Guide, 2022), p. 2, available at: https://stateparks.oregon.gov/index.cfm?do=v.publication&d

=park_guide_2022; Oregon Department of Forestry, *Lands Managed by the State Forests* (Webpage Map, May 3, 2019), available at: https://www.oregon.gov/odf /working/documents/StateForestsLandsMap.pdf; Oregon Department of Fish and Wildlife, *Visit ODFW Wildlife Areas* (Webpage, 2022), available at: https:// myodfw.com/visit-odfw-wildlife-areas; Noel Bacheller, Ecologist/Natural Resource Coordinator, Oregon Parks and Recreation Department, email correspondence (June 6, 2022); Oregon Department of State Lands, *State of Oregon State Land Inventory System Report* (Fact Sheet, September 7, 2021), available at: https://www .oregon.gov/dsl/Land/Documents/1SLIOwnershipStatewide.pdf.

Pennsylvania: Pennsylvania Department of Conservation and Natural Resources, *2020–24 Pennsylvania Statewide Outdoor Recreation Plan: Recreation for All* (Report, 2019), p. 23, available at: https://www.dcnr.pa.gov/Recreation/PAOut doorRecPlan/Pages/default.aspx; Pennsylvania Department of Conservation and Natural Resources, Bureau of Forestry, *Guidelines and Definitions for Natural Areas and Wild Areas* (Document, June 2016), available at: http://elibrary.dcnr.pa.gov /PDFProvider.ashx?action=PDFStream&docID=1742466&chksum=&rev ision=0&docName=MP2015_WNA_Definitions_Guidelines&nativeExt=pdf &PromptToSave=False&Size=1143132&ViewerMode=2&overlay=0; Paul Zeph, Chief, Planning Section, Pennsylvania Department of Conservation and Natural Resources, Bureau of State Parks, email correspondence (June 1, 2022).

Rhode Island: Rhode Island Department of Environmental Management, Division of Parks, (Homepage, 2022), available at: https://www.riparks.com/; Rhode Island Department of Environmental Management, *State Land Conservation Totals to Date* (Interactive Map, December 6, 2022), available at: https:// ridemgis.maps.arcgis.com/apps/opsdashboard/index.html#/85a4b90da40147e 8818cc072a28917cf.

South Carolina: South Carolina Department of Parks, Recreation, and Tourism, *South Carolina Statewide Comprehensive Outdoor Recreation Plan 2019* (Report, 2019), pp. 39, 42–44, available at: https://p.widencdn.net/bzuwqi/2019-South -Carolina-SCORP-FINAL; Samantha Queen, Director of Corporate Communications, South Carolina Department of Parks, Recreation, and Tourism, email correspondence (June 27, 2022); South Carolina Department of Parks, Recreation, and Tourism, *Caesar's Head State Park* (Webpage, 2022), available at: https:// southcarolinaparks.com/caesars-head.

South Dakota: South Dakota Game, Fish, and Parks, *2018–2022 South Dakota Statewide Comprehensive Outdoor Recreation Plan* (Report, 2017), p. 1.13, available at: https://gfp.sd.gov/userdocs/docs/scorp18.pdf; Paul Coughlin, Terrestrial Habitat Program Administrator, South Dakota Game, Fish, and Parks, email correspondence (May 26, 2022); South Dakota Game, Fish, and Parks, *Find a State Park* (Webpage, 2022), available at: https://gfp.sd.gov/parks/findpark/.

Tennessee: Tennessee Advisory Commission on Intergovernmental Relations, *Improving Management of Government-Owned Real Property in Tennessee* (Report, January 2019), pp. 8–9, available at: https://www.tn.gov/content/dam/tn/tacir /2019publications/2019ImprovingMgmtGovtOwnedRealProperty.pdf; Tennessee State Parks, *Interpretive and Recreation Program Plan: 2018–2023 Updated Process* (Report, June 2018), p. 7, available at: https://tnstateparks.com/assets/pdf /additional-content/6.1_Recreation_Interpretive_Program_Plan_signed_.pdf; Tennessee Department of Agriculture, Division of Forestry, *Plan 2020: Harvest Plan for Sustainable State Forests* (Report, November 2011), p. 4, available at: https://www.tn.gov/content/dam/tn/agriculture/documents/forestry/2018/Ag ForSF2020_Plan.pdf; Wally Akins, Assistant Chief—Habitat Section, Wildlife and Forestry Division, Tennessee Wildlife Resources Agency, email correspondence (June 13, 2022); Natural Areas Association, *State Natural Areas Program Roundtable: State Reports* (Tennessee State Natural Areas Video Report, November 17, 2021), available at: https://www.naturalareas.org/2021_state_natural_ar eas_progr.php.

Texas: Texas Parks and Wildlife Department, *Official Guide*, 18th edition (Guide, March 2022), p. 3, available at: https://tpwd.texas.gov/publications/pwdpubs /media/pwd_bk_p4000_0000aa.pdf; Texas Parks and Wildlife Department, Wildlife Information, email correspondence (June 1, 2022); Texas A&M Forest Service, *Texas State Forests and Arboretums* (Webpage, undated), available at: https://tfsfrd.tamu.edu/storymaps/texasstateforests/; State of Minnesota, Office of the Legislative Auditor, *School Trust Land Management and Oversight* (Report, May 2020), p. 7, available at: https://www.auditor.leg.state.mn.us/sreview/schoo ltrust.pdf; Texas Parks and Wildlife Department, *2018 Texas Outdoor Recreation Plan* (Report, 2017), chap. 4, p. 4, available at: https://tpwd.texas.gov/business /grants/pwd_rp_p4000_1673_TORP.pdf.

Utah: Ellie Leydsman McGinty, *Range Resources of Utah* (Utah State University Cooperative Extension Service Report, 2009), pp. 19–21, 138; Chelsea Duke, Wildlife Lands Coordinator, Utah Division of Wildlife Resources, email correspondence (June 6, 2022).

Vermont: Vermont Agency of Natural Resources, Department of Forests, Parks, and Recreation, *State Lands Management* (Webpage, 2022), available at: https://fpr.vermont.gov/forest/state-forests/state-lands-management; Vermont Agency of Natural Resources, Fish and Wildlife Department, *State Lands and Managed Lands* (Webpage, 2020), available at: https://vtfishandwildlife.com/con serve/lands-and-habitats/state-lands-and-state-managed-lands; Vermont Agency of Natural Resources, Department of Forests, Parks, and Recreation, *State Lands List—FPR State Forests* (Webpage, 2022), available at: https://fpr.vermont .gov/state_lands/land-records/state-lands-list#FPR%20State%20Forests; Vermont Agency of Natural Resources, Department of Forests, Parks, and Recre-

ation, *Vermont Natural Areas* (Webpage, 2022), available at: https://fpr.vermont
.gov/vermont-natural-areas; Jordan Smith, Anna Miller, and Yu-Fai Leung, *2019
Outlook and Analysis Letter* (National Association of State Park Directors Report,
February 2020), p. 54.

Virginia: Virginia Department of Conservation and Recreation, *Virginia Conservation Lands Database* (Webpage, November 4, 2022), available at: https://www
.dcr.virginia.gov/natural-heritage/clinfo; Virginia Department of Conservation
and Recreation, *Fun Facts* (Webpage, July 11, 2022), available at: https://www
.dcr.virginia.gov/state-parks/fun-facts; Virginia Department of Forestry, *State
Forests* (Webpage, 2022), available at: https://dof.virginia.gov/education-and-rec
reation/state-forests/; Virginia Department of Wildlife Resources, *Wildlife Management Areas* (Fact Sheet, undated), available at: https://dwr.virginia.gov/wp-con
tent/uploads/media/wma-locator.pdf; Virginia Department of Conservation and
Recreation, *Virginia Natural Area Preserves* (Webpage, August 4, 2022), available
at: https://www.dcr.virginia.gov/natural-heritage/natural-area-preserves/.

Washington: Washington State Recreation and Conservation Office, *All Public
Lands* (Interactive GIS Map, December 6, 2022), available at: https://wa-rco
.maps.arcgis.com/apps/opsdashboard/index.html#/2f8aa05d2a074cc0b4e18cb
0b88006ab; Washington Department of Fish and Wildlife, *WDFW Lands* (Web-
site, 2022), available at: https://wdfw.wa.gov/about/wdfw-lands; Washington
State Department of Natural Resources, *Forest and Trust Lands* (Webpage, 2022),
available at: https://www.dnr.wa.gov/managed-lands/forest-and-trust-lands;
Washington State Department of Natural Resources, *Washington State's Natural
Areas Program* (Fact Sheet, April 13, 2022), available at: https://www.dnr.wa.gov
/publications/em_fs10_009_natural_areas_program.pdf; Washington Communities and Schools Network, *Trust Lands 101* (Webpage, undated), available at:
https://dnrtrustlands.org/trust-lands/trust-lands-101/.

West Virginia: West Virginia Division of Natural Resources, *Annual Report
2020–2021* (Report, 2020), p. 33, available at: https://wvdnr.gov/wp-content
/uploads/2022/01/2022.01.10-DNRAnnualReport_2020-2021.pdf; Tracie
Spencer, Wildlife Resources Section, West Virginia Division of Natural Resources, email correspondence (June 6, 2022); West Virginia Division of Natural Resources, *West Virginia Wildlife Management Areas* (Webpage, 2022), available at:
https://wvdnr.gov/lands-waters/wildlife-management-areas/; Natural Areas Association, *State Natural Areas Program Roundtable: State Reports* (West Virginia State
Natural Areas Video Report, November 17, 2021), available at: https://www
.naturalareas.org/2021_state_natural_areas_progr.php.

Wisconsin: Ann Scott, Land Records Officer, Wisconsin DNR, email correspondence (June 6, 2022); Wisconsin Department of Natural Resources, *State
Natural Areas Program* (Webpage, September 26, 2022), available at: https://dnr

.wi.gov/topic/Lands/NaturalAreas/index.asp; Wisconsin Board of Commissioners of Public Lands, *Who We Are and What We Do* (Webpage, undated), available at: https://bcpl.wisconsin.gov/Pages/Home.aspx.

Wyoming: Wyoming Department of State Parks and Cultural Resources, *Wyoming Statewide Comprehensive Outdoor Recreation Plan 2019–2023* (Report, 2019), p. 23, available at: https://wyoparks.wyo.gov/index.php?preview=1&option=com_dropfiles&format=&task=frontfile.download&catid=536&id=433&Itemid=1000000000000; Jon Cicarelli, GIS Analyst, Wyoming State Parks and Cultural Resources, email correspondence (June 23, 2022); Wyoming Game and Fish Department, *Comprehensive Management System Annual Report* (Report, 2021), p. 61, available at: https://wgfd.wyo.gov/WGFD/media/content/PDF/About%20Us/Commission/WGFD_ANNUALREPORT_2021.pdf; Wyoming Office of State Lands and Investments, *Business Plan and Annual Report* (Report, 2021), p. 3, available at: https://drive.google.com/file/d/1b5Xufa5RZgyTNTE5Gsw476GZKiru2z9d/view.

Notes

PREFACE

1. Alex Brown, "Flush with Cash, States Invest in their Crowded Parks" in *Pew Stateline* (June 23, 2021).

2. William Rice and Bing Pan, "Understanding Changes in Park Visitation During the COVID-19 Pandemic" in *Wellbeing, Space and Society* (Vol. 2, May 2021), p. 6; Heather Hansman, "COVID-19's Legacy in Parks and Public Lands" in *Sierra* (March 29, 2022).

3. "Maryland Parks Deserve a Second Look: Are They Adequate?" in *Baltimore Sun* (September 2, 2021); Taylor DeVille, "Visits to State Parks, Including Patapsco Valley, Up Sharply, as Gyms and Most Recreational Facilities Remain Closed" in *Baltimore Sun* (June 1, 2020).

4. Kelly House, "Michigan Parks Look Increasingly Likely to Get Big COVID Funding Boost" in *Bridge Michigan* (October 28, 2021).

5. Bradley Karkkainen, "Biodiversity and Land" in *Cornell Law Review* (Vol. 83, No. 1, 1997), p. 44.

6. James Miller and Richard Hobbs, "Conservation Where People Live and Work" in *Conservation Biology* (Vol. 16, No. 2, April 2002).

7. Margaret Walls, *Parks and Recreation in the United States: State Park Systems* (Resources for the Future Report, January 2009), p. 8.

8. Sally Fairfax, "Thinking the Unthinkable: States as Public Land Managers" in *Hastings Environmental Law Journal* (Vol. 14, No. 1, Winter 2008), p. 524.

9. Jon A. Souder and Sally K. Fairfax, *State Trust Lands: History, Management, and Sustainable Use* (Lawrence: University of Kansas Press, 1996); Ney Landrum, *The State Park Movement in America: A Critical Review* (Columbia, MO: University of Missouri Press, 2004); Freeman Tilden, *The State Parks: Their Meaning in American Life* (New York: Knopf, 1962); Rebecca Conard, *Places of Quiet Beauty: Parks,*

Preserves, and Environmentalism (Iowa City: University of Iowa Press, 1997); Thomas Cox, *The Park Builders: A History of State Parks in the Pacific Northwest* (Seattle: University of Washington Press); Tomas Koontz, *Federalism in the Forest: National versus State Natural Resource Policy* (Washington, DC: Georgetown University Press, 1989).

10. See, for example, Richard Louv, *Last Child in the Woods* (Chapel Hill, NC: Algonquin Books, 2005); Howard Frumkin et al., "Nature Contact and Human Health: A Research Agenda" in *Environmental Health Perspectives* (Vol. 125, No. 7, July 31, 2017); Gregory Bratman et al., "Nature and Mental Health: An Ecosystem Service Perspective" in *Science Advances* (Vol. 5, No. 7, July 24, 2019).

CHAPTER 1

1. Carol Hardy Vincent, Laura Hanson, and Lucas Bermejo, *Federal Land Ownership: Overview and Data* (Congressional Research Service Report R42346, February 21, 2020), p. 1.

2. *Ibid.*, pp. 7–8.

3. For all state land acreage data, see appendix.

4. Sally Fairfax, "Thinking the Unthinkable: States as Public Land Managers" in *Hastings Environmental Law Journal* (Vol. 14, No. 1, Winter 2008), p. 524.

5. *Ibid.*, pp. 517–519.

6. See, for example, Robert Nelson, *State-Owned Lands in the Eastern United States: Lessons from State Land Management in Practice* (PERC Public Lands Report, March 2018).

7. Fairfax, p. 518

8. *Ibid.*

9. For an assessment of this recurring idea, see, Martin Nie and Patrick Kelly, "State and Local Control of Federal Lands: New Developments in the Transfer of Federal Lands Movement" in *Ecology Law Currents* (August 21, 2018).

10. A few caveats are in order here. First, these figures cannot help but be a mere snapshot of an extremely dynamic domain in which states are constantly adding new acquisitions and occasionally divesting of others. As a result, these findings were technically obsolete from the moment they were written down; fortunately, in most cases, these inevitable inaccuracies will likely remain marginal for quite some time and thus are more than adequate in giving a reliable sense of how states compare. The other caveat is that this table only shows acreage directly owned by states—what in real estate terms is called *fee simple*. However, many millions more acres are *managed* but not owned by state natural resource agencies. They are most often leased, though various types of conservation easements are also becoming increasingly common. While the latter can be quite permanent, the former tends to be a much more unstable and ephemeral arrangement, often with less managerial control than fee simple lands, and so they are not included in Table 1.1. However, where leased lands are most prominent (in state parks and, especially, wildlife management areas), greater efforts are made to account for them in later chapters and tables that deal specifically with these areas.

11. Technically, Hawaii's grant was former royal lands dating from before Hawaii was colonized by the U.S. The federal government kept these lands intact and gave them back to the new state at statehood. Hawaii Department of Land and Natural Resources, *Hawaii Statewide Comprehensive Outdoor Recreation Plan 2015 Update* (Report, May 2015), p. 15, available at: https://www.recpro.org/assets/Library/SCORPs/hi_scorp_2015.pdf.

12. Daniel Elazar, *American Federalism: A View from the States*, 2nd edition (New York: Thomas Y. Crowell, 1972); Wesley Leckrone, "State and Local Political Culture" in Michael Shally-Jensen (editor), *American Political Culture: An Encyclopedia* (Santa Barbara, CA: ABC-CLIO, 2015); Daniel Fudge, "Geographic Differences of Individual Views toward the Role of Government" in *American Review of Politics* (Vol. 37, No. 2, 2020), pp. 71–96.

13. Steven Davis, *In Defense of Public Lands* (Philadelphia: Temple University Press, 2018), pp. 150–157.

14. Scott Lehmann, *Privatizing Public Land* (New York: Oxford University Press, 1995), p. 31.

15. While the federal government has the main jurisdiction for dealing with Native nations, their relationship to state governments and state public lands is much more variable and complex. In many states, tribal members are granted no special privileges, while in others, like Wisconsin, they have special hunting and harvesting privileges due to treaty rights on the ceded lands and are consulted at a peer-government level on certain natural resource decisions. In Minnesota, meanwhile, tribal members get free state park passes to access the land that was once theirs. Walker Orenstein, "Starting in 2022, Tribal Members Will Get Free Permits to Minnesota State Parks" in *Minnpost* (September 23, 2021). Minnesota's legislature also voted in 2023 to close the 1,280-acre Upper Sioux Agency State Park and transfer it to the control of a local community of the Sioux tribe whose ancestors are buried there. Although the DNR has been instructed to find equivalent acreage in the area to replace lost recreation, this transfer has proven to be quite controversial. Patrick Durkin, "Minnesota Public-Land Transfer Stirs Historical Debate" in *The Meateater* (July 28, 2023).

16. Erin Pounds, "State Trust Lands: Static Management and Shifting Value Perspectives" in *Environmental Law* (Vol. 41, 2011), p. 1334.

17. Sean O'Day, "School Trust Lands: The Land Manager's Dilemma between Educational Funding and Environmental Conservation, a Hobson's Choice?" in *NYU Environmental Law Journal* (Vol. 8, 1999), pp. 167, 179.

18. *Ibid.*, p. 167.

19. *Ibid.*, p. 164, note 5.

20. Chelsea Liddell and Mark Haggerty, *State Trust Lands in Transition: States' Treatment of Permanent Funds* (Headwaters Economics Report, November 2019), p. 2; Pounds, p. 1335, note 9.

21. Of the eastern states, only Minnesota, Wisconsin, Mississippi, Alabama, and Louisiana retain any school trust lands.

22. Ney Landrum, *The State Park Movement in America: A Critical Review* (Columbia, MO: University of Missouri Press, 2004).

23. Incidentally, national forests in those same states largely had the same tax forfeiture origins. The same is true of Wisconsin and Minnesota's extensive county forest systems. William Shands, *The Lands Nobody Wanted* (Washington, DC: Conservation Foundation, 1977); Steven Davis, "The Forests Nobody Wanted: The Politics of Land Management in the County Forests of the Upper Midwest" in *Journal of Land Use and Environment Law* (Vol. 28, No. 2, Spring 2013), p. 198.

24. Landrum, p. 168.

25. Land and Water Conservation Fund Act of 1965, Public Law 88-578 (September 3, 1964), 78 Stat. 897. SCORP stands for State Comprehensive Outdoor Recreation Plan.

26. Carol Hardy Vincent and Bill Heniff Jr., *Land and Water Conservation Fund (LWCF): Frequently Asked Questions* (Congressional Research Service, May 3, 2019), p. 2.

27. Carol Hardy Vincent, Laura Comay, and Bill Heniff Jr., *The Great American Outdoors Act, P.L. 116–152* (Congressional Research Service, November 19, 2020).

28. Alex Brown, "Flush with Cash, States Invest in Their Crowded Parks" in *Pew Stateline* (June 23, 2021).

29. Daniel Press and Nicole Nakagawa, "Local Open Space Preservation in the United States" in Daniel Mazmanian and Michael Kraft (editors), *Towards Sustainable Communities*, 2nd edition (Cambridge, MA: MIT Press, 2009), p. 143.

30. Ballotpedia, *Missouri Sales Tax for Parks and Conservation, Amendment 1—2016* (Webpage, 2022), available at: https://ballotpedia.org/Missouri_Sales_Tax_for_Parks _and_Conservation,_Amendment_1_(2016).

31. Doug Phillips, *Forever Wild Land Trust* (Encyclopedia of Alabama, May 21, 2018), available at: http://encyclopediaofalabama.org/ARTICLE/h-1125.

32. Ballotpedia, *Texas Proposition 5, Sales Tax on Sporting Goods Dedicated to Parks, Wildlife, and Historical Agencies Amendment—2019* (Webpage, 2022), available at: https:// ballotpedia.org/Texas_Proposition_5,_Sales_Tax_on_Sporting_Goods_Dedicated _to_Parks,_Wildlife,_and_Historical_Agencies_Amendment_(2019); Joan Moses, *Conservation Funding Protected in Montana* (Western Resource Advocates Press Release, July 7, 2021), available at: https://westernresourceadvocates.org/timeline/conservation -funding-protected-in-montana/.

33. New Jersey Department of Environmental Protection, *Green Acres Program* (Report, August 2003), available at: https://www.nj.gov/dep/newsrel/releases/03 _0150presspak.pdf; Kelly Pohl and Megan Lawson, *Minnesota's Legacy Fund* (Outdoor Industry Association Report, September 2017), available at: http://headwaters economics.org/wp-content/uploads/state-rec-MN.pdf; Peter McGuire, "State Budget Includes Huge Boost for Land Preservation" in *Portland Press Herald* (July 11, 2021); Connecticut Department of Energy and Environmental Protection, *Open Space and Watershed Land Acquisition Grant Program* (Webpage, 2022), available at: https://portal.ct.gov/DEEP/Business-and-Financial-Assistance/Grants-Finan cial-Assistance/Open-Space-and-Watershed-Land-Acquisition-Grant-Program.

34. Nelson, p. 37.

35. *Ibid.*

36. Mackinac Center, *Land Ho! Should Government Be Landlord?* (Report, February 15, 1999), available at: https://www.mackinac.org/1856.

37. Jeff Alexander, "Interview with Senator Casperson" in *Bridge Michigan* (August 23, 2012).

38. *Ibid.*

39. *Ibid.*

40. Lisa Speckhard, "Wisconsin DNR Identifies 128 Properties to Sell, 12 in Dane County" in *Capital Times* (June 27, 2016).

41. Wisconsin Policy Forum, "Public Property: State Faces Deadline for Conservation" in *Wisconsin Taxpayer* (Vol. 87, No. 6, 2019), p. 5.

42. Wilderness Act, Public Law 88-577, 16 U.S.C. 1131-1136 (September 3, 1964); Multiple-Use Sustained-Yield Act, Public Law 86-517, 16 U.S.C. 28-531 (June 12, 1960).

43. See, for example, the recommendations in Joel Smith and William Travis, *Adaptation to Climate Change in Public Lands Management* (Resources for the Future Issue Brief 10-04, February 2010).

44. Washington, Minnesota, and Colorado are the notable exceptions to this rule as their state DNRs manage both trust and nontrust lands.

CHAPTER 2

1. State parks make up only 7% of all state lands, or 14% if we take Alaska's huge unassigned land grant out of the calculation. See Table 2.1.

2. Alex Brown, "Flush with Cash, States Invest in their Crowded Parks" in *Pew Stateline* (June 23, 2021); Margaret Walls, *Parks and Recreation in the United States: State Park Systems* (Resources for the Future Report, January 2009), p. 8.

3. Jordan Smith, Anna Miller, and Yu-Fai Leung, *2019 Outlook and Analysis Letter* (National Association of State Park Directors Report, February 2020), p. 3; Juha Siikamäki, *State Parks: Assessing Their Benefits* (Resources for the Future Report, February 15, 2012), p. 29.

4. Thomas Cox, *The Park Builders: A History of State Parks in the Pacific Northwest* (Seattle: University of Washington Press), p. xi.

5. Indiana also includes a land category called *state reservoirs* in its park system. Many other states lease land from around federal reservoirs from the Army Corps of Engineers and manage these units as state parks. Other states, like Massachusetts and Wisconsin, manage their reservoir lands as multiple use areas more akin to state forests and so they are not included in their park systems. Finally, some states, like West Virginia, New Hampshire, and Wisconsin, consider (for management purposes) at least some of their state forest units that are more heavily oriented toward recreation to be part of their park systems, although they have some clear distinctions in terms of management goals. For the purposes of this study, however, state parks and state forests are considered as strictly separate systems.

6. Grady Gammage Jr. and Nancy Welch, *The Price of Stewardship: The Future of Arizona's State Parks* (Morrison Institute for Public Policy Report, October 2009), p. 34.

7. A few other states, such as Michigan (Mackinac) and Georgia (Jekyll Island), also have quasi-independent park units with their own governing boards, but these are isolated and much smaller than New York and Maine's massive special status

parks. Also, the very significant 71,000-acre Custer State Park in South Dakota was, for most of its history, an independently governed special status park until its board was dissolved and it was folded into the regular state park system. Ney Landrum, *The State Park Movement in America: A Critical Review* (Columbia, MO: University of Missouri Press, 2004), pp. 64, 214.

8. New York Department of Environmental Conservation, *New York's Forest Preserve* (Webpage, undated), available at: https://www.dec.ny.gov/lands/4960.html.

9. Baxter State Park, *History* (Webpage, undated), available at: https://baxterstate park.org/shortcodes/history/.

10. New York Department of Environmental Conservation webpage. The entire Adirondack Park is closer to 6 million acres as more than half of the land within its boundaries is private and includes many towns and developments. Adirondack Park is a unique preserve in that there is so much private land within the preserve boundaries, though it is subject to fairly strict land use regulations. Adirondack Park Agency, *More about the Adirondack Park . . .* (Webpage, undated), available at: https://apa .ny.gov/About_Park/more_park.html. Furthermore, the public land within the park boundaries, unlike nearly all other public land in the U.S., pays property taxes to local governments. Robert Nelson, *State-Owned Lands in the Eastern United States: Lessons from State Land Management in Practice* (PERC Public Lands Report, March 2018), p. 12.

11. Again, this includes New York's special status parklands. If only the regular park system is considered, the figure drops to a mere 8% of all state land.

12. Rebecca Conard, *Places of Quiet Beauty: Parks, Preserves, and Environmentalism* (Iowa City: University of Iowa Press, 1997), p. 8.

13. Landrum (2004), p. 35.

14. *Ibid.*, p. 39.

15. Conard, p. 8.

16. Landrum (2004), pp. 40–56.

17. Noel Sherry, "Adirondack History: New York State to the Rescue" in *New York Almanack* (November 15, 2022), available at: https://www.newyorkalmanack .com/2022/11/twitchell-lake-history-new-york-state-to-the-rescue/.

18. Adirondack Park Agency, *History of the Adirondack Park* (Webpage, undated), available at: https://apa.ny.gov/About_Park/history.htm.

19. New York Constitution, Article XIV, § 1.

20. Walls (2009), p. 1.

21. Conard, p. 2.

22. *Ibid.*, 9; Landrum (2004), pp. 58, 65; Cox, pp. 33–37.

23. Landrum (2004), pp. 81–89.

24. *Ibid.*, p. 110.

25. *Ibid.*, pp. 81–89.

26. *Ibid.*, p. 1.

27. *Ibid.*, p. 88.

28. Conard, pp. 4–5.

29. Cox, p. 175.

30. *Ibid.*, p. 12.

31. The only public lands that were available for African Americans to recreate on were the federal lands, which had largely been desegregated from the start. William O'Brien, "The Strange Career of a Florida State Park: Uncovering a Jim Crow Past" in *Historical Geography* (Vol. 35, 2007), p. 165. It should be noted, however, that national parks were not particularly plentiful or easily accessed in the South during the Jim Crow era.

32. Andrew Kahrl, "The 'Achilles' Heel' of Jim Crow: A Review of Landscapes of Exclusion" in *Southern Spaces* (April 4, 2017).

33. Walls (2009), p. 2.

34. Landrum (2004), p. 133.

35. *Ibid.*, p. 134.

36. *Ibid.*, p. 138.

37. It is very important to note, however, that segregationist Jim Crow policies in many southern states kept many state parks and their facilities off-limits to African Africans until later in the 1960s.

38. *Ibid.*, pp. 167–168.

39. Walls (2009), p. 2.

40. See, for example, Phyllis Myers and Sharon Green, *State Parks in a New Era: A Look at the Legacy* (Washington, DC: Conservation Foundation, 1986).

41. Brown (2021).

42. Landrum (2004), p. 223.

43. Smith, Miller, and Leung, p. 3.

44. *Ibid.*

45. Carol Hardy Vincent et al., *Federal Land Management Agencies: Appropriations and Revenues* (Washington, DC: Congressional Research Service, December 10, 2014), pp. 6–7.

46. Margaret Walls, *Paying for State Parks: Evaluating Alternative Approaches for the 21st Century* (Resources for the Future Report, January 28, 2013), p. 7; Yu-Fai Leung, Jordan Smith, and Anna Miller, *Statistical Report of State Park Operations: 2014–2015 Annual Information Exchange* (National Association of State Park Directors, Vol. 37, March 2016), p. 27.

47. Walls (2013), p. 7; Leung, Smith, and Miller, p. 40.

48. Jordan Smith, Emily Wilkins, and Yu-Fai Leung, "Attendance Trends Threaten Future Operations of America's State Park Systems" in *Proceedings of the National Academy of Sciences* (Vol. 116, No. 26, June 25, 2019), p. 12775.

49. Myles Dannhausen Jr. and Jackson Parr, "Can Self-Sustaining Funding Model Work for Wisconsin State Parks" in *Peninsula Pulse* (April 21, 2017).

50. Erin Luhrman, "Bailout or Bonus" in *Wisconsin Watch* (State of the Parks Series, June 9, 2013); Dannhausen and Parr.

51. Mike Maciag, "Struggling State Parks Seek New Ways to Survive" in *Governing* (November 21, 2016).

52. Leung, Smith, and Miller, p. 29.

53. *Ibid.*, p. 29.

54. Walls (2013), pp. 9, 11.

55. *Ibid.*, p. 13; Gammage and Welch, p. 8.

56. Gammage and Welch, p. 36.

57. Walls (2013), p. 26; Leung, Smith, and Miller, p. 27.

58. Walls (2013), p. 9.

59. Jodi Peterson, "State Park Problems" in *High Country News* (October 18, 2011).

60. Gammage and Welch, pp. 4, 8.

61. Walls (2013), p. 26.

62. U.S. Census Bureau, *From Municipalities to Special Districts, Official Count of Every Type of Local Government in 2017 Census of Governments* (Report, October 29, 2019), p. 4, available at: https://www.census.gov/content/dam/Census/library/visualizations/2019/econ/from_municipalities_to_special_districts_america_counts_october_2019.pdf.

63. Rebecca Retzlaff, "The Illinois Forest Preserve District Act of 1913 and the Emergence of Metropolitan Park System Planning in the USA" in *Planning Perspectives* (Vol. 25, No. 4, October 2010); Steven Davis, "The Politics of Urban Natural Areas Management at the Local Level: A Case Study" in *Kentucky Journal of Equine, Agriculture, and Natural Resources Law* (Vol. 2, No. 2, 2010), p. 130.

64. Walls (2013), p. 2.

65. *Ibid.*

66. *Ibid.*, p. 26.

67. *Ibid.*, p. 9.

68. Ballotpedia, *How Much Does It Cost to Go to a State Park?* (Webpage, April 2018), available at: https://ballotpedia.org/How_much_does_it_cost_to_go_to_a_state_park.

69. Maciag.

70. Dannhausen and Parr.

71. *Ibid.*

72. *Ibid.*

73. See, for example, Pahre's meticulous accounting of how a full-on revenue-generation model is entirely unworkable for all but the most highly visited parks. Robert Pahre, "Privatizing Isle Royale? The Limits of Free Market Environmentalism" in *The George Wright Forum* (Vol. 25, No. 3, 2008).

74. Thomas More, "From Public to Private: Five Concepts of Park Management and Their Consequences" in *The George Wright Forum* (Vol. 22, No. 2, 2005), pp. 14–15.

75. Landrum (2004), p. 250.

76. *Ibid.*, p. 251.

77. Alex Brown, "Privatizing State Parks Can Save Them—Or Wreck Them" in *Pew Stateline* (December 3, 2019).

78. Walls (2013), p. 1.

79. Dannhausen and Parr.

80. Landrum (2004), p. 246.

81. This figure is an average of all states, which range from a high of 0.54% in South Dakota to 0.05% in Wisconsin. Leung, Smith, and Miller, p. 31.

82. Mancur Olson, *The Logic of Collective Action: Public Goods and the Theory of Groups* (Cambridge, MA: Harvard University Press, 1971). Regarding federal land management agencies, Clarke and McCool make essentially the same argument for the budget woes of the NPS and the USFWS with their very diffuse and disorganized user bases. Jeanne Clarke and Daniel McCool, *Staking Out the Terrain: Power and Performance among Natural Resource Agencies*, 2nd edition (Albany: State University of New York Press, 1996).

83. Brown (2021).

84. Smith, Wilkins, and Leung, p. 12778.

85. *Ibid.*, p. 12779.

86. Brown (2019).

87. Peter Fimrite and Wyatt Buchanan, "70 California State Parks Fall to Budget Ax" in *San Francisco Chronicle* (May 13, 2011); Leonard Gilroy, Harris Kenny, and Julian Morris, *Parks 2.0: Operating State Parks through Public-Private Partnerships* (Buckeye Institute Policy Study No. 419, December 2013), p. 1.

88. *Ibid.*

89. Paul Rodgers, "Is Brown's Plan to Close State Parks All a Political Gimmick?" in *San Jose Mercury News* (January 15, 2012).

90. Siikamäki; Richard Dolesh, "State Park Crisis" in *Parks and Recreation* (January 31, 2012).

91. Washington state park commissioner quoted in Dolesh.

92. Hibah Ansari, "Funding Cuts, Staff Reductions Lead to Staff Shortages at High Cliff State Park" in *Appleton Post-Crescent* (July 29, 2019).

93. *Ibid.*

94. *Ibid.*

95. Rhode Island Division of Statewide Planning and Rhode Island Department of Environmental Management, *Ocean State Outdoors: Rhode Island's Comprehensive Outdoor Recreation Plan* (Report No. 122, August 29, 2019), p. 22, available at: https://dem .ri.gov/sites/g/files/xkgbur861/files/programs/bpoladm/plandev/pdf/scorp19-d.pdf.

96. Geoff Pender, "Move to Privatize State Parks Halted—for Now—Amid Heated Debate" in *Mississippi Today* (February 5, 2021).

97. William Petroski, "Budget Cuts Raise Worries That Some Iowa Parks Will Have 'Closed' Signs" in *Des Moines Register* (May 16, 2017).

98. See, for example, Christos Siderelis and Jordan Smith, "Ecological Settings and State Economies as Factor Inputs in the Provision of Outdoor Recreation" in *Environmental Management* (Vol. 52, 2013), pp. 699–711.

99. Uma Outka, "State Lands in Modern Public Land Law" in *Stanford Environmental Law Journal* (Vol. 36, 2017), p. 150.

100. *Ibid.*, p. 205.

101. "Bill Allowing Logging in State Parks Falls Apart" in *MetroNews* (January 23, 2018), available at: https://wvmetronews.com/2018/02/23/bill-allowing-log ging-in-state-parks-falls-apart/.

102. Emily Guerin, "A Tale of Two Parks: How the Bakken Boom Transformed a Landscape" in *High Country News* (November 27, 2017).

103. Luhrman.

104. *Ibid.*; Ansari.

105. Ansari.

106. Luhrman.

107. Peterson.

108. Joe Wertz, "The Death of OK's Lake Texoma State Park and the Promises of Privatization" in *NPR State Impact* (June 11, 2012), available at: https://stateimpact.npr.org/oklahoma/2012/06/11/oklahomas-lake-texoma-bought-and-paid-for/.

109. Peterson.

110. Adam Roy, "The Alaskan Non-Profit Saving State Parks" in *Backpacker* (January 16, 2018).

111. More, pp. 15–17.

112. Russ Harding, *Privatization in Michigan State Parks* (Mackinac Center for Public Policy, October 27, 2005).

113. "Liberty State Park Is Not for Sale. At Any Price" in *New Jersey Star-Ledger* (December 5, 2019).

114. Lee Bergquist, "Wisconsin DNR and Kohler Plan Land Swap to Allow Company to Use State Park Land for Golf Course" in *Milwaukee Journal Sentinel* (February 17, 2018).

115. Brown (2019).

116. Steven Greenhut, "How Budget Cutbacks Are Helping California Parks" in *Reason* (March 16, 2012).

117. Gilroy, Kenny, and Morris, pp. 1, 14.

118. Pender.

119. Gilroy, Kenny, and Morris, pp. 10–12.

120. Aaron Barkley, "Cost and Efficiency in Government Outsourcing: Evidence from the Dredging Industry" in *American Economic Journal: Microeconomics* (Vol. 13, No. 4, 2021), pp. 514–547.

121. Argentino Pressoa, *Outsourcing and Public Sector Efficiency: How Effective Is Outsourcing in Dealing with Impure Public Goods?* (FEP Working Papers, Universidade do Porto, 2009).

122. Joseph Stiglitz, *The Harms of Infrastructure Privatization: A Step Backward in Progressive Policymaking* (Roosevelt Institute, July 26, 2021), available at: https://rooseveltinstitute.org/2021/07/26/the-harms-of-infrastructure-privatization-a-step-backward-in-progressive-policymaking/.

123. See, for example, Jon Luoma, "The Privatisation of Water" in *The Ecologist* (March 1, 2004).

124. Greg Mankiw, *Monuments as Natural Monopoly* (Greg Mankiw's Blog, May 18, 2006), available at: https://gregmankiw.blogspot.com/search?q=national+monuments.

125. Walls (2013), p. 9.

126. Ney Landrum, "Entrepreneurism in America's State Parks" in *The George Wright Forum* (Vol. 22, No. 2, 2005), p. 30.

127. Brown (2019).

128. Mary Brooks, "Privatizing State Parks Doesn't Work" in *Wyoming County Report* (February 28, 2022). To be fair, some more diligent contract writers actually do the opposite and require very specific investment and expenditure as the price of being awarded a contract. But this is, admittedly, a much tougher sell. Brown (2019).

129. Andy Davis and Chance Raso, "Investments in West Virginia's Public Lands Are Attracting Visitors and Income: Let's Not Risk It" in *WV News* (March 11, 2022).

130. Brooks.

131. Brown (2019).

132. See, for example, the very honest appraisal in Arizona's park privatization report. Arizona State Parks Foundation, *Arizona State Park Privatization and Efficiency Plan* (Report, December 2010), p. 18.

133. Kate Prengaman, "Crown Jewels Sustain State Parks" in *Wisconsin Watch* (State Park Series, May 26, 2013).

134. Arizona State Parks Foundation, pp. 5–8, 18.

135. Pender.

136. Andrew Mowen et al., "What Factors Shape Visitor Support for the Privatization of Park Service and Amenities?" in *Journal of Park and Recreational Administration* (Vol. 27, No. 2, April 2009), p. 33, 39.

137. *Ibid.*, p. 40.

138. *Ibid.*

139. *Ibid.*

140. National Park Service, *The NPS Mission* (Common Learning Portal Webpage, September 10, 2019), available at: https://mylearning.nps.gov/library-resources/nps-mission/.

141. Robert Douglass, "History of Outdoor Recreation and Nature-Based Tourism in the United States" in H. Ken Cordell et al. (editors), *Outdoor Recreation in American Life: A National Assessment of Demand and Supply Trends* (Champaign, IL: Sagamore Publishing, 1999), pp. 15–24.

142. Landrum (2004), p. 178.

143. Landrum (2005), p. 27.

144. *Ibid.*

145. Conard, p. 234.

146. Landrum (2004), pp. 235–236.

147. *Ibid.*, p. 240.

148. Leung, Smith, and Miller, pp. 12–13.

149. Landrum (2004), pp. 20–21, 236.

150. J. Mark Morgan, "Resources, Recreationists, and Revenues. A Policy Dilemma for Today's State Park Systems" in *Environmental Ethics* (Vol. 18, No. 3, Fall 1996), p. 282.

151. Landrum (2004), p. 259.

152. Dannhausen and Parr.

153. Morgan, p. 282.

154. "Private Sector Could Benefit Oklahoma's State Parks" in *The Oklahoman* (November 18, 2018).

155. Brown (2019).

156. Morgan, p. 283.

157. *Ibid.*, pp. 284–285.

158. *Ibid.*, p. 285.

159. *Ibid.*

160. *Ibid.*, p. 283.

161. Kathleen Andereck documents some of these direct impacts, including air and water pollution, soil compaction and erosion, solid waste disposal, fragmentation of wildlife habitat, noise pollution, and excess water consumption. Kathleen Andereck, "The Impact of Tourism on Natural Resources" in *Parks and Recreation* (Vol. 28, No. 6, June 1993).

162. See, for example, Nick Haddad et al., "Habitat Fragmentation and Its Lasting Impact on Earth's Ecosystems" in *Science Advances* (Vol. 1, No. 2, March 20, 2015); Almo Farina, *Principles and Methods in Landscape Ecology: Towards a Science of the Landscape* (Dordrecht, Netherlands: Kluwer Academic Press, 2006); Christer Nilsson and Gunnell Grelsson, "The Fragility of Ecosystems: A Review" in *Journal of Applied Ecology* (Vol. 32, No. 4, November 1995), pp. 677–692; William Laurance et al., "Rainforest Fragmentation Kills Big Trees" in *Nature* (Vol. 404, April 20, 2001), p. 836.

163. National Park Service, *About Us—Parks/Units* (Webpage, December 5, 2022), available at: https://www.nps.gov/aboutus/national-park-system.htm.

164. Walls (2009), p. 1.

165. Steven Davis, "Preservation, Resource Extraction, and Recreation on Public Lands: A View from the States" in *Natural Resources Journal* (Vol. 48, No. 2, Spring 2008), p. 334.

166. Leung, Smith, and Miller, p. 12.

167. Nora Hertel and Andrea Casey, "Campgrounds Getting More Electric" in *Wisconsin Watch* (State of the Parks Series, May 26, 2013).

168. Walls (2009), p. 4.

169. Landrum (2004), p. 225.

170. North Carolina Division of Parks and Recreation, *Systemwide Plan for North Carolina State Parks* (Report, 2018), pp. 1.11, 2.4, available at: https://www.ncparks.gov/media/1341/open.

171. Landrum (2004), p. 225.

172. *Ibid.*, p. 224.

173. Lowell Caneday, Debra Jordan, and Yating Liang, "Management Policy in and Typology of State Park Systems" in *American Journal of Environmental Sciences* (Vol. 5, No. 2, 2009), p. 195.

174. Landrum (2004), pp. 253, 257.

175. *Ibid.*, p. 258.

176. *Ibid.*, p. 257.

177. *Ibid.*, p. 254; Morgan, p. 288.

178. Landrum (2004), p. 260.

179. Aldo Leopold quoted in Morgan, p. 288.

180. Christos Siderelis et al., "A Nationwide Production Analysis of State Park Attendance in the United States" in *Journal of Environmental Management* (Vol. 99, 2012), p. 25.

181. Gammage and Welch, p. 31.

182. Davis (2018), pp. 110–111.

183. Samuel Robinson, "State Parks, Trails Would Receive $250 Million in Federal Stimulus under Whitmer Plan" in *Ann Arbor News* (June 10, 2021); West Virginia Division of Natural Resources, *Annual Report 2015–2016* (Report, 2016), p. 44; Maine Department of Agriculture, Conservation and Forestry, *The Case for Maine State Parks* (Webpage, January 2021), available at: https://legislature.maine .gov/doc/5156.

184. Nelson, p. 41.

185. John Bergstrom et al., "Economic Impacts of State Parks on State Economies in the South" in *Southern Journal of Agricultural Economics* (Vol. 22, No. 2, 1990), p. 75.

186. *Ibid.*

187. Jeffrey Prey, David Marcouiller, and Danya Kim, *Economic Impacts of the Wisconsin State Park System: Connections to Gateway Communities* (Wisconsin Department of Natural Resources Report PR-487-2013, November 2013), pp. 9, 29.

188. Siikamäki, p. 29.

189. Maciag.

190. For a good description, see Rudolf De Groot, Matthew Wilson, and Roelof Boumans, "A Typology for the Classification, Description and Valuation of Ecosystems Functions, Goods and Services" in *Ecological Economics* (Vol. 41, No. 3, 2002), pp. 393–408.

191. David Holzman, "Accounting for Nature's Benefits: The Dollar Value of Ecosystem Services" in *Environmental Health Perspectives* (Vol. 120, No. 4, April 2012), p. 153.

192. Like its much larger special status park sibling in the Adirondacks, the Catskill preserve has a large boundary line that encompasses both public and private land, with the latter under certain more restrictive zoning. The Catskill preserve contains 705,500 acres within its boundaries, of which 287,500 acres (41%) are state owned and 40,500 acres (6%) are New York City owned or leased watershed lands. New York Department of Environmental Conservation, *Catskill Park State Land Master Plan* (Planning Report, August 2008, amended 2014), p. i.

193. Margaret Walls and Anne Riddle, *Biodiversity, Ecosystem Services, and Land Use Comparing Three Federal Policies* (Resources for the Future Report, February 2012), p. 12.

194. Tania Briceno and Johnny Mojica, *A Model for Measuring the Benefits of State Parks for the Washington State Parks and Recreation Commission* (Earth Economics Report, January 2016), p. 23. The inflation-adjusted figures were calculated from 2015, which is the date when the data in the study was measured.

CHAPTER 3

1. John Muir, *A Thousand-Mile Walk to the Gulf* (Cambridge, MA: Riverside Press, 1916), p. 77.

2. Robert Marshall quoted in Roderick Nash, *Wilderness and the American Mind* (New Haven, CT: Yale University Press, 1967), p. 203.

3. Aldo Leopold, *A Sand County Almanac* (New York: Random House, 1986), p. xviii.

4. Leopold was the director of the University of Wisconsin–Madison Arboretum (which he designed as a collection of native landscapes, not individual plant species), and there he did groundbreaking work on reestablishing tallgrass prairies and other native ecosystems on formerly barren farm fields. University of Wisconsin–Madison Arboretum, *History* (Webpage, 2022), available at: https://arboretum .wisc.edu/about-us/history/.

5. Leopold, p. 260.

6. Aldo Leopold, *Round River* (New York: Oxford University Press, 1993), pp. 145–146.

7. New York State Law, Environmental Conservation (ENV), Ch. 43-B, Article 45, State Nature and Historical Preserve Trust, § 45-0117, Jurisdiction and Administration.

8. See, for example, the early efforts encapsulated within The Nature Conservancy, *Preserving Our Heritage: Volume II—State Activities* (Washington, DC: U.S. Department of the Interior Report, 1977).

9. Rebecca Conard, *Places of Quiet Beauty: Parks, Preserves, and Environmentalism* (Iowa City: University of Iowa Press, 1997), p. 242.

10. Perhaps the closest category to the SNA in the federal inventory is in the national forest system, where the USFS has the power to designate certain limited areas as research natural areas. However, these lands tend to be much less visible and more subject to administrative whims.

11. Richard Thom and Mike Leahy, *Status of State Natural Area Programs 2015* (Natural Areas Association Report, 2015), p. 9.

12. *Ibid.*, pp. 7–9.

13. *Ibid.*, p. 8.

14. In some states, local, federal, and private land can be granted protective SNA status with the owner's blessing. All the data sources for the information in Table 3.1 discussed in this chapter can be found in the appendix.

15. This figure is intended as a proportion or ratio rather than a literal measurement of how much state land has an SNA designation—it is important to remember that some states include SNAs on local, federal, and private land, so, for example, Wisconsin, with many nonstate lands protected in its SNA program, scores 25.6% on this measure, but there is not technically a quarter of state land as SNAs but closer to 13.7%.

16. North Carolina Division of Parks and Recreation, *Systemwide Plan for North Carolina State Parks* (Report, 2018), pp. 1.11, 2.4, available at: https://www.ncparks .gov/media/1341/open.

17. Minnesota Department of Natural Resources, *Minnesota Scientific and Natural Areas Sanctuaries—Restricted Entry* (Webpage, 2022), available at: https://www .dnr.state.mn.us/snas/sanctuaries.html.

18. See, for example, Chelsey Lewis, "Parfrey's Glen, Pewits Nest, Rock Island to Open for Visitors Again" in *Milwaukee Journal-Sentinel* (April 13, 2021); Natural Areas Association, *State Natural Areas Program Roundtable: State Reports* (Wisconsin

State Natural Areas Video Report, November 17, 2021), available at: https://www
.naturalareas.org/2021_state_natural_areas_progr.php.

19. Laura Holson, "Is Geotagging on Instagram Ruining Natural Wonders?
Some Say Yes" in *New York Times* (November 29, 2018).

20. Natural Areas Association, Wisconsin video report.

21. *Ibid.* This is a theme present in most of the video reports from state natural
areas directors to the Natural Areas Association roundtable.

22. To get a sense of the scale and scope of the effort to restore SNAs and/or keep
them ecologically healthy, see, Missouri Department of Natural Resources, *Missouri
Natural Areas Inspection Report 2018–2019* (2019), available at: https://www.natural
areas.org/docs/Missouri_Natural_Areas_Inspection_Report_20182019_final.pdf.

23. Natural Areas Association video reports.

24. In fact, starting in the 1970s, restorationists working in the county forest
preserve systems of the Chicago area and northeastern Illinois were perhaps the
pioneers of the volunteer-led ecological restoration movement and "wrote the
book," so to speak, on restoring tallgrass prairies and closed and open oak savannas.
For a detailed profile of their efforts and achievements, see, William Stevens, *Miracle under the Oaks* (New York: Pocket Books, 1995).

25. Wisconsin Department of Natural Resources, *2021 SNA Volunteer Report*
(2022), p. 3, available at: https://widnr.widen.net/s/bpqnjh97dc/sna_2021_volunteer
_report.

26. *Ibid.* and Stevens. Perhaps one of the very best examples of citizen volunteer
groups developing powerful partnerships to achieve things the public agency alone
cannot would be Wisconsin's Ice Age Trail Alliance. Not only does this group plan
and advocate for the completion of Wisconsin's 1,200-mile Ice Age National Scenic
Trail, but they do extensive trail maintenance, habitat restoration, land acquisition,
land management (of their own preserves along key spots on the trail), and fundraising. See, Ice Age Trail Alliance (Homepage, 2023), available at: https://www.iceage
trail.org/.

27. See, for example, the story of how grassroots restoration volunteers rallied
when the Cook County, Illinois, Board placed a moratorium on all restoration
activities on forest preserve lands after complaints from well-connected landowners living adjacent to the preserves. Steven Davis, "The Politics of Urban Natural
Areas Management at the Local Level: A Case Study" in *Kentucky Journal of Equine,
Agriculture, and Natural Resources Law* (Vol. 2, No. 2, 2010), pp. 143–144.

28. Mississippi Valley Conservancy, *Conservation Easements* (Webpage, 2022),
available at: https://mississippivalleyconservancy.org/land-protection/conservation
-easements.

29. North Shore Land Alliance, *Purchase of Development Rights* (Webpage, undated), available at: https://northshorelandalliance.org/land-conservation/purchase-of
-development-rights/.

30. For a good example of this process, see, The Nature Conservancy, *Quincy
Bluff and Wetlands* (Webpage, 2022), available at: https://www.nature.org/en-us
/get-involved/how-to-help/places-we-protect/quincy-bluff-and-wetlands/. This process is precisely what Bruce Yandle and other free marketers object to regarding pri-

vate conservation, despite it being a form of conservation that would seem ought to please a free marketer. See, Bruce Yandle, "Land Trusts or Land Agents?" in *PERC Bulletin* (Vol. 17, No. 4, Winter 1999).

31. Anne Riddle and Katie Hoover, *Wilderness: Overview, Management, and Statistics* (Congressional Research Service Report, July 29, 2022), p. 3.

32. John Muir, *My First Summer in the Sierra*, illustrated edition (New York: Houghton Mifflin Harcourt, 2011), p. 100.

33. Nash, pp. 141–160.

34. Riddle and Hoover, pp. 3–4.

35. Moreno Di Marco, Simon Ferrier, Tom Harwood, Andrew Hoskins and James Watson "Wilderness Areas Halve the Extinction Risk of Terrestrial Biodiversity" in *Nature* (Vol. 573, September 18, 2019), pp. 582–585; T. Ryan McCarley and Jocelyn Aycrigg, "Biodiversity within the National Wilderness Preservation System: How Well Do Wilderness Areas Represent Species Richness across the Contiguous United States?" in *International Journal of Wilderness* (Vol. 20, No. 3, December 2020).

36. Curiously, all prior studies that attempt to inventory state wilderness systems (Stankey, Petersen, Propst and Dawson, and Holeton and Takacs) ignore Pennsylvania's state "wild areas" program as they all seem to have determined that the program does not meet the criteria to be considered a wilderness system. However, in terms of prohibition of extractive activities and motorized transportation, minimum preserve size, and other aspects of management goals, these preserves are very much akin to any other wilderness areas. The sticking point seems to be existing roads and buildings like cabins. Pennsylvania guidelines ban driving and building new roads or cabins but allow existing infrastructure to remain in place, even if unused. For the purposes of this study, that is similar enough to the goals of wilderness management to include here, especially since so few states go to the trouble of having *any* category even slightly close to purposely managed wilderness. See, Pennsylvania Department of Conservation and Natural Resources, Bureau of Forestry, *Guidelines and Definitions for Natural Areas and Wild Areas* (Report, June 2016), available at: http://elibrary .dcnr.pa.gov/PDFProvider.ashx?action=PDFStream&docID=1742466&chk sum=&revision=0&docName=MP2015_WNA_Definitions_Guidelines&native Ext=pdf&PromptToSave=False&Size=1143132&ViewerMode=2&overlay=0; Miranda Holeton and David Takacs, "U.S. State-Based Wilderness Law: An Evaluation" in *Hastings Environmental Law Journal* (Vol. 28, No. 1, Winter 2022), pp. 25–28; Blake Propst and Chad Dawson, "State-Designated Wilderness in the United States: A National Review" in *International Journal of Wilderness* (Vol. 14, No. 1, April 2008), pp. 19–24; Mark Peterson, "Wilderness by State Mandate: A Survey of State-Designated Wilderness Areas" in *Natural Areas Journal* (Vol. 16, No. 3, 1996), pp. 192–197; George Stankey, "Wilderness Preservation Activity at the State Level: A National Survey" in *Natural Areas Journal* (Vol. 4, No. 4, 1984), pp. 20–28.

37. These ad hoc wilderness areas are not necessarily less permanent than those embedded within established systems as a number of these ad hoc units have been designated as a result of legislative action. See, Holeton and Takacs.

38. *Ibid.*, pp. 42–43.

39. *Ibid.*, pp. 43–44.

40. *Ibid.*, pp. 38–39.

41. Baxter State Park (Homepage, undated), available at: https://baxterstatepark .org.

CHAPTER 4

1. IN Code § 14-23-4-1 (2021).

2. Most prominent in this line of critique is Charles Reich, *Bureaucracy and the Forests* (Santa Barbara, CA: Center for the Study of Democratic Institutions, 1962). See also, William Alverson, Don Waller, and Walter Kuhlmann, *Wild Forests: Conservation Biology and Public Policy* (Washington, DC: Island Press, 2013), pp. 136–150.

3. Alaska Department of Natural Resources, Division of Forestry and Fire Protection, *Alaska's State Forests* (Webpage, undated), available at: https://forestry.alaska .gov/stateforests.

4. In the former, this might be explained by a scarcity in forestlands, but in the West, it is probably better explained by the presence of so much national forest land in their states, along with state land inventories dominated by trust lands.

5. For a good overview of the forest history of this period, see, Douglas MacCleery, *American Forests: A History of Resiliency and Recovery* (Forest History Society, 2011), pp. 13–28.

6. Forest Stearns, "History of the Lake States Forests: Natural and Human Impacts" in J. M. Webster (editor), *Lake States Regional Forest Resources Assessment: Technical Papers* (USDA Forest Service General Technical Report NC-189, 1997), pp. 8–29.

7. The notable exception to this pattern was Wisconsin, which kept county ownership and management of tax-forfeited land but with close state oversight. Steven Davis, "The Forests Nobody Wanted: The Politics of Land Management in the County Forests of the Upper Midwest" in *Journal of Land Use and Environment Law* (Vol. 28, No. 2, Spring 2013).

8. Oregon Department of Forestry, *About Oregon's State Forests* (Webpage, undated), available at: https://www.oregon.gov/ODF/Working/Pages/StateForests .aspx (histories found under each individual state forest).

9. The extent to which Minnesota mixes and merges its regular land management classifications and its trust lands is quite unique as most states with extensive trust holding manage them strictly segregated from their other lands due to the built-in fiduciary duties they imply, which seem to be at odds with true multiple use principles.

10. Robert Nelson, *State-Owned Lands in the Eastern United States: Lessons from State Land Management in Practice* (PERC Public Lands Report, March 2018), p. 20.

11. The former law authorized the USFS to purchase land within headwaters of navigable waterways, while the latter extended federal land acquisition to pretty much anywhere. Lincoln Bramwell and James Lewis, "The Law That Nationalized the US Forest Service" in *Forest History Today* (Spring–Fall 2011), pp. 8–16.

12. Michael Berry, "'Up for Grabs' Chronicles the Complicated History of Maine's Public Reserved Lands" in *Portland Press Herald* (November 14, 2021).

13. *Ibid.*

14. Jon Van Dyke, "What Are the 'Ceded Lands' of Hawaii?" in *Honolulu Civil Beat* (October 25, 2010).

15. Lacy Hamner, Statehood Entitlement Manager, Alaska DNR, Division of Mining, Land, and Water, email correspondence (June 8, 2022).

16. Friends of Florida State Forests, *Florida State Forests History* (Webpage, 2022), available at: https://development.floridastateforests.org/florida-state-forests-history/.

17. See, for example, Mac Aubrey, "The Cutting Controversy of Logging in Indiana State Forests" in *The Horizon* (February 6, 2019).

18. This is from timber revenue. Nelson, p. 28. In Michigan, gas, oil, and mineral revenues go to a state park trust fund and general revenues.

19. Anne Riddle, *Timber Harvesting on Federal Lands* (Congressional Research Service Report #R45688, October 25, 2022), pp. 7–8.

20. Robert Leverett, "Definitions and History" in Mary Davis (editor), *Eastern Old-Growth Forests: Prospects for Rediscovery and Recovery* (Washington, DC: Island Press, 1996), pp. 3–17.

21. Bruce G. Marcot and Jack Ward Thomas, *Of Spotted Owls, Old Growth, and New Policies: A History since the Interagency Scientific Committee Report* (USDA Forest Service, General Technical Report PNW-GTR-408, September 1997), pp. 9–12.

22. Tomas Koontz, *Federalism in the Forest* (Washington, DC: Georgetown University Press, 2002).

23. Oregon has a modest system of county and community forests at the local level. Of that 4% figure cited, 3% is state forest, 1% is locally owned.

24. Nelson, pp. 15, 23, 27–28; Holly Fretwell and Shawn Regan, *Divided Lands: State vs. Federal Management in the West* (PERC Public Lands Report, March 3, 2015), pp. 9–10, 14–16.

25. Nelson, p. 22.

26. Generally, a mature forest is understood as older than about 80 years.

27. See, for example, Holly Fretwell, *Do We Get What We Pay For?* (PERC Report, 1999).

28. See, for example, Robert Mitchell et al., "Old Forests and Endangered Woodpeckers: Old-Growth in the Southern Coastal Plain" in *Natural Areas Journal* (Vol. 29, No. 3, 2009), pp. 301–310; Jared Nunery and William Keeton, "Forest Carbon Storage in the Northeastern United States: Net Effects of Harvesting Frequency, Post-Harvest Retention, and Wood Products" in *Forest Ecology and Management* (Vol. 259, No. 8, March 31, 2010), pp. 1363–1375.

29. Davis, p. 215. These federal protected categories include wilderness areas, wilderness study areas, old-growth areas, research natural areas, special management areas, and semi-primitive nonmotorized areas. That last category allows only very limited selective logging and no roads or motorized vehicles, while the other categories generally prohibit all logging.

30. Davis, pp. 205–206, note 43.

31. Tomas Koontz, "Differences between State and Federal Public Forest Management: The Importance of Rules" in *Publius: The Journal of Federalism* (Vol. 27, No. 1, Winter 1997), p. 29.

32. See, for example, Indiana Department of Natural Resources, *The Role of Forest Openings* (Issue Paper, undated), available at: https://www.in.gov/dnr/forest ry/files/fo-Role_of_Forest_Openings.pdf.

33. See, for example, Carl Jordan, "Ecological Effects of Forest Clearcutting" in National Research Council, *Ecological Knowledge and Environmental Problem-Solving: Concepts and Case Studies* (Washington, DC: National Academies Press, 1986), pp. 345–357.

34. David Cleland, Larry Leefers, and Donald Dickmann, "Ecology and Management of Aspen: A Lake States Perspective" in Wayne Shepperd et al. (editors), *Sustaining Aspen in Western Landscapes: Symposium Proceedings* (USDA Forest Service Proceedings, RMRS-P-18, 2001), pp. 81–100.

35. Nelson, p. 30.

36. Ted Sickinger, "Forestry Board Moves Ahead with Controversial Habitat Conservation Plan for State Forests" in *The Oregonian* (October 8, 2020).

37. Alex Baumhardt, "OR Supreme Court Declines Logging Case" in *Corvallis Advocate* (September 23, 2022).

38. Sickinger.

39. Evan Bush, "What Is the Future of Washington State's Forests?" in *Aberdeen Daily World* (December 30, 2019).

40. MT Code § 77-5-116 (2021).

41. Jonathan Mohr, "Forestry Subcommittee Considers New Timber Target" in *Session Daily* (Minnesota House of Representatives News Site, March 7, 2018), available at: https://www.house.leg.state.mn.us/SessionDaily/Story/13062.

42. Danielle Kaeding, "Northern Wisconsin Residents Claim DNR Is Violating Its Own Standards to Protect Water Quality" in *Wisconsin Public Radio* (July 18, 2022).

43. *Ibid.*

44. Nelson, p. 29.

45. *Ibid.* Nelson argues that this discrepancy may be due to the fact that the Michigan DNR gets to keep this leasing revenue, while the USFS does not—it goes to the U.S. Treasury. This tends to disincentive the approval of energy products on national forests. This should be no surprise; for federal managers, the prospect of intensive energy production on national forest land is all the downside of damage and pollution with none of the upside (revenue).

46. Nelson, p. 29.

47. Uma Outka, "State Lands in Modern Public Land Law" in *Stanford Environmental Law Journal* (Vol. 36, 2017), p. 207.

48. Pennsylvania Office of the Governor, *PA Governor Rendell Signs Moratorium Protecting Sensitive State Forest Land from Future Natural Gas Leases* (Press Release, October 26, 2010), available at: https://www.prnewswire.com/news-releases/pa-gover nor-rendell-signs-moratorium-protecting-sensitive-state-forest-land-from-future -natural-gas-leases-105793788.html.

49. Outka, p. 208.

50. *Ibid.*, p. 206.

51. Ben Elgin, "U.S. Public Forests Are Cashing In on Dubious Carbon Offsets" in *Bloomberg* (April 28, 2022); Debra Kahn and Jordan Wolman, "Red and Blue States See Green in Forest Offsets" in *Politico* (April 18, 2023).

52. Elgin.

53. *Ibid.*

54. *Ibid.*

55. Tomas Koontz, "Federal and State Public Forest Administration in the New Millenium: Revisiting Herbert Kaufman's *The Forest Ranger*" in *Public Administration Review* (January/February 2007), p. 20.

56. Wilderness Act of 1964, Public Law 88-577, § 1 (September 3, 1964), 78 Stat. 890; National Environmental Policy Act of 1969 (83 Stat. 852) [42 U.S.C. 4321 et seq.]; Endangered Species Act of 1973, 16 U.S.C., Ch. 35, §1531 et seq.; National Forest Management Act of 1976, Public Law 94-588 (October 22, 1976), 90 Stat. 2949.

57. Outka, p. 197.

58. *Ibid.*

59. *Ibid.*, pp. 197–198.

60. In fact, it was this element of NFMA, and not the Endangered Species Act, that was invoked in Judge Dwyer's monument ruling on the spotted owl in 1991.

61. Koontz (1997), p. 28.

62. *Ibid.*, p. 17.

63. Defenders of Wildlife, *State Forestry Laws* (Report, July 2000), available at: https://defenders.org/sites/default/files/publications/state_forestry_laws.pdf.

64. Koontz (2007), p. 156.

65. Koontz (1997), p. 24.

66. Multiple-Use Sustained-Yield Act of 1960, Public Law 86-517 (June 12, 1960), 74 Stat. 215 (16 U.S.C. 531 § 4 a.).

67. Koontz (2007), p. 156.

68. Pinchot Institute Report quoted in Nelson, p. 23.

69. Sally Fairfax, "Thinking the Unthinkable: States as Public Land Managers" in *Hastings Environmental Law Journal* (Vol. 14, No. 1, Winter 2008), p. 527.

70. William Niro, "Constitutional Law—Standing to Sue in Environmental Litigation: Sierra Club v. Morton" in *DePaul Law Review* (Vol. 22, No. 2, Winter 1973).

71. Koontz (2007), p. 156.

72. David Erickson, "Forest Service-Funded Study: Timber Sale Lawsuits Impact Local Jobs, Tax Revenue" in *Missoulian* (May 8, 2015). To be clear, though, a sale that is being challenged is not necessarily being blocked. A different estimate of Region 1 finds that ultimately only 4% of sales acreage are actually enjoined, despite ongoing lawsuits. Glenn Kessler, "Montana Senator Twice Gets His Facts Wrong on Timber Sales and Litigation" in *Washington Post* (February 25, 2015).

73. U.S. Government Accountability Office, *Public Timber: Federal and State Programs Differ Significantly in Pacific Northwest* (GAO/RCED-96-108, May 1996), p. 10.

74. Amanda Miner, Robert Malmsheimer, and Denise Keele, "Twenty Years of Forest Service Land Management Litigation" in *Journal of Forestry* (Vol. 112, No. 1, January 2014), pp. 33–36.

75. *Ibid.*, pp. 35–38.

76. *Ibid.*, p. 40. This conclusion has also been reached by Elise Jones and Cameron Taylor, "Litigating Agency Change: The Impact of the Courts and the Ad-

ministrative Appeals Process on the Forest Service" in *Policy Studies Journal* (Vol. 23, No. 3, Summer 1995), pp. 310–336.

77. Koontz (1997), p. 30.

78. Koontz (2007), p. 157.

79. Koontz (1997), p. 36.

80. *Ibid.*, p. 31.

81. U.S. Government Accountability Office, pp. 4, 7.

82. Koontz (1997), p. 37.

83. Herbert Kaufman, *The Forest Ranger: A Study in Administrative Behavior* (Baltimore, MD: Johns Hopkins University Press, 1960).

84. Koontz (2007), p. 159.

85. National Association of Forest Service Retirees, *Increasing Workforce Capacity to Increase the Pace and Scale of Restoration on National Forest System Lands* (Report, July 25, 2019), pp. 3–4, available at: https://www.nafsr.org/advocacy/2019/072619%20 Workforce%20Capacity%20Study.pdf.

86. Lynne Westphal et al., "USDA Forest Service Employee Diversity during a Period of Workforce Contraction" in *Journal of Forestry* (Vol. 120, No. 4, 2022), pp. 434–452. While the USFS has made great strides in diversifying its ranks, this is still a work in progress as the agency has been accused of still fostering a hostile work environment for women and people of color. See, for example, James Lewis, *The Greatest Good: A Centennial History of the Forest Service* (Durham, NC: Forest History Society, 2005), pp. 163–185.

87. For USFS 1960 statistics, see, Koontz (2007), p. 153. For 2018 statistics, see, National Association of Forest Service Retirees, p. 5.

88. *Ibid.*, p. 157.

89. National Association of State Foresters, *State Foresters by the Numbers* (Report, December 2021), p. 7, available at: https://www.stateforesters.org/wp-content /uploads/2022/01/2020-State-Foresters-by-the-Numbers-01272022.pdf.

90. *Ibid.*, p. 159.

91. *Ibid.*, p. 158.

92. Greg Brown and Charles C. Harris, "The United States Forest Service: Changing of the Guard" in *Natural Resources Journal* (Vol. 32, No. 3, Summer 1992), p. 455.

93. Koontz (2007), p. 162.

94. *Ibid.*, p. 157.

95. Davis, pp. 218–219. This county system is bigger than Wisconsin state forest acreage as well as the state's national forest acreage.

96. Koontz (2007), p. 157.

97. *Ibid.*, p. 160.

CHAPTER 5

1. While the purpose and scope of this volume preclude a detailed legal analysis of the debate over federal versus state primary in wildlife law, suffice it say that Sandra Zellmer, Martin Nie, and their colleagues have forcefully challenged the

state supremacy model of wildlife management as reflected in the opening quote from the Association of Fish and Wildlife Agencies. They argue that especially when it comes to the 28% of America that is federal land, federal wildlife managers have at least coequal jurisdiction as "co-trustees" to manage not just habitat but wildlife populations themselves. And, of course, the federal government maintains primacy in areas where Congress has granted full jurisdiction, such as endangered species, marine mammals, and migratory birds. Others, such as Lane Kisonak, have strenuously rebutted Nie's assertions that states are not the primary actors in managing wildlife within their state's borders. Sandra Zellmer, Martin Nie, Christopher Barnes, Jonathan Haber, Julie Joly, and Kenneth Pitt, "Fish and Wildlife Management on Federal Lands: Debunking State Supremacy" in *Environmental Law* (Vol. 47, 2017), pp. 797–936; Lane Kisonak, "Fish and Wildlife Management on Federal Lands" in *Environmental Law* (Vol. 50, No. 4, 2020), pp. 935–971.

2. The very first state agencies were created in New Hampshire and California, both in 1878. Edward E. Langenau Jr. and Charles W. Ostrom Jr., "Organizational and Political Factors Affecting State Wildlife Management" in *Wildlife Society Bulletin* (Vol. 12, No. 2, Summer 1984), p. 108.

3. Joan Van Tol, "The Public Trust Doctrine: A New Approach to Environmental Preservation" in *West Virginia Law Review* (Vol. 81, No. 3, April 1979), p. 460.

4. Langenau and Ostrom, p. 108.

5. Robert Nelson, *State-Owned Lands in the Eastern United States: Lessons from State Land Management in Practice* (PERC Public Lands Report, March 2018), p. 42.

6. There is great diversity in what states call their wildlife lands, including wildlife management areas, wildlife areas, conservation areas, game refuges, wildlife sanctuaries, critical habitat areas, management areas, fishery areas, wildlife habitat areas, game production areas, and ecological reserves. Because *wildlife management areas* is the most common term, this is used as the default term for this category throughout Chapter 5.

7. However, owning perpetual conservation easements, rather than merely having a simple lease, is something of a middle ground that makes long-term investment more attractive.

8. Sean McCain, "Political Polarization Is Bad for State Wildlife Management" in *Hunt Science* (Blog, June 13, 2018), available at: https://huntscienceus.wordpress .com/2018/06/13/political-polarization-has-bad-implications-for-state-wildlife -management/.

9. *Ibid.*

10. Association of Fish and Wildlife Agencies, *The State Conservation Machine* (Report, 2017).

11. Langenau and Ostrom, p. 107.

12. Michael Manfredo et al., *America's Wildlife Values: The Social Context of Wildlife Management in the U.S.* (Colorado State University Department of Human Dimensions of Natural Resources, 2018), p. 14.

13. Manfredo et al. (2018), pp. 13–14.

14. Michael Manfredo et al., "The Changing Sociocultural Context of Wildlife Conservation" in *Conservation Biology* (Volume 34, No. 6, 2020), pp. 1554–1558.

15. Manfredo et al. (2018), pp. 21, 32.

16. National Caucus of Environmental Legislators, *State Wildlife Agency Funding* (Fact Sheet, undated), available at: https://www.ncelenviro.org/app/uploads/2022/10 /Cons.-State-Wildlife-Agency-Funding-Fact-Sheet.pdf.

17. Fred Koontz, "State Wildlife Agencies Should Protect All Wildlife" in *Wildland Network Blog* (Blog, May 31, 2018), available at: https://wildlandsnetwork.org /news/state-wildlife-agencies-should-protect-all-wildlife.

18. Manfredo et al. (2018), p. 75.

19. Melissa Koval and Angela Mertig, "Attitudes of the Michigan Public and Wildlife Agency Personnel toward Lethal Wildlife Management" in *Wildlife Society Bulletin* (Vol. 32, No. 1, Spring 2004), pp. 232–243.

20. Cynthia Jacobson et al., "State Fish and Wildlife Agency Culture: Access Points to Leverage Major Change" in *Conservation Science and Practice* (Vol. 4, No. 2, February 2022), pp. 1–2.

21. Ayeisha Brinson and Delwin Benson, *Values and Attitudes of National Wildlife Refuge Managers and Biologists: Report to Respondents* (U.S. Department of the Interior, U.S. Geological Survey, Open File Report OF 02-459, 2002), p. 13.

22. *Ibid.*, p. 6.

23. Manfredo et al. (2018), pp. 78, 80; U.S. Fish and Wildlife Service, *U.S. Fish and Wildlife Service Work Environment Survey* (Supplemental Statistical Report, September 29, 2017), pp. 27–28.

24. Robert Fischman, "The Significance of National Wildlife Refuges in the Development of U.S. Conservation Policy" in *Journal of Land Use and Environmental Law* (Vol. 21, No. 1, 2005), pp. 16–17.

25. *Ibid.*, p. 16.

26. *Ibid.*

27. Langenau and Ostrom, p. 115.

28. Bruce Rocheleau, "The Politics of State Wildlife Management: Why Anti-Conservation Forces Usually Win" in *Medium* (August 14, 2019), available at: https:// medium.com/@brucerocheleau/the-politics-of-state-wildlife-management-why -anti-conservation-forces-usually-win-26bfae92bca1#_edn53.

29. Wildlife for All, *State Wildlife Commissions* (Webpage, 2023), available at: https:// wildlifeforall.us/resources/overview-state-wildlife-management/state-wildlife -commissions/.

30. Wildlife for All, *Solution* (Webpage, 2023), available at: https://wildlifefor all.us/what-we-do/solution/.

31. Emma Cotton, "Wild Divide: A Debate Over Wildlife Management in Vermont Runs Deep" in *VT Digger* (May 7, 2024).

32. Jacobson et al., pp. 4–5.

33. Manfredo et al. (2020), pp. 1551–1552.

34. Manfredo et al. (2018), pp. 48–51.

35. Nathan Rott, "Decline in Hunters Threatens How U.S. Pays for Conservation" in *NPR News* (Webpage, March 20, 2018), available at: https://www.npr .org/2018/03/20/593001800/decline-in-hunters-threatens-how-u-s-pays-for-cons ervation. The percentage of hunters varies by region from 10% in the south-central

states to 3% in the Pacific Coast and New England. U.S. Fish and Wildlife Service, *2022 National Survey of Fishing, Hunting, and Wildlife-Associated Recreation* (Report, September 2023), pp. 22–23. The percentage of Americans 16 years old and older who hunt was calculated by averaging the male and female percentages at the 97:100 male-female ratio that marks the U.S. population.

36. Rott.

37. U.S. Fish and Wildlife Service, *2022 National Survey of Fishing, Hunting, and Wildlife-Associated Recreation*, p. 30.

38. *Ibid.*, pp. 36–37, 42.

39. *Ibid.*, p. 4.

40. See, as examples, David Hewitt, "Public Attitudes and Predator Control: The Biologist's Puppeteer?" in *The Role of Predator Control as a Tool in Game Management* (Kerrville, TX, Symposium, Extension Publication SP-113, April 18–19, 2001), available at: http://agrilife.org/texnat/files/2010/09/007.pdf; Michael Manfredo et al., "Public Acceptance of Wildlife Trapping in Colorado" in *Wildlife Society Bulletin* (Vol. 27, 1999), pp. 499–508; Tara Teel, Richard Krannich, and Robert Schmidt, "Utah Stakeholders' Attitudes toward Selected Cougar and Black Bear Management Practices" in *Wildlife Society Bulletin* (Vol. 30, No. 1, Spring 2002), pp. 2–15; Rebecca Niemiec et al., "Rapid Changes in Public Perception Toward a Conservation Initiative" in *Conservation Science and Practice* (Vol. 4, No. 4, April 2022); Rocheleau.

41. Rocheleau.

42. Wayne Pacelle, "Forging a New Wildlife Management Paradigm: Integrating Animal Protection Values" in *Human Dimensions of Wildlife: An International Journal* (Vol. 3, No. 2, 1998), p. 47.

43. Rocheleau.

44. *Ibid.*

45. Jeanne Clarke and Daniel McCool, *Staking Out the Terrain: Power and Performance among Natural Resource Agencies*, 2nd edition (Albany: State University of New York Press, 1996). Conversely, though, while the USFWS is somewhat weak, its broad constituency is not nearly as intensely focused as state agencies are on the demands of hunters and anglers, and thus the agency seems freer to adopt ecosystem-based approaches and allocate many more resources to nongame species.

46. Rocheleau.

47. Manfredo et al. (2018), p. 58.

48. Depending on the regional population, this occurred between 2011 and 2020.

49. Ted Joosse, "Wolf Populations Drop as More States Allow Hunting" in *Scientific American* (September 7, 2021). A separate and much rarer subspecies, the Mexican wolf, barely holds on in the desert Southwest.

50. Cassidy Randall, "For Wolves, the Culture War Is Extremely Deadly" in *Rolling Stone* (April 5, 2022).

51. Joosse.

52. In December 2023, the first batch of 5 wolves was released on public land in Grand County after several unsuccessful court challenges to the referendum

result. Ultimately, the plans are for about 50 wolves to be released over the next few years. Elliot Wenzler, "Colorado Releases First 5 Wolves as Controversial Reintroduction Gets Underway" in *Vail Daily* (December 19, 2023).

53. Dana Hoeg et al., *Economic Wins and Losses from Reintroducing Wolves in Colorado* (Regional Economic Development Institute Report, April 2023), available at: https://csuredi.org/wp-content/uploads/2023/04/REDI-Report-Apr23-Wolf-Reintroduction-1.pdf.

54. Ted Williams, "America's New War on Wolves and Why It Must Be Stopped" in *Yale Environment 360* (February 17, 2022), available at: https://e360.yale.edu/features/americas-new-war-on-wolves-and-why-it-must-be-stopped.

55. The gray wolf has been on a roller-coaster of ESA listings and delistings since the ESA was first passed. Here is a very brief timeline: January 1974—wolves put on endangered species list; 1995–1996—wolves reintroduced to Yellowstone and central Idaho; February 2007—USFWS delists the Great Lakes population; February 2008—USFWS delists the Northern Rockies population; July 2008—federal court overturns Rockies delisting, wolves back under ESA protection; September 2008—federal court overturns Great Lakes delisting; April 2011—Congress passes law overruling ESA and delisting Rockies population, except for Wyoming; December 2011—USFWS delists Great Lakes population; August 2012—USFWS delists Wyoming population; September 2014—federal court orders Wyoming population back on ESA; December 2014—federal court orders Great Lakes population back on ESA; March 2017—federal appeals court restores Wyoming population delisting decision; October 2020—Trump administration orders all wolf populations delisted; February 2022—federal courts order all wolves except Rockies population (because of legislative delisting) back on ESA. Humane Society of the U.S., *Timeline: Gray Wolves and the Endangered Species Act* (Fact Sheet, September 22, 2021), available at: https://blog.humanesociety.org/wp-content/uploads/2021/09/Wolf-timeline-9-22-21.pdf.

56. Williams.

57. William Funk, "Wyoming Is Waging a War on Wolves" in *Sierra Magazine* (April 2, 2018).

58. Randall; Jennifer Sherry, *Six of the Worst States to Be a Wolf* (Natural Resources Defense Council Experts Blog, May 17, 2021), available at: https://www.nrdc.org/bio/jennifer-sherry/six-worst-states-be-wolf.

59. Jon Waterman, "Alaska's Slaughter of Bears Must Stop" in *New York Times* (August 24, 2023).

60. *Ibid.*

61. Sherry.

62. Rocheleau.

63. Joosse.

64. *Ibid.*

65. Paul Smith, "In an Unprecedented Move of Rejecting a Natural Resources Board Decision, the DNR Has Announced a Quota of 130 for the Wolf Hunt" in *Milwaukee Journal-Sentinel* (October 4, 2021). It is not fully clear if the DNR actually has the legal authority to reject the Natural Resources Board's imposed quota,

as this had never happened before, but it is a measure of how fanatically hostile to the welfare of the wolf the board's decision was that a fairly conservative agency felt it necessary to reject the decision on principle.

66. In the interim, the DNR has finalized a new wolf management plan in October 2023 that, to the dismay of antiwolf activists, lifts the former unrealistically low population cap of 350. While no formal cap is stated in the plan, the new unofficial goal is said to be between 800 and 1,200 wolves. This would mean fairly modest wolf hunting quotas when the Great Lakes wolf is removed from endangered species protection. Henry Redman, "Wisconsin DNR Board Votes to Approve Wolf Management Plan without Numerical Population Goal" in *Wisconsin Examiner* (October 25, 2023).

67. Williams. It should also be mentioned that along with old-line hunting and sportsman organizations that stress hunting ethics and fair chase, there are also some newer organizations, like Backcountry Hunters of America, that stress responsible hunting and strong support of public land and its ecological health.

68. Manfredo et al. (2020), p. 1558.

69. Association of Fish and Wildlife Agencies, p. 9.

70. *Ibid.*; Andrew Moore, "The Role of Hunting in Wildlife Conservation, Explained" in *NC State College of Natural Resources News* (February 24, 2021), available at: https://cnr.ncsu.edu/news/2021/02/the-role-of-hunting-in-wildlife-conservation -explained/.

71. Association of Fish and Wildlife Agencies, p. 9.

72. Alex Brown, "A Bipartisan Push Could Change State Wildlife Protection" in *Michigan Advance* (March 5, 2021).

73. Bruce Stein et al., *Reversing America's Wildlife Crisis* (National Wildlife Federation Report, March 2018).

74. Kenneth Rosenberg et al., "Decline of the North American Avifauna" in *Science* (Vol. 366, No. 6461, September 19, 2019), pp. 120–124.

75. Association of Fish and Wildlife Agencies, *State Wildlife Action Plans-Blueprints for Conserving Our Nation's Fish and Wildlife* (Webpage, undated), available at: https://www.fishwildlife.org/afwa-informs/state-wildlife-action-plans.

76. Brown.

77. Ruth Musgrave, *Fish and Wildlife Conservation: Agency Relevance and Funding* (NCEL Presentation, November 12, 2019), p. 5, available at: https://www.ncelenviro .org/app/uploads/2021/07/Fish-and-Wildlife-Conservation-Agency-Relevance -and-Funding-Presentation-2019.pdf.

78. Rocheleau; Rott.

79. Association of Fish and Wildlife Agencies, p. 9.

80. National Caucus of Environmental Legislators; National Wildlife Federation, *Mechanisms for State-Level Wildlife Funding* (Fact Sheet, October 2019), available at: http://statewildlifetoolkit.nwf.org/wp-content/uploads/2019/10/Wildlife -Funding-Mechanisms.pdf.

81. David Lien, *State Wildlife Areas Deserve Everyone's Support* (Backcountry Hunters and Anglers Blog, July 15, 2020), available at: https://www.backcountry hunters.org/state_wildlife_areas_deserve_everyone_s_support.

82. Miles Blumhardt, "Planning a Trip to a Colorado State Wildlife Area? Now There's a Pass for That" in *The Coloradan* (March 30, 2021).

83. Responsive Management, *Significant Majority of Americans Support the Recovering America's Wildlife Act* (Press Release, September 2022), available at: https://responsivemanagement.com/wp-content/uploads/2022/09/rawa_news.pdf.

84. Except perhaps in Missouri and Rhode Island, where they explicitly are considered multiple use lands.

85. Fischman, pp. 16–17.

86. Florida Division of State Lands, *Management of Florida's State-Owned Lands* (Presentation, October 23, 2012), p. 10, available at: https://www.myflorida.com /myflorida/cabinet/agenda12/1023/LandManagement102312.pdf.

87. Nelson, p. 24.

88. *Ibid.*, p. 25.

89. *Ibid.*

90. J. R. Lind, "Activists Rally against Proposed White County Clear-Cutting" in *Nashville Scene* (September 29, 2021); Michael Ray Taylor, "Hardwoods v. Hard Cash: TWRA's Faustian Bargain Protects Some Forests and Dooms Others" in *Nashville Scene* (October 8, 2021).

91. Anita Wadhwani, "Wildlife Officials Release Details of Controversial Plan to Clearcut Wilderness Area" in *Tennessee Lookout* (January 13, 2022).

92. *Ibid.*

93. Taylor.

94. Lind; Taylor.

95. Anita Wadhwani, "Wildlife Officials Scale Down Deforestation Plans in White County" in *Tennessee Lookout* (February 3, 2022).

96. Anita Wadhwani, "After Controversy, Shakeup at Tennessee Wildlife Resources Agency" in *Tennessee Lookout* (May 26, 2022).

97. Christopher Maag, "New Jersey Environmental Agency Accuses Itself of Harming Bird Habitats" in *New York Times* (April 15, 2023).

98. John Myers, "Rift within DNR over Logging in State Wildlife Areas" in *Duluth News Tribune* (August 12, 2019).

99. *Ibid.*

100. Minnesota Department of Natural Resources, *Sustainable Timber Harvest Analysis and Wildlife Management Areas: Frequently Asked Questions* (Fact Sheet, November 7, 2019), available at: https://files.dnr.state.mn.us/forestry/subsection/harvest-analysis/stha-wma-faq.pdf.

101. Myers.

102. Benji Jones, "The US Was Poised to Pass the Biggest Environmental Law in a Generation. What Went Wrong?" in *Vox* (January 11, 2023), available at: https:// www.vox.com/down-to-earth/2023/1/11/23546413/recovering-americas-wildlife-act-congress-2023; Brown.

103. While most mainstream sportsmen's groups support RAWA, including the National Wildlife Federation, many affiliated state wildlife federations, Backcountry Hunters and Anglers, and Ducks Unlimited, there are other hunting groups, according to Rocheleau, that resist the expansion into new funding sources as they

fear it would dilute their standing as the premier constituent of wildlife agencies. He argues that "many hunters want to keep their dominance of funding for their state wildlife agencies and oppose broadening the funding for fear of losing control over them." Rocheleau.

104. Jacobson et al., pp. 3–7.

105. *Ibid.*, p. 8.

CHAPTER 6

1. Jon Souder and Sally Fairfax, *State Trust Lands: History, Management, and Sustainable Use* (Lawrence: University of Kansas Press, 1996), p. 1.

2. Sally Fairfax, "Thinking the Unthinkable: States as Public Land Managers" in *Hastings Environmental Law Journal* (Vol. 14, No. 1, Winter 2008), p. 509.

3. Melinda Bruce and Teresa Rice, "Controlling the Blue Rash: Issues and Trends in State Land Management" in *Land and Water Law Review* (Vol. 29, No. 1, 1994), pp. 23, 25.

4. Peter Culp et al., *State Trust Lands in the West: Fiduciary Duty in a Changing Landscape* (Lincoln Institute of Land Policy, Policy Focus Report, 2015), p. 11.

5. Alaska Department of Natural Resources, Division of Forestry, *Who Owns/Manages Alaska* (Webpage Map, 2007), available at: http://forestry.alaska.gov/Assets/pdfs/posters/07who_owns_alaska_poster.pdf; Lacy Hamner, Statehood Entitlement Manager, Alaska DNR, Division of Mining, Land, and Water, email correspondence (June 8, 2022).

6. Fairfax, p. 509.

7. Culp et al., p. 8.

8. Sean O'Day, "School Trust Lands: The Land Manager's Dilemma between Educational Funding and Environmental Conservation, a Hobson's Choice?" in *NYU Environmental Law Journal* (Vol. 8, 1999), p. 167.

9. *Ibid.*, p. 172.

10. Texas was the exception to this rule. Because it was a sovereign nation before annexation and statehood, it merely kept the lands it already owned and was granted none by the federal government. It developed its own school trust lands system from this land it already owned. Alan Hager, "State School Lands: Does the Federal Trust Mandate Prevent Preservation?" in *Natural Resources and Environment* (Vol. 12, No. 1, Summer 1997), p. 39.

11. O'Day, p. 164, note 5; Chelsea Liddell and Mark Haggerty, *State Trust Lands in Transition: States' Treatment of Permanent Funds* (Headwaters Economics White Paper, November 2019), p. 2.

12. Erin Pounds, "State Trust Lands: Static Management and Shifting Value Perspectives" in *Environmental Law* (Vol. 41, 2011), p. 1334.

13. *Ibid.*, p. 1335.

14. O'Day, p. 183.

15. Fairfax, p. 524.

16. O'Day, p. 163.

17. Sally Fairfax, Jon Souder, and Gretta Goldenman, "The School Trust Lands: A Fresh Look at Conventional Wisdom" in *Environmental Law* (Vol. 22, 1992), p. 833.

18. O'Day, pp. 179–180.

19. *Ibid.*, p. 185.

20. The one exception is California's rather modest 459,000 acres of trust lands, which, since 1980, have been instructed by the state legislature to be managed according to multiple use principles. Hager, pp. 44–45.

21. Bruce and Rice, p. 6, note 23.

22. *Ibid.*, p. 7.

23. Mark Haggerty and Chelsea Liddell, *State Trust Lands in Transition: Understanding the Trust Model* (Headwaters Economics White Paper, November 2019), p. 4.

24. John Myers, "Report Finds Vast Acres of Minnesota Public Land Off-Limits to Public" in *Duluth News Tribune* (August 9, 2020).

25. Bruce and Rice, p. 19. The authors do point out the one possible exception to the difficulties they outline here and that is that numerous scattered parcels might actually increase the chances of hitting a lode of minerals. Bruce and Rice, p. 7.

26. *Ibid.*, p. 7, note 25. In Washington's case, it should be noted that most of this consolidation occurred in the forested western part of the state, while the more arid eastern half still has a checkerboard of widely scattered trust land parcels.

27. Culp et al., p. 10.

28. There have been some court cases and local battles in a few states such as Colorado and Washington that have challenged this basic notion of immediate revenue maximization in favor of broader and more long-term conceptions of value and maximization. This is discussed in more detail further on in the chapter.

29. Stephanie Bertaina et al., *Collaborative Planning on State Trust Lands* (Sonoran Institute and Lincoln Institute of Land Policy Report, April 2006), p. 11.

30. Bruce and Rice, p. 45.

31. Bertaina et al., p. 11. This figure does not necessarily denote exclusive use as some grazing land also holds energy leases or produces timber.

32. Anna Smith, "How States Generate Money from the Land They Own" in *High Country News* (November 27, 2017).

33. Bruce and Rice, p. 56.

34. Smith.

35. Tania Lown-Hecht, *3 Major Differences between State Lands and Public Lands* (Outdoor Alliance Blog Post, April 5, 2016), available at: https://www.outdooralliance.org/blog/2016/3/16/sqirba7p80kpbt808e7fktik3y5iwe.

36. Philip Cook, Michelle Benedum, and Dennis Becker, *Recreation Access and Leasing of State Endowment Lands* (University of Idaho College of Natural Resources, Issue Brief No. 19, September 2016), p. 4.

37. Culp et al., p. 20. Interestingly, Colorado, Utah, and New Mexico also include their state park systems among the trust beneficiaries.

38. Haggerty and Liddell, p. 3.

39. *Ibid.*, p. 9.

40. Bruce and Rice, p. 30–31.

41. New Mexico State Land Office, *Trust Beneficiaries* (Webpage, undated), available at: https://www.nmstatelands.org/about/trust-beneficiaries; Bruce and Rice, p. 18, note 119; Sonoran Institute/Lincoln Institute of Land Policy, *Wyoming Trust Lands and Education Funding* (Report, October 2, 2007), available at: https://sonoran institute.org/files/pdf/wyoming-trust-lands-a-education-funding-10022007.pdf; Wyoming Legislative Service Office, *Wyoming School Land Revenues* (Presentation, May 24, 2022), p. 6, available at: https://wyoleg.gov/InterimCommittee/2022/05 -202206062-01WyomingStateSchoolLandsRevenues_AgStatePublicLandsWater ResCommittee_FINAL.pdf.

42. Bruce and Rice, p. 18; Evan Bush, "What Is the Future of Washington State's Forests?" in *Aberdeen Daily World* (December 30, 2019).

43. Pounds, p. 1340.

44. Pounds, p. 1370; O'Day, p. 168. The first of these cases was *Ervien v. United States*, which strongly confirmed that the New Mexico/Arizona enabling acts did indeed require states to hold their school lands in an actual trust arrangement. O'Day, pp. 168–169.

45. Fairfax, p. 525.

46. Pounds, p. 1349.

47. Fairfax, pp. 527–528.

48. Hager, pp. 44–45.

49. *Ibid.*, p. 45.

50. *Ibid.*

51. Chelsea Liddell and Mark Haggerty, *State Trust Lands in Transition: Challenges from New Uses and Demands* (Headwaters Economics White Paper, November 2019), p. 2.

52. *Ibid.*, p. 3.

53. *Ibid.*, p. 4.

54. Pounds, p. 1359.

55. Pounds, pp. 1351–1354.

56. Liddell and Haggerty, *State Trust Lands in Transition: Challenges from New Uses and Demands*, p. 4.

57. Pounds, p. 1337.

58. Liddell and Haggerty, *State Trust Lands in Transition: Challenges from New Uses and Demands*, p. 3.

59. Liddell and Haggerty, *State Trust Lands in Transition: States' Treatment of Permanent Funds*, pp. 10–18.

60. *Ibid.*, p. 24.

61. *Ibid.*, p. 28.

62. *Ibid.*, p. 21.

63. Wade Budge, "Changing the Focus: Managing State Trust Lands in the Twenty-First Century" in *Journal of Land, Resources, and Environmental Law* (Vol. 19, No. 223, 1999), pp. 244–245.

64. Michael Loring and John Workman, "The Relationship between Land Ownership and Range Condition in Rich County, Utah" in *Journal of Range Management* (Vol. 40, July 4, 1987), pp. 291–293.

65. Cally Carswell, "Threatened Plants on State Lands Have Few Protections" in *High Country News* (November 27, 2017).

66. *Ibid.*

67. *Ibid.*

68. Western Environmental Law Center, *NM State Trust Lands Bonding Report Reveals Monumental Oil and Gas Industry Clean-Up Assurance Shortfall* (News Release, May 20, 2021), available at: https://westernlaw.org/nm-state-trust-lands-bonding -report-reveals-monumental-oil-gas-industry-clean-assurance-shortfall/.

69. Pounds, p. 1336.

70. Bruce and Rice, p. 19.

71. *Ibid.*, p. 35.

72. Isaac Stanley-Becker, Joshua Partlow, and Yvonne Sanchez, "How a Saudi Firm Tapped a Gusher of Water in Drought-Stricken Arizona" in *Washington Post* (July 16, 2023).

73. There is some debate, however, over whether the leases truly were market rate. A 2018 study found the Butler Valley lease to be five times less per acre than market rate ($25 vs. $125). While this would indeed be a violation of the trust doctrine, the difference is a pittance compared to the real value in water being captured for free. Fondomonte points out the tens millions of dollars it has invested in improvements, local wages, and taxes, but this should be irrelevant on trust land since none of that goes to the trust beneficiaries—only the miniscule amount of rent does. Whether or not this transaction is indeed a grotesque violation of the trust doctrine, a glide path for this lease and Fondomonte's subsequent actions were certainly set up by the very powerful and politically connected lobbyists they have employed to secure these arrangements. Stanley-Becker, Partlow, and Sanchez.

In October 2023, Governor Katie Hobbs, a Democrat elected in 2022, decided to terminate one of Fondomonte's leases in the Butler Valley and let three others lapse when they came up for renewal in February 2024. Stacey Barchenger, "Saudi Company with Alfalfa Farms in Arizona to Appeal Governor's Move to Revoke Groundwater Deal" in *Arizona Republic* (October 3, 2023).

74. Liddell and Haggerty, *State Trust Lands in Transition: Challenges from New Uses and Demands*, p. 13.

75. *Ibid.*

76. *Ibid.*

77. Pounds, p. 1362.

78. Gregory Hicks, "Managing State Trust Lands for Ecosystem Health: The Case of Washington State's Range and Agricultural Lands" in *Hastings Environmental Law Journal* (Vol. 6, No. 1, Fall 1999), pp. 1–3.

79. *Ibid.*, pp. 4–6.

80. Culp et al., p. 23.

81. Robert Nelson, *State-Owned Lands in the Eastern United States: Lessons from State Land Management in Practice* (PERC Public Lands Report, March 2018), p. 33.

82. Northwoods Land Trust, *Old-Growth Forest Protection at Sack Lake* (Newsletter, Spring 2020), available at: https://northwoodslandtrust.org/wp-content /uploads/2023/03/2020Spring.pdf.

83. Budge, p. 241.

84. Nathan Rice, "States Work Conservation into Trust Lands Management" in *High Country News* (June 22, 2011).

85. Fairfax, p. 529.

86. Ironically, this forest used to be part of the much-bigger Siuslaw National Forest that surrounds it, but 91,000 acres were transferred to the state in the 1920s as part of an exchange of trust lands with the federal government so Oregon could consolidate some of its scattered holdings. Andy Kerr, "Converting State Trust Lands into Public Lands, Part 2: Focus on Oregon" in *Andy Kerr's Public Lands Blog* (Blog, August 28, 2020), available at: https://www.andykerr.net/kerr-public-lands-blog /2020/8/28/converting-state-trust-lands-into-public-lands-part-2-focus-on-oregon.

87. Smith.

88. "Elliott State Forest Proposal a Win for Oregon" in *The Oregonian* (February 6, 2022).

89. Kerr, "Converting State Trust Lands into Public Lands, Part 2: Focus on Oregon."

90. Andy Kerr, "What to Do with Stranded State Trust Lands in Federal Conservation Areas?" in *Andy Kerr's Public Lands Blog* (Blog, August 14, 2020), available at: https://www.andykerr.net/kerr-public-lands-blog/2020/8/14/what-to-do-with -stranded-state-trust-lands-in-federal-conservation-areas.

91. John Ruple, "The Transfer of Public Lands Movement: The Battle to Take 'Back' Lands That Were Never Theirs" in *Colorado Natural Resources, Energy and Environmental Law Review* (Vol. 29, No. 1, 2018), p. 75.

92. Budge, pp. 237–239.

93. *Ibid.*

94. *Ibid.*, p. 238.

95. Minnesota Office of School Trust Lands, *Boundary Waters Land Exchanges* (Webpage, undated), available at: https://mn.gov/school-trust-lands/projects/bound ary-waters/.

96. Susan Culp and Joe Marlow, *Conserving State Trust Lands: Strategies for the Intermountain West* (Lincoln Institute of Land Policy, Policy Focus Report PF 038, 2015), p. 46.

97. If those concerns seem merely theoretical, consider that Project BOLD, an ambitious state attempt in the 1980s to consolidate Utah's fragmented trust holdings, was scuttled by opposition from well-connected commodity-user groups who felt that if isolated trust sections were excised from federal lands, those interests would lose their influence over federal management. Budge, pp. 238–239.

98. Stephen Trimble, "Culture Wars and an Embattled Utah Monument" in *Writers on the Range* (March 25, 2024); Amy O'Donoghue, "Utah Says 'I Don't Think So' to Federal Land Exchange at Bears Ears" in *Deseret News* (February 6, 2024).

99. O'Day, p. 225.

100. Haggerty and Liddell, p. 8.

101. Backcountry Hunters and Anglers, *Colorado State Trust Land Access Report* (July 2019), p. 8, available at: https://d3n8a8pro7vhmx.cloudfront.net/backcount ryhunters/pages/7885/attachments/original/1583366570/CO_STL_Access_Re port_Final_-_21_Dec_2019_.pdf?1583366570.

102. O'Day, p. 224.

103. Andrew McKean, "Are State Lands Really Public?" in *Outdoor Life* (October 1, 2019).

104. Culp and Marlow, p. 17.

105. Ballotpedia, *Arizona Proposition 303, State Funds for Open Space Land Amendment (1998)* (Webpage, undated), available at: https://ballotpedia.org/Arizona_Proposition_303,_State_Funds_for_Open_Space_Land_Amendment_(1998).

106. Culp and Marlow, p. 16.

107. Rice.

108. Culp and Marlow, pp. 22–23.

109. *Ibid.*

110. Sonoran Institute, *Analysis of Ecosystem Services Potential on Colorado State Trust Lands* (Report, February 2012), p. 4.

111. Culp and Marlow, p. 38.

112. *Ibid.*, pp. 32–34.

113. Adam Davis, *State Trust Lands: The Ecosystem Services Report* (Lincoln Institute of Land Policy Working Paper WP07AD1, 2006), p. 3.

114. *Ibid.*, p. 3.

115. Ada Montague, Samuel Panarella, and Peter Yould, "Renewable Energy Development on State Trust Lands" in *Duke Environmental Law and Policy Forum* (Vol. 32, No. 2, Spring 2022), p. 12.

116. *Ibid.*, p. 81.

117. *Ibid.*

118. *Ibid.*, pp. 14–22.

119. *Ibid.*, p. 33.

CHAPTER 7

1. Regarding policy diffusion, see, Jack Walker, "The Diffusion of Innovations among the American States" in *American Political Science Review* (Vol. 63, 1969), pp. 880–899; Everett Rogers, *Diffusion of Innovations*, 4th edition (New York: Free Press, 1995).

2. Sally Fairfax, "Thinking the Unthinkable: States as Public Land Managers" in *Hastings Environmental Law Journal* (Vol. 14, No. 1, Winter 2008), p. 524, note 48.

3. Mitchell Schmidt, "2020 Election Again Shows Lopsided Republican Legislative Maps" in *Wisconsin State Journal* (November 12, 2020). This might all change in 2024, as a newly elected state supreme court justice changed the composition of the courts, which promptly revisited Wisconsin's gerrymandered state legislative maps, found them unconstitutional, and ordered them redrawn in time for the 2024 elections.

4. Stan Morrison, "McCurtain County Preserve Retains Primeval Mantle" in *The Oklahoman* (July 12, 1987).

5. Steven Davis, *In Defense of Public Lands* (Philadelphia: Temple University Press, 2018), pp. 19–23.

6. For an analysis of these legal theories, see John Ruple, "The Transfer of Public Lands Movement: The Battle to Take 'Back' Lands That Were Never Theirs" in

Colorado Natural Resources, Energy and Environmental Law Review (Vol. 29, No. 1, 2018), pp. 3–79.

7. *Ibid.*, pp. 4–7. Ruple is doubtful that Utah's legal theories underlying their transfer demands would withstand scrutiny should the state ever decide to take the federal government to court for ignoring their transfer legislation of 2012.

8. *Ibid.*, pp. 7–8.

9. Jeff Mapes, *GOP Platform Supports Transferring Western Public Lands to States* (Oregon Public Broadcasting, July 19, 2016), available at: http://www.opb.org/news /series/election-2016/republican-platform-public-land-privatization/.

10. Martin Nie and Patrick Kelly, "State and Local Control of Federal Lands: New Developments in the Transfer of Federal Lands Movement" in *Ecology Law Currents* (August 21, 2018); Brooke Larsen, "Why Utah is Suing the U.S. for Control of Public Land" in *High Country News* (August 23, 2024).

11. Nie and Kelly.

12. Robert Nelson, *State-Owned Lands in the Eastern United States: Lessons from State Land Management in Practice* (PERC Public Lands Report, March 2018), p. 7.

13. *Ibid.*, p. 5.

14. Fairfax, p. 509.

15. *Ibid.*, p. 526.

16. Holly Fretwell and Shawn Regan, *Divided Lands: State vs. Federal Management in the West* (PERC Public Lands Report, February 2015), p. 5.

17. *Ibid.*, pp. 14, 17, 22.

18. Randall O'Toole, "Congress Should Turn Federal Lands into Trusts" in *Should Federal Lands Be Transferred to Western States?* (PERC Forum, July 27, 2017), available at: https://www.perc.org/2017/07/27/should-federal-lands-be-transferred -to-western-states/; Fairfax, p. 532.

19. This would notably leave out the energy-rich 1.87-million-acre Grand Staircase-Escalante National Monument, which, like many more recently designated monuments, is administered by the BLM and would be transferred if Utah had its way.

20. Ruple, pp. 4–5.

21. Robert Keiter and John Ruple, *The Transfer of Public Lands Movement: Taking the 'Public' out of Public Lands* (University of Utah Wallace Stegner Center White Paper No. 2015-01, January 28, 2015), p 4.

22. *Ibid.*, pp. 4–5.

23. *Ibid.*, p. 8.

24. *Ibid.*, p. 5.

25. Jay O'Laughlin, *Would a Transfer of Federal Lands to the State of Idaho Make or Lose Money?* (University of Idaho College of Natural Resources, Issue Brief No. 16, November 2014), pp. 2, 4, available at: https://legislature.idaho.gov/wp-content /uploads/sessioninfo/2014/interim/fedl_olaughlin.pdf.

26. David Bergendorf, *FY 2022 Agency Timber Target* (USDA Forest Service Report, April 27, 2022), available at: https://www.fs.usda.gov/sites/default/files /fy2022-agency-timber-target-report.pdf.

27. Mark Haggerty and Chelsea Liddell, *State Trust Lands in Transition: Implications for Federal Land Transfer* (Headwaters Economics White Paper, November 2019), pp. 5–6.

28. *Ibid.*, p. 3.

29. Wes Siler, "Why You Don't Want the States Managing Public Land" in *Outside* (November 2, 2017).

30. Haggerty and Liddell, pp. 4–6.

31. *Ibid.*, p. 1.

32. *Ibid.*

33. Carol Hardy Vincent, Laura Hanson, and Lucas Bermejo, Federal Land Ownership: Overview and Data, (Congressional Research Service Report R42346, February 21, 2020), pp. 7–8.

34. Uma Outka, "State Lands in Modern Public Land Law" in *Stanford Environmental Law Journal* (Vol. 36, 2017), p. 215.

35. *Ibid.*, p. 215.

36. Perhaps the closest federal analog to a state natural area would be USFS special management areas or scientific areas, but these are still quite different from a typical SNA program.

37. Ney Landrum, *The State Park Movement in America: A Critical Review* (Columbia, MO: University of Missouri Press, 2004), p. 260.

38. Gregg Krupa, "Michigan Owns 12% of State's Land and Water. But Is It Too Much?" in *Detroit News* (August 29, 2020).

39. *Ibid.*

40. Baylor Spears, "Wisconsin Legislature Approves Final Version of Brewers Stadium Deal" in *Wisconsin Examiner* (November 15, 2023).

41. University of Wisconsin–Milwaukee Institute for Survey and Policy Research, *The Economic Impact of the Milwaukee Brewers* (Report, January 2005), p. 2.

42. Jeffrey Prey, David Marcouiller, and Danya Kim, *Economic Impacts of the Wisconsin State Park System: Connections to Gateway Communities* (Wisconsin Department of Natural Resources Report PR-487-2013, November 2013), pp. 7, 9.

43. Ricardo Torres, "What's Happening at the Foxconn Site in Wisconsin Five Years after the Company Announced Its Plans" in *Milwaukee Journal-Sentinel* (March 23, 2023). Ultimately, the main facility was never built by Foxconn and only a tiny fraction of the promised jobs materialized. However, Governor Tony Evers, a Democrat, replaced Walker in 2018 and renegotiated the deal with stricter benchmarks for achieving tax benefits, and as a result, very few have ultimately been granted. However, hundreds of millions of dollars in ultimately unneeded infrastructural improvements were spent.

44. Laura Schulte, "A New Report Looks at Outdoor Recreation and Land Conservation in Wisconsin. Here's What It Says about How We Rank with Other States" in *Milwaukee Journal-Sentinel* (March 29, 2023).

45. Danielle Kaeding, "Report: State Tax Funding for Conservation and Parks has Steadily Eroded over Decades" in Wisconsin Public Radio (March 24, 2023).

46. Schulte.

Selected Bibliography

This bibliography includes only the sources more central to this book's theoretical and empirical arguments.

Andereck, Kathleen, "The Impact of Tourism on Natural Resources" in *Parks and Recreation* (Vol. 28, No. 6, June 1993).

Association of Fish and Wildlife Agencies, *The State Conservation Machine* (Report, 2017).

Bergstrom, John, Ken Cordell, Alan Watson, and Gregory Ashley, "Economic Impacts of State Parks on State Economies in the South" in *Southern Journal of Agricultural Economics* (Vol. 22, No. 2, 1990).

Bertaina, Stephanie, Alden Boetsch, Emily Kelly, Eirin Krane, Jessica Mitchell, Lisa Spalding, Matt Stout, Drew Vankat, and Steve Yaffee, *Collaborative Planning on State Trust Lands* (Sonoran Institute and Lincoln Institute of Land Policy Report, April 2006).

Bratman, Gregory, Christopher Anderson, Marc Berman, Bobby Cochran, Sjerp De Vries, Jon Flanders, Howard Frumkin, James Gross, and Gretchen Daily, "Nature and Mental Health: An Ecosystem Service Perspective" in *Science Advances* (Vol. 5, No. 7, July 24, 2019).

Briceno, Tania, and Johnny Mojica, *A Model for Measuring the Benefits of State Parks for the Washington State Parks and Recreation Commission* (Earth Economics Report, January 2016).

Brinson, Ayeisha, and Delwin Benson, *Values and Attitudes of National Wildlife Refuge Managers and Biologists: Report to Respondents* (U.S. Department of the Interior, U.S. Geological Survey, Open File Report OF 02-459, 2002).

Brown, Alex, "Privatizing State Parks Can Save Them—Or Wreck Them" in *Pew Stateline* (December 3, 2019).

Brown, Greg, and Charles C. Harris, "The United States Forest Service: Changing of the Guard" in *National Resources Journal* (Vol. 32, No. 3, Summer 1992).

Bruce, Melinda, and Teresa Rice, "Controlling the Blue Rash: Issues and Trends in State Land Management" in *Land and Water Law Review* (Vol. 29, No. 1, 1994).

Budge, Wade, "Changing the Focus: Managing State Trust Lands in the Twenty-First Century" in *Journal of Land, Resources, and Environmental Law* (Vol. 19, No. 223, 1999).

Clarke, Jeanne, and Daniel McCool, *Staking Out the Terrain: Power and Performance among Natural Resource Agencies*, 2nd edition (Albany: State University of New York Press, 1996).

Conard, Rebecca, *Places of Quiet Beauty: Parks, Preserves, and Environmentalism* (Iowa City: University of Iowa Press, 1997).

Cox, Thomas, *The Park Builders: A History of State Parks in the Pacific Northwest* (Seattle: University of Washington Press, 1989).

Culp, Peter, Andy Laurenzi, Cynthia Tuell, and Alison Berry, *State Trust Lands in the West: Fiduciary Duty in a Changing Landscape* (Lincoln Institute of Land Policy, Policy Focus Report, 2015).

Culp, Susan, and Joe Marlow, *Conserving State Trust Lands: Strategies for the Intermountain West* (Lincoln Institute of Land Policy, Policy Focus Report PF 038, 2015).

Dannhausen, Miles, Jr., and Jackson Parr, "Can Self-Sustaining Funding Model Work for Wisconsin State Parks" in *Peninsula Pulse* (April 21, 2017).

Davis, Adam, *State Trust Lands: The Ecosystem Services Report* (Lincoln Institute of Land Policy Working Paper WP07AD1, 2006).

Davis, Steven, "The Forests Nobody Wanted: The Politics of Land Management in the County Forests of the Upper Midwest" in *Journal of Land Use and Environment Law* (Vol. 28, No. 2, Spring 2013).

———. *In Defense of Public Lands* (Philadelphia: Temple University Press, 2018).

———. "The Politics of Urban Natural Areas Management at the Local Level: A Case Study" in *Kentucky Journal of Equine, Agriculture, and Natural Resources Law* (Vol. 2, No. 2, 2010).

———. "Preservation, Resource Extraction, and Recreation on Public Lands: A View from the States" in *Natural Resources Journal* (Vol. 48, No. 2, Spring 2008).

De Groot, Rudolf, Matthew Wilson, and Roelof Boumans, "A Typology for the Classification, Description and Valuation of Ecosystems Functions, Goods and Services" in *Ecological Economics* (Vol. 41, No. 3, 2002).

Elgin, Ben, "U.S. Public Forests Are Cashing In on Dubious Carbon Offsets" in *Bloomberg* (April 28, 2022).

Fairfax, Sally, "Thinking the Unthinkable: States as Public Land Managers" in *Hastings Environmental Law Journal* (Vol. 14, No. 1, Winter 2008).

Fairfax, Sally, Jon Souder, and Gretta Goldenman, "The School Trust Lands: A Fresh Look at Conventional Wisdom" in *Environmental Law* (Vol. 22, 1992).

Fischman, Robert, "The Significance of National Wildlife Refuges in the Development of U.S. Conservation Policy" in *Journal of Land Use and Environmental Law* (Vol. 21, No. 1, 2005).

Fretwell, Holly, and Shawn Regan, *Divided Lands: State vs. Federal Management in the West* (PERC Public Lands Report, March 3, 2015).

Gilroy, Leonard, Harris Kenny, and Julian Morris, *Parks 2.0: Operating State Parks through Public-Private Partnerships* (Buckeye Institute Policy Study No. 419, December 2013).

Hager, Alan, "State School Lands: Does the Federal Trust Mandate Prevent Preservation?" in *Natural Resources and Environment* (Vol. 12, No. 1, Summer 1997).

Haggerty, Mark, and Chelsea Liddell, *State Trust Lands in Transition: Understanding the Trust Model* (Headwaters Economics White Paper, November 2019).

Hicks, Gregory, "Managing State Trust Lands for Ecosystem Health: The Case of Washington State's Range and Agricultural Lands" in *Hastings Environmental Law Journal* (Vol. 6, No. 1, Fall 1999).

Holeton, Miranda, and David Takacs, "U.S. State-Based Wilderness Law: An Evaluation" in *Hastings Environmental Law Journal* (Vol. 28, No. 1, Winter 2022).

Holzman, David, "Accounting for Nature's Benefits: The Dollar Value of Ecosystem Services" in *Environmental Health Perspectives* (Vol. 120, No. 4, April 2012).

Jacobson, Cynthia, Leeann Sullivan, Mark Gasta, Michael Manfredo, Judy Camuso, Peter Novotny, Rick Jacobson, and Kendra Witthaus, "State Fish and Wildlife Agency Culture: Access Points to Leverage Major Change" in *Conservation Science and Practice* (Vol. 4, No. 2, February 2022).

Joosse, Ted, "Wolf Populations Drop as More States Allow Hunting" in *Scientific American* (September 7, 2021).

Kaufman, Herbert, *The Forest Ranger: A Study in Administrative Behavior* (Baltimore, MD: Johns Hopkins University Press, 1960).

Keiter, Robert, and John Ruple, *The Transfer of Public Lands Movement: Taking the 'Public' out of Public Lands* (University of Utah Wallace Stegner Center White Paper No. 2015-01, January 28, 2015).

Koontz, Tomas, "Differences between State and Federal Public Forest Management: The Importance of Rules" in *Publius: The Journal of Federalism* (Vol. 27, No. 1, Winter 1997).

———. "Federal and State Public Forest Administration in the New Millenium: Revisiting Herbert Kaufman's *The Forest Ranger*" in *Public Administration Review* (January/February 2007).

———. *Federalism in the Forest* (Washington, DC: Georgetown University Press, 2002).

Koval, Melissa, and Angela Mertig, "Attitudes of the Michigan Public and Wildlife Agency Personnel toward Lethal Wildlife Management" in *Wildlife Society Bulletin* (Vol. 32, No. 1, Spring, 2004).

Landrum, Ney, "Entrepreneurism in America's State Parks" in *George Wright Forum* (Vol. 22, No. 2, 2005).

———. *The State Park Movement in America: A Critical Review* (Columbia, MO: University of Missouri Press, 2004).

Langenau, Edward, Jr., and Charles Ostrom Jr., "Organizational and Political Factors Affecting State Wildlife Management" in *Wildlife Society Bulletin* (Vol. 12, No. 2, Summer 1984).

Leopold, Aldo, *Round River* (New York: Oxford University Press, 1993).
———. *A Sand County Almanac* (New York: Random House, 1986).
Leung, Yu-Fai, Jordan Smith, and Anna Miller, *Statistical Report of State Park Operations: 2014–2015 Annual Information Exchange* (National Association of State Park Directors, Vol. 37, March 2016).
Liddell, Chelsea, and Mark Haggerty, *State Trust Lands in Transition: Challenges from New Uses and Demands* (Headwaters Economics White Paper, November 2019).
———. *State Trust Lands in Transition: States' Treatment of Permanent Funds* (Headwaters Economics White Paper, November 2019).
Loring, Michael, and John Workman, "The Relationship between Land Ownership and Range Condition in Rich County, Utah" in *Journal of Range Management* (Vol. 40, July 4, 1987).
Lowell, Debra, and Yating Liang, "Management Policy in and Typology of State Park Systems" in *American Journal of Environmental Sciences* (Vol. 5, No. 2, 2009).
MacCleery, Douglas, *American Forests: A History of Resiliency and Recovery* (Durham, NC: Forest History Society, 2011).
Maciag, Mike, "Struggling State Parks Seek New Ways to Survive" in *Governing* (November 21, 2016).
Manfredo, Michael, Cynthia Pierce, David Fulton, Jennifer Pate, and Bruce Gill, "Public Acceptance of Wildlife Trapping in Colorado" in *Wildlife Society Bulletin* (Vol. 27, 1999).
Manfredo, Michael, Tara Teel, Andrew Don Carlos, Leeann Sullivan, Alan Bright, Alia Dietsch, Jeremy Bruskotter, and David Fulton, "The Changing Sociocultural Context of Wildlife Conservation" in *Conservation Biology* (Vol. 34, No. 6, 2020).
Manfredo, Michael, Tara Teel, Alia Dietsch, Jeremy Bruskotter, Mark Duda, Andrew Don Carlos, and Leeann Sullivan, *America's Wildlife Values: The Social Context of Wildlife Management in the U.S.* (Report, Colorado State University Department of Human Dimensions of Natural Resources, 2018).
Miller, James, and Richard Hobbs, "Conservation Where People Live and Work" in *Conservation Biology* (Vol. 16, No. 2, April 2002).
Miner, Amanada, Robert Malmsheimer, and Denise Keele, "Twenty Years of Forest Service Land Management Litigation" in *Journal of Forestry* (Vol. 112, No. 1, January 2014).
Montague, Ada, Samuel Panarella, and Peter Yould, "Renewable Energy Development on State Trust Lands" in *Duke Environmental Law and Policy Forum* (Vol. 32, No. 2, Spring 2022).
More, Thomas, "From Public to Private: Five Concepts of Park Management and their Consequences" in *George Wright Forum* (Vol. 22, No. 2, 2005).
Morgan, J. Mark, "Resources, Recreationists, and Revenues: A Policy Dilemma for Today's State Park Systems" in *Environmental Ethics* (Vol. 18, No. 3, Fall 1996).
Nelson, Robert, *State-Owned Lands in the Eastern United States: Lessons from State Land Management in Practice* (PERC Public Lands Report, March 2018).

Nie, Martin, and Patrick Kelly, "State and Local Control of Federal Lands: New Developments in the Transfer of Federal Lands Movement" in *Ecology Law Currents* (August 21, 2018).

O'Day, Sean, "School Trust Lands: The Land Manager's Dilemma Between Educational Funding and Environmental Conservation, A Hobson's Choice?" in *NYU Environmental Law Journal* (Vol. 8, 1999).

O'Laughlin, Jay, *Would a Transfer of Federal Lands to the State of Idaho Make or Lose Money?* (University of Idaho College of Natural Resources, Issue Brief No. 16, November 2014).

Outka, Uma, "State Lands in Modern Public Land Law" in *Stanford Environmental Law Journal* (Vol. 36, 2017).

Pahre, Robert, "Privatizing Isle Royale? The Limits of Free Market Environmentalism" in *George Wright Forum* (Vol. 25, No. 3, 2008).

Peterson, Mark, "Wilderness by State Mandate: A Survey of State-Designated Wilderness Areas" in *Natural Areas Journal* (Vol. 16, No. 3, 1996).

Pounds, Erin, "State Trust Lands: Static Management and Shifting Value Perspectives" in *Environmental Law* (Vol. 41, 2011).

Prey, Jeffrey, David Marcouiller, and Danya Kim, *Economic Impacts of the Wisconsin State Park System: Connections to Gateway Communities* (Wisconsin Department of Natural Resources Report PR-487-2013, November 2013).

Propst, Blake, and Chad Dawson, "State-Designated Wilderness in the United States: A National Review" in *International Journal of Wilderness* (Vol. 14, No. 1, April 2008).

Randall, Cassidy, "For Wolves, the Culture War Is Extremely Deadly" in *Rolling Stone* (April 5, 2022).

Rocheleau, Bruce, "The Politics of State Wildlife Management: Why Anti-Conservation Forces Usually Win" in *Medium* (August 14, 2019).

Rosenberg, Kenneth, Adriaan Dokter, Peter Blancher, John Sauer, Adam Smith, Paul Smith, Jessica Stanton, Laura Helft, Michael Parr, and Peter Marra, "Decline of the North American Avifauna" in *Science* (Vol. 366, No. 6461, September 19, 2019).

Ruple, John, "The Transfer of Public Lands Movement: The Battle to Take 'Back' Lands That Were Never Theirs" in *Colorado Natural Resources, Energy and Environmental Law Review* (Vol. 29, No. 1, 2018).

Siderelis, Christos, Roger Moore, Yu-Fai Leung, Jordan Smith, "A Nationwide Production Analysis of State Park Attendance in the United States" in *Journal of Environmental Management* (Vol. 99, 2012).

Siderelis, Christos, and Jordan Smith, "Ecological Settings and State Economies as Factor Inputs in the Provision of Outdoor Recreation" in *Environmental Management* (Vol. 52, 2013).

Siikamäki, Juha, *State Parks: Assessing Their Benefits* (Resources for the Future Report, February 15, 2012).

Smith, Jordan, Anna Miller, and Yu-Fai Leung, *2019 Outlook and Analysis Letter* (National Association of State Park Directors Report, February 2020).

Smith, Jordan, Emily Wilkins, and Yu-Fai Leung, "Attendance Trends Threaten Future Operations of America's State Park Systems" in *Proceedings of the National Academy of Sciences* (Vol. 116, No. 26, June 25, 2019).

Souder, Jon, and Sally Fairfax, *State Trust Lands: History, Management, and Sustainable Use* (Lawrence: University of Kansas Press, 1996).

Stankey, George, "Wilderness Preservation Activity at the State Level: A National Survey" in *Natural Areas Journal* (Vol. 4, No. 4, 1984).

Stearns, Forest, "History of the Lake States Forests: Natural and Human Impacts" in J. M. Webster (editor), *Lake States Regional Forest Resources Assessment: Technical Papers* (USDA Forest Service General Technical Report NC-189, 1997).

Stein, Bruce, Naomi Edelson, Lauren Anderson, John Kanter, and Jodi Stemler, *Reversing America's Wildlife Crisis* (National Wildlife Federation Report, March 2018).

Stevens, William, *Miracle under the Oaks* (New York: Pocket Books, 1995).

Teel, Tara, Richard Krannich, and Robert Schmidt, "Utah Stakeholders' Attitudes toward Selected Cougar and Black Bear Management Practices" in *Wildlife Society Bulletin* (Vol. 30, No. 1, Spring, 2002).

Thom, Richard, and Mike Leahy, *Status of State Natural Area Programs 2015* (Natural Areas Association Report, 2015).

U.S. Department of the Interior, U.S. Fish and Wildlife Service, *2016 National Survey of Fishing, Hunting, and Wildlife-Associated Recreation* (Report #FHW/16-NAT[RV], revised October 2018).

U.S. Government Accountability Office, *Public Timber: Federal and State Programs Differ Significantly in Pacific Northwest* (GAO/RCED-96-108, May 1996).

Walker, Jack, "The Diffusion of Innovations among the American States" in *American Political Science Review* (Vol. 63, 1969).

Walls, Margaret, *Parks and Recreation in the United States: State Park Systems* (Resources for the Future Report, January 2009).

———. *Paying for State Parks: Evaluating Alternative Approaches for the 21st Century* (Resources for the Future Report, January 28, 2013).

Westphal, Lynne, Michael Dockry, Laura Kenefic, Sonya Sachdeva, Amelia Rhodeland, Dexter Locke, Christel Kern, Heidi Huber-Stearns, and Michael Coughlan, "USDA Forest Service Employee Diversity during a Period of Workforce Contraction" in *Journal of Forestry* (Vol. 120, No. 4, 2022).

Williams, Ted, "America's New War on Wolves and Why It Must Be Stopped" in *Yale Environment 360* (February 17, 2022).

Zellmer, Sandra, Martin Nie, Christopher Barnes, Jonathan Haber, Julie Joly, and Kenneth Pitt, "Fish and Wildlife Management on Federal Lands: Debunking State Supremacy" in *Environmental Law* (Vol. 47, 2017).

Index

Steven Davis is Professor of Political Science and Environmental Studies at Edgewood College in Madison, Wisconsin, and author of *In Defense of Public Lands: The Case against Privatization and Transfer* (Temple).

www.ingramcontent.com/pod-product-compliance
Lightning Source LLC
Chambersburg PA
CBHW030837300326
41935CB00037B/464